ArtScroll Series®

D1495603

Rabbi Nosson Scherman / Rabbi Meir Zlotowitz
General Editors

POSITIVE

by
RABBI ABRAHAM J. TWERSKI, M.D.
URSULA SCHWARTZ, PH.D.

PARENTING

DEVELOPING YOUR CHILD'S POTENTIAL

Published by

Mesorah Publications, ltd

FIRST EDITION
First Impression . . . May 1996
Second Impression . . . November 1996

Published and Distributed by
MESORAH PUBLICATIONS, Ltd.
4401 Second Avenue
Brooklyn, New York 11232

Distributed in Europe by
J. LEHMANN HEBREW BOOKSELLERS
20 Cambridge Terrace
Gateshead, Tyne and Wear
England NE8 1RP

Distributed in Israel by
SIFRIATI / A. GITLER — BOOKS
10 Hashomer Street
Bnei Brak 51361

Distributed in Australia & New Zealand by
GOLDS BOOK & GIFT CO.
36 William Street
Balaclava 3183, Vic., Australia

Distributed in South Africa by
KOLLEL BOOKSHOP
22 Muller Street
Yeoville 2198, Johannesburg, South Africa

ISBN:
0-89906-644-5 (hard cover)
0-89906-645-3 (paperback)

Printed in the United States of America by Noble Book Press Corp.
Bound by Sefercraft Quality Bookbinders, Ltd., Brooklyn, N.Y.

Table of Contents

Section IV: Toward a Toolbox for Jewish Parents

Section V: Putting It All to Work

Section VI: Bringing Basics Together

POSITIVE PARENTING

Introduction:
Why This Book

Approaching the writing of a new book, one is reminded of the words of the wisest of all men, "Be extremely cautious, my son, making books to no end" (*Ecclesiastes* 12:12). Sometimes a new book can be easily justified, as when it contains new material not available elsewhere. It is more difficult to justify another book when there are already volumes available on the subject. One may rightfully ask: What need is there for another book on parent-child relationships? The subject seems to have been thoroughly covered in many secular popular books and periodicals, and several fine books have been written regarding the Torah-halachic concept of parenting. Why, then, another book?

Whether in giving or attending lectures, it is rare that one walks away with truly new data. Yet these lectures have value because they may enhance one's knowledge considerably. Material may be organized a bit differently or presented from another perspective, enabling it to be better understood and applied more effectively. This is what the Talmud means, "There is no session in the House of Study that is devoid of something new" (*Chagigah* 3a), because although the data itself may not be new, the method in which it is handled is new.

While there is no assurance that a new book, regardless of how well the subject is covered, will resolve the many difficult problems of parenting, there is no question that both parents and children can use help from whatever source possible. Cultural and social changes have made the tasks both of parenting and growing up incredibly more difficult. Just in the past few decades many values, at least in the secular world, have fallen by the wayside. Concepts of moral right and wrong have undergone revolutionary changes. Respect for authority of all kinds has disintegrated, governments at all levels are virtually powerless over crime, young people are trapped in alcoholism and drug addiction, and the media bombard both young and old with unspeakable violence and inappropriate interests.

The Torah world has tried in various ways to circle the wagons, to insulate itself from these demoralizing forces, but the fact is that none of the defenses are impermeable. Secular influences have impacted even on Torah-observant families, taking greater or lesser tolls. Some of the current literature on parenting is actually supportive of the cultural-social changes, advocating allowing a child to grow up with a minimum of restraints and restrictions, and leaving him to "make up his own mind." This naive approach fails to recognize that behavior patterns may become so ingrained in childhood that even after the maturing person reaches the age of reason and wishes to make some changes, whatever intellectual strength he may try to apply is no match for established habits.

Furthermore, there is a plethora of parenting concepts that are mutually contradicting, all the way from advocating firm discipline to broad permissiveness, with each authority implying that deviation from this particular course may result in the child becoming neurotic. The well-read parent may be confused by this cacophony of voices, and may develop an inconsistent approach, or may try to alternate parenting techniques, switching from one to another when the desired behavior is not immediately forthcoming. Such confusion can be ruinous, and essentially results from trying to apply techniques of parenting rather than allowing a methodology of parenting to emerge from a thorough understanding of what parenting is all about and why.

Trying to raise a physically-emotionally-morally healthy child in today's environment is thus a herculean task, and in search of a reliable and consistent approach, parents should turn to Torah authorities for clarification of what Torah says about parenting. This is certainly a wise step, but the desired solutions may not be readily forthcoming. The Torah and its wisdom are so vast that a rabbi may be exceptionally learned and authoritative in many areas, but will not necessarily be expert in what the Torah teaches about practical aspects of child behavior. The solutions to such problems are surely to be found in Torah literature, as is stated in *Ethics of the Fathers*, "Review it (Torah) and review it again, for everything is therein" (5:26), but not every sage has translated them into practical application.

While there may not be specific instructions in Torah literature what to do if a child refuses to go to school, lies, or throws tantrums, there are healthy concepts of parenting which can result in a home environment that will minimize the incidence of such problems, and make the parents more capable of dealing with them effectively.

There are some specific problems with which rabbis may not be familiar. In the past, it was a given that alcoholism and drug abuse (even of prescription and over the counter drugs) were not Jewish problems, with the understandable result that most rabbis have not dealt with these problems. Times have changed, however, and Jews are no longer immune to the dangers of alcohol, cocaine, heroin, marijuana, and prescription drugs.

Although the media is inundated with cases of spousal abuse, the problem as a whole is still largely covered up among observant families. The penchant for secrecy about family problems and emotional and often physical illnesses has resulted in concealment which has often precluded effective resolution of problems. Families may be living in turmoil, presenting a facade of bliss to the public, while children suffer helplessly and silently. Child abuse, at one time unthinkable within a Jewish family, is unfortunately a reality. Even when consulting professionals, information that would be considered a "*shanda*" is often withheld.

While parents are certainly concerned about their child's welfare, the cultural tendency toward concealment may be so great that it may actually overwhelm their considerations for the child. In sharp contrast to the frequent recourse which parents may have to physicians for treating any physical problems the child may manifest, they may ignore psychological symptoms. This may be at a conscious or unconscious level; i.e., either the "*shanda*" complex renders them oblivious to these problems, or they consciously set it aside, deceiving themselves with rationalizations such as, "It really isn't that bad. It's a phase and it will go away by itself." While there are indeed symptoms that are transitory and disappear spontaneously, there are others that are more permanent, and consultation with someone who has the expertise to distinguish the two is necessary.

Some parents may consult a psychologist and withhold essential information, either about the child's behavior, situations in the home, or a family history of emotional problems. Parents sometimes withhold important information about a child's learning problems or behavior from the school, hoping that these will not surface or will not be detected.

The same holds true when parents consult their rabbi for help, and do not volunteer what they consider to be stigmatizing data. The rabbi may proceed on the basis of what he was told, not having been able to elicit important data from reluctant clients. Consequently, rabbis have given advice which they thought to be correct, sometimes collaborating with the family's concealment, especially when there is concern that exposure would be a *chilul Hashem*, a public disgrace. Unfortunately, even the recent failure of presidents to succeed in cover-ups has not convinced people that concealment is futile.

The reason for emphasizing the lack of broad-based knowledge in the training of some rabbis to counsel effectively in problems of a social-cultural nature is because Torah-observant families confronted with situations that can impact on parent-child relationships, or in need of competent guidance to establish a healthy family environment, may turn to the rabbi, as they should, as a Torah authority. If the rabbi is an accomplished Torah scholar, yet has not been adequately prepared to deal with problems of this kind, he may not have the proper vehicle whereby to transmit his Torah knowledge to people in need of it in a manner whereby they can apply it in their lives.

It is axiomatic that although the *Shulchan Aruch* has four sections, a Torah authority must have the fifth section, which consists of an understanding of the realities of the life of his congregants. No rabbi is permitted to deliver halachic decisions on the basis of book learning alone, and must undergo *shimush*, or an apprenticeship with a halachic authority, to observe how these halachic principles are put into practice. Given the role of the contemporary rabbi as a counselor and possibly even therapist as well as a *posek*, he must often delve into chapters of the "fifth section" that may not be easily available.

This book is therefore intended not only to enlighten the reader to psychological-Torah approaches to parenting, but also to alert the spokespeople of halachah that there is a need for them to become more effective transmitters of their Torah wisdom to their flock.

Psychological-Torah approach? Is there such an entity? Is not much of psychology in contradiction to vital Torah principles? We will discuss this question in an ensuing chapter. We can indeed derive much valuable guidance from Torah literature, but we need our Torah scholars to help us fetch from this eternal well.

Most of the books on parenting are "how to" books, and while they have merit, their application is rather limited. One cannot possibly remember all the specific instructions, and certainly one cannot run to the books to look up what to do when the 4-year-old has just stuck his finger in the baby's eye, or the 6-year-old has spilled milk onto the table after repeatedly being told to be careful. What is needed is an understanding of *principles* of parenting, and parents will have to use their ingenuity to apply these principles in specific instances.

Parenting is a weighty responsibility, perhaps the most important task of one's entire lifetime. Yet most people approach this awesome responsibility with the assumption that all parents intuitively know how to raise their children and do not require any special preparation and knowledge. Some people operate according to the myth that "You either have it or you don't"; i.e., one is either a natural-born parent who does not need any education in parenting, or one does not have the capacity for healthy parenting, in which case education will be of no use. There is also the myth that "If you can do it with one child, you can do it with all children," which is in stark defiance of the reality that children can be very different, and what works with one will not work with another. In some families, people marry very young, and have children when they are still emotionally immature, without having had any preparation for parenting. Again, we cannot have recourse to practices of the past, because as pointed out above, the challenges and stresses of modern-day parenting are both qualitatively and quantitatively greater than those confronting previous generations.

In earlier times, if the child was brought up to a great degree by the community rather than solely by the parents, this was essentially a positive influence. The street may not have been perfect, but a sense of decency and morality generally prevailed. There was a general consensus on values in the community, the neighborhood, the extended family, and the nuclear family, who, for all intents and purposes, spoke with one voice. The parents' efforts at guidance were reinforced by the environment.

This has all changed radically. The street today is toxic, and parents face the challenge of combating the environmental influences. *Parenting can no longer be viewed as a supplementary task but is a full-time job*, and a very taxing one at that. In the past, parental tasks could be seen as planting, cultivating, and watering the young shoots, whereas today, parents have a major weeding job. Modern life may have been made easier in the sense of our having many technological conveniences, but our prime responsibility, that of raising children, has been made much, much more difficult. We should be aware that raising a child is work, hard work, creative rather than routine work, requiring considerate thought and deliberation.

As parents we are entrusted with caring for both the physical and emotional development of our children. No parent would take a child in need of health care to someone who had no medical training. Yet few parents realize that they themselves may lack the skills to be optimal parents. While it is true that we often learn by mistakes, it is tragic when these mistakes are wrought on our children, because these mistakes are not easily, if at all, undone. For example, a distraught mother may scream at her children, "I can't take this anymore! If you keep this up, Mommy's going to go away and never come back." Some children are insecure and already have a fear of abandonment, and this only serves to reinforce it. Such mistakes are avoidable, and it is the parents' responsibility to prevent as many mistakes as possible.

There is a fascinating phenomenon which is rather difficult to understand, and that is the generational perpetuation of negative behavior. Children who suffered abuse and who harbor bitter resentments about how they had been mistreated would seem to be the last to behave similarly to their children. Logic dictates that having experienced such suffering, they would not want to inflict it on their children. But as with so many emotional issues, logic does not always prevail and when children grow up and become parents, they may repeat the mistakes in parenting that they had experienced. Hence it is not sufficient for people who recognize that they were victims of inadequate parenting to simply be determined not to repeat the mistakes that were done to them. Something more is necessary to avoid such generational perpetuation of mistakes. Hopefully we can provide some guidelines to avoid this apparent self-perpetuating pattern.

There is no microwave to hasten development of parenting skills. It is a long and often tedious course, requiring a great deal of patience. This book is not intended to replace the authoritative books on parenting, but rather to complement them. It is not intended to shorten the process of becoming a better parent, but rather to increase the awareness of what constitutes better parenting, and to facilitate the execution of this weighty responsibility.

Section I

Approaching the Task

Chapter One

What Is the Goal?

t the risk of appearing absurd, I must ask prospective parents the question: "Why do you want to have children?" In every other venture in life, our methodology is generally determined by the goal we desire. For example, my goal is to build a house. I must then decide on a plan. Do I have enough money? Can I obtain a mortgage? How do I go about finding a reliable contractor? How do I wish the house furnished? Many questions may arise, and they will all be dealt with in the light of my ultimate goal for this particular project. There should thus be a tripartite composition to our behavior: (A) a goal; (B) a plan; and (C), action. If we begin to act without a goal or plan, we will end up with a chaotic situation. Just a bit of thought will reveal that we go through a similar process for every undertaking even though we may not be conscious of this.

The nature of the plan and the action may well be different according to our reason for the end product. If I wish to build a house for commercial purposes, to lease to tenants rather than as a personal dwelling, I may well choose a different design, different building materials, and different furnishings. To look for a plan before one has a clear understanding of the goal is both unwise and totally confusing.

It is therefore not quite as absurd as it may seem at first in discussing techniques of parenting to ask, "Why do you wish to be a parent?" This is one time where the stakes are too great to accept the answer, "Because."

I have had the occasion to talk with young women who are distressed because after two years of marriage they have not yet conceived. While their concern is easily understandable, they invariably mention how distressed they are that all their peers are pushing baby carriages, and they have nothing to display. While I truly feel for them and can identify with their distress, there is no escaping the conclusion that while this is by far not the major factor, nonetheless, for them having a child is at least partially an "ego" thing. The child's fulfilling an ego need of the parent is perfectly normal, but this must be recognized and considered in the parenting process. Having a child to satisfy an ego need may still be operative when the child is 8, 12, or 16, as well as when he is an infant in the carriage. Thus, while perfectly normal, it can affect parenting.

There is a very enlightening episode in the Torah, where the matriarch Rachel, who was childless, was envious of her sister Leah, and in desperation cried out to Jacob, "If I cannot have children, then I might as well be dead." Jacob, who loved Rachel intensely, responds to her angrily (*Genesis* 30:1-2). A bit later, the Torah states that G-d remembered Rachel and she conceived Joseph (ibid. 30:22). Rashi comments that Rachel merited a child because she had selflessly yielded her beloved Jacob to her sister Leah, and although the Divine wisdom had deprived her of children until now, it was this virtue that was her salvation. We may not be capable of achieving the great spirituality of the patriarchs and matriarchs, yet they are meant to serve as models of the idea.

What the Torah is teaching us is that the saintly matriarch Rachel had momentarily been overcome by a personal interest to have a child, and this is why Jacob replied with rebuke, that one must submit to the supreme will of G-d. Rachel quickly recovered her lofty spiritual status of total selflessness as had been characterized by her willingness to yield her beloved Jacob to her sister rather than to allow Leah to be publicly humiliated. Having shed her personal interest and having returned to her lofty spiritual level, she was then given a child, who indeed became Joseph the *tzaddik*. The average mother cannot be Rachel, and does have an ego interest in being a parent. Again I must stress, this is perfectly normal, yet should be reckoned with.

It is too simplistic to say that language determines thought, but on the other hand, language certainly influences thought or, at the very least, gives us clues to levels of meanings that may not be obvious or points out assumptions that are not immediately evident.

The phrase "to have children" is a very interesting one. Let's take some time to listen closely. How many children do you "have"? Do you want to "have" children? When do you plan to "have" a child? Do you want to "have" a boy or a girl?" "Having" implies a possession, something that we own, something that we acquire out of our own volition. In and of itself, "having" something implies a state. To "have" a house implies that I own it, that it is mine to do as I please, that a transaction has taken place, and that I am in full control over this acquisition. Since I chose to make this acquisition it enhances me, and if it does not, my goal may be to exchange this acquisition for something that suits me better. In addition, the relationship between an owner and his possession is a simple two-way relationship, the owner and the object owned.

From a Jewish perspective, having children is first of all not a matter of a possession, and secondly it is not a matter of a two-way relationship between parent and child. The Talmud says that there are three partners in every child: G-d, the father, and the mother (*Kiddushin* 30b). The same way that G-d is involved in a Jewish marriage, in our kitchens, in our sleeping and awakening, so is He also involved in the enterprise of parenting. This means that there needs to be space in our child rearing equation for G-d.

With G-d as an intimate partner in parenting, we can no longer talk of "having" a child in the simple possessive fashion implied by ordinary language. Rather, having a child means to be entrusted with a responsibility. A child is a gift of G-d chosen for us specifically and entrusted to us for safekeeping to be raised and treasured. As a gift from G-d, a child — any child — cannot be looked upon at as an accident or a mistake. Rather, we need to believe — hard as this may be at times — that our children are a perfect match for us and we for them. The same way that a marriage holds in it potential for growth for each partner, it is precisely in the affirmation of this match that there is the potential for good and for growth.

The task for parents is not simply to teach children manners or to get them to behave properly. This is not at all minimizing good manners and civilized ways. On the contrary, *middos* and *derech eretz* (decency) are extremely important, but these are qualities that become lasting attributes of a child's character and personality only if they are embedded in a vision of the world that is imbued with Torah values. In *Ethics of the Fathers* (3:17) we read "If there is no Torah there is no *derech eretz*, and if there is no *derech eretz* there is no Torah." The two are interdependent.

The job of the parent involves much more than simply "training" the child to do things the right way. Training is merely a method of teaching that does not require understanding and simply rests on an association between a stimulus and a response that has been reinforced. Raising Jewish children means that the parents instill in them a view of the world where events and actions are seen through Torah eyes; where words are heard with Torah ears; where words are spoken with Torah thoughts in mind. In a sense, then, it is our job to construct the world for them as one of Torah and to build up with them and for them a map of life and the world that will guide them for the rest of their lives. It is a task that transcends our own existence on earth. The Torah is indeed a "map." It is the master plan whereby G-d created the universe, as stated in the Zohar, "G-d looked into the Torah, and created the universe according to it" (*Zohar Terumah* 161a).

But giving our children a map of the world does not ensure that their actions will be appropriate at all times. A map is a guide. It tells us when we are on track and when we are off track. Most importantly, it allows us to move closer to our destination. If we get lost, it allows us to turn around and to redirect ourselves. So too, raising a child is to transmit to him our map of the world so that at some point in time he can embark on the journey by himself. The parent who transmits a map gives the child tools that transcend by far any automatic conditioning of good behavior.

For the Torah-observant couple, the *mitzvah* of procreating is important, and bringing a child into the world should be the fulfillment of an important *mitzvah*. Yet we would be wise not to deceive ourselves, because self-deception never has positive results. If an ego element is present, one should not deny it and try to conceal it under some other factors.

Again, it is certainly not wrong to have an ego investment in a child, and common sense tells us that it cannot be otherwise. We are, after all, human beings, and not spiritual angels. But the ego investment in a child can be either positive or negative, and if we recognize its presence, we are in a position to direct it positively.

Raising children is a goal-directed and purposeful task and demands a concentrated sustained effort on the parents' part. It really is hard work.

Parenting may also be said to be "absorbing," which means that this task can be successfully accomplished only if we connect to it and to the child in a deep and lasting fashion, overcoming immediate frustrations, setbacks, disappointments, and fatigue. In this sense, parenting is quite similar to the study of Torah, which is an encounter with the word of G-d, and it, too, is often fraught with frustrations, questions, and difficulties. At the same time, learning opens up to the student delights that only a fellow learner can understand. Similarly, when a child says a first word, takes a first step, has a first recognition of the *aleph-beis,* makes the first moral decision based on Torah law, these are the delights that only a parent can truly savor.

G-d gave us a head start with the *mitzvah* of parenting by giving us the capability of feeling a deep bond with our children right from birth, and by embellishing the newborn with capabilities that allow him to connect with us immediately. We know that optimal vision for newborns and young infants is at approximately 12 inches, just about the distance to his mother's face when he is nursing or being held. Studies indicate that a baby is indeed "wired" for speech: For example, even newborns can distinguish between "B" and "P" sounds, which shows that they are particularly attuned to human voices. Research has also shown that as early as a few weeks, the infant gazes longer at his mother's face than that of a stranger, and is also capable of differentiating between the voice of his mother and that of a stranger. Given the challenges that young children pose from infancy throughout childhood, including the sleepless or interrupted nights, and their seemingly irrational behavior, crying, "I want the blue cup and not the yellow cup!," the stability of this bond is just short of amazing, and is due only to the *chesed* which G-d has granted to parents.

The commitment to a child can indeed bring out the best in a parent. By investing themselves completely in their child, parents are capable of acting purely in the service of the child, and for the moment their own selves become subsumed to the needs of the child. We might say that at such a moment the parent loses his self and his resources in the service of the child.

An example from clinical practice comes to mind. A couple who could not have children was finally able to adopt a healthy little baby boy, just a few weeks old. As the child grew older, he became increasingly more difficult to manage and seemed to have great difficulty communicating and socializing. This progressed to the point where he became a threat to their second child, a son born to them about two years after they had adopted their first child. The painful diagnosis was finally made that their adopted child was autistic. These parents have continued to amaze me in their dedication to this child and their lack of regrets at having adopted him, and their firm belief that G-d gave them this child and that he was meant to be their own. The child's progress in therapy is no doubt due to a great degree to their attitude which allows them to give freely of themselves and to meet his needs.

Let us avoid a possible major pitfall. Putting oneself at a child's disposal by no means implies that the parent is asked to become a shadow-like presence, catering to every whim of the child. Rather, it means that the parent puts all of his inner resources in the service of raising this child. Looking at it this way resolves a paradox. A parent needs to be strong, determined, caring, focused — hardly a doormat or a menial worker. The role of the Jewish mother has been aptly likened to that of a *rosh yeshivah*. Just as the *rosh yeshivah* guides his pupils and watches over them for their own benefit, the parents' investment in their children is not for the sake of the parent, but a means to bring their children to reach their fullest potential as individuals and as Jews, and to bring them closer to G-d. Both with a parent and the *rosh yeshivah*, it is a determination that does not have as its goal the celebration of one's ego. This analogy is clearly stated in the Talmud. "Whoever teaches a child Torah is as though he has given birth to him" (*Sanhedrin* 19b).

Let us therefore draw a distinction between "ego involvement" and "self-investment." Ego involvement in a child's upbringing views the child primarily as a source of parental enhancement. The *nachas* that children, G-d willing, bring to the parents, are experienced as tributes to parental competence, or are indicators of social status and personal superiority. The parent feels entitled to these gifts from the child and needs them to preserve his own self-esteem. In contrast, the parent who has little "ego involvement" but high "self-investment" can experience the *nachas* that a child brings as expressions of the child's growth as a Jew and as feedback that he is on the right track as a parent. The result is enjoyment of the child for his own sake, and gratitude to G-d for His blessings.

The parent who is primarily driven by ego involvement interprets the same experience very differently than the parent who has invested himself in the parental task. When parental expectations and needs correspond to the child's natural inclinations, talents, and capabilities, this relationship, although flawed, can work. But the ego boost that one gets from "My son the Talmud whiz" or "My daughter the well-known educator" are but fortuitous coincidences and in constant need of reaffirmation. One patient complained to his therapist, "I am sick and tired of being a *nachas* machine." The wise Solomon cautioned, "Train the child according to *his* way" (*Proverbs* 22:6). The child's makeup and needs must be understood.

Children are often very much aware of their parents' needs and their role in fulfilling them. As adults, they pose a challenge in therapy of having to work through a sense of alienation of themselves and their identity. When the parents are primarily ego driven, this house of cards tends to fall apart if the child does not correspond to the parents' image and is "different" or truly makes mistakes. Since the parental ego is so tied to the child's success, it becomes extremely difficult for such parents to acknowledge a problem, to get help, and to disclose the extent of their difficulties. Often this results in denial, covering up, and blaming everyone else. The child, unfortunately, gets lost in all of this.

Given our frailties as human beings, it is not astonishing that all of us, perhaps with the exception of a few saintly persons, are involved with our children at some level of ego involvement. This should not cause us to feel guilty. Rather, the task is for us to become aware of our particular weaknesses and blind spots, our ego-driven goals and expectations for the child, and our difficulties in accepting even positive traits in our children when they do not correspond to our wishes and needs.

Self-awareness results in self-knowledge. This allows a parent to change a destructive ego-driven wish and helps to overcome selfish needs that can be detrimental to the child. If this does not happen, parents and children can get stuck in a destructive circle of fear, disappointment, resentment, and misunderstanding. We need to be clear in our minds that *our task as parents is to invest ourselves in our children without entangling ourselves in a self-centered way*. Sometimes our ego involvement is easily evident; other times it is covered up and hidden.

Ego involvement does not necessarily refer to a drive for feeling superior to others, as when we say, "He has a huge ego." Rather, it may refer to certain needs of our own which are not necessarily those of the child, and may conceivably even be contrary to the child's interests.

One mother was driven to distraction by one of her sons, who from the earliest days was fiercely independent, insisting on doing things by himself and learning by his own mistakes. He would not accept help or guidance, and his most famous words were "Don't worry, Ima," which was precisely when she began worrying. She was extremely frustrated by having to restrain herself from offering any help unless he asked for it. This should not have posed so severe a problem, since many children are highly individualistic in every sense of the word, and prefer self-sufficiency with all its drawbacks rather than being helped.

In therapy it emerged that this woman's father was a self-made man, eminently practical, an organizer, and a leader. He was domineering, and lectured to his children who had to be a passive, receptive audience. As a child, this woman was frustrated by her father's lack of receptivity to her juvenile ideas and wishes, and her child's attitude of fierce independence triggered an association to her frustration with her father. She was essentially carrying over to her child her own early childhood attitudes toward her father. When she realized this, she was able to think through her reactions toward him, and the parenting process was greatly facilitated.

This, too, is ego involvement; i.e., not reacting to the child's independence objectively, but being affected by a personal attitude, a remnant from her own feelings of frustration that had never been completely resolved.

A fairly reliable sign of ego involvement is the degree of hurt, upset, or anger we feel toward a child. When our feelings are out of proportion to the offense or the problem at hand, we can be pretty sure that we are dealing with a considerable degree of ego involvement. Even when a problem is really significant and a child has gotten himself into actual trouble, we can become aware of our ego involvement when we notice that we are more concerned with what this means for us ("I won't be able to show my face in *shul*!"), and when our own reaction prevents us from constructive problem solving and getting help to a child in trouble. Self-reflection and self-awareness are the prerequisites for putting our ego in the background. Being aware of our own foibles allows us to bracket our own issues and keep them separate. This enables us as parents to deal with the issue constructively and in the child's best interest. Self-awareness allows a parent to invest his self into the child for the child's good.

This description of parenting is no doubt daunting and formidable. It is a task that demands the best in us and at its best becomes for the parent a stepping stone toward self-growth and increased closeness to G-d.

It goes without saying that for most of us parenting is fraught with mistakes, misjudgments made in the heat of anger and disappointment, and difficulties relating to our children in a constructive fashion. To a good degree, this is so because we are not completely cognizant of what parenting entails. Unclear ideas allow the *yetzer hara* to affect us without our being fully aware of it. With lack of clarity, conceptual confusion, and half-thought-through ideas, the *yetzer hara* manages to get us to do things that under better illumination and closer scrutiny would be less possible, and that we would at least wish to change. A clear and well-articulated vision is critical to successful parenting.

Some parents may shy away from wanting to face the challenges inherent in parenting. For them, a clear vision may be the cause of self-incrimination and despair at their own shortcomings and personal self-reproach. This may cause them to close their eyes to important parenting issues. However, is this not what being Jewish is all about? Just because we are not perfect or even near perfect does not mean that we should give up and feel that we are not good enough or entitled to shoot for the top. The Talmud is replete with stories of our great personalities. We tell our children the stories of the lives of our *tzaddikim*, their growing up, their saintly deeds, and their successful struggles. We know that we will never be like the saintly Reb Zusia, who lived in a hovel in poverty and who in reality had no notion of what suffering was. Reb Zusia truly regarded himself as blessed and in need of nothing. Why do we read such stories and why do we remember them in the comforts of our beautiful homes? It is because a story such as this paints a vision of where we should move spiritually. It points out to us that we need to grow in gratefulness and tells us that there exists a view of oneself in this world that views everything as good, and although we are not at this highly spiritual level, this is the goal toward which we should strive.

A young woman whose child was born with Down's Syndrome related that at the *shalom zachor* (gathering on the Friday night after the birth) one guest told her a story from our tradition that became a guiding metaphor for her during the coming years with all the difficulties that she encountered. Stories of our great men and women, great leaders, hidden *tzaddikim*, with their deep trust, sacrifice, and love for Torah are examples of the finest kind. These are more than moral lessons. Rather, precisely because they often show extreme situations, reactions out of the ordinary, and ways of viewing things in a truly transcendent way, they more effectively communicate the vision of Judaism. When we teach our children of the humble beginnings of Rabbi Akiva, who at age 40 was starting to learn the *aleph-beis*, we allow them to become part of and identify with an unforgettable example of how a person can transcend seemingly fixed and awesome circumstances. When we tell them about his wife Rachel, we connect them with the ideal model of conjugal love and inspiration. These stories are not quaint folk tales from a repository of cultural traditions and lore, but lessons in Jewish living, and are indispensable tools for optimum parenting.

Let me now cite an example of a case of an ego factor which was not constructive.

I once received an emergency visit from a desperate father, who told me that his 17-year-old son had been arrested in a drug raid. He said that this came like a bolt from the blue, because he had no inkling that his son had been using drugs. He wished to have his son hospitalized immediately for treatment.

This occurred at a time when there were no drug treatment facilities in our city. I explained this to the father, and told him that I knew of two treatment centers elsewhere that might be available, but that it would take one or two days to arrange an admission. The father concurred, but requested that I admit the son promptly to our psychiatric hospital while awaiting these arrangements. I pointed out to him that there was nothing to be accomplished by such hospitalization, and that he could wait out the short period at home.

"You don't understand," the father said. "The desk sergeant said that if I could get him into a hospital immediately, he would not have to press charges or keep him in jail."

"I can understand your concern," I said, "but believe me, it will not hurt your son in the least to realize the consequences of his behavior. Spending the night in jail might actually be to his advantage, and you should be able to transfer him to a treatment center within a day or so."

"But I can't let that happen," the father said. "If they press charges, then it will get into the paper, and I don't want my name dragged into this."

I was a bit upset, because it was evident that the urgency for treatment was not primarily for the son's benefit. To the contrary, a night in jail might have better suited the son's treatment, but I responded calmly.

"I truly empathize with you," I said. "I think that after working hard for so long to establish a reputation of dignity and respectability in the community, your son has no right to cast aspersions on the family.

"But I must tell you that I think it is highly unlikely that your son did not provide sufficient telltale signs that he was using drugs. You did not panic about this, and either consciously or unconsciously remained oblivious to this as long as it did not impinge upon you. Your present panic is not because of what drugs might do to your *son*, but what the adverse publicity may do to *you*.

"I am ready to go along with your request for your sake and admit your son immediately to avoid charges, but on the condition that you be up front with him. You must bring him into this office and say, 'Son, as long as you were only harming yourself, it didn't bother me that much. But now your drug use is going to hurt me, and I don't deserve that. Therefore you are now going to be admitted to the hospital primarily to preserve my good reputation from being besmirched by your reckless behavior.'

"You must be truthful with your son, and not pretend that you are primarily seeking his welfare. I will then gladly admit him." At that the father arose angrily and left the office, slamming the door in his rage. I did, to a degree, empathize with the father who did not wish his family to be stigmatized, but I was not about to be party to a deception.

At this point I am not making a value judgment whether or not a child should be raised to suit the parents' ego, but rather that to the degree that this is so, it should be acknowledged. There are few things that are as destructive to the parent-child relationship as dishonesty and deception. If we are aware of our parental ego, we can utilize it constructively, and we can set it aside if it is not in the child's best interest.

One's attitudes toward his child may undergo variation, even from day to day. Since our ability to learn is best served from rather extreme examples, let us consider the feelings of parents who have a child with either physical or mental handicaps. This is certainly a very difficult ordeal for the parents, yet how they accept and react to it can fluctuate significantly.

The Baal Shem Tov's students once asked him about an apparent contradiction in the Talmud, which states that a person's livelihood is determined on Rosh Hashanah (*Beitzah* 16b), but elsewhere it is stated that a person's livelihood is determined each day (*Rosh Hashanah* 16a).

The Baal Shem Tov responded by beckoning the water carrier to come close. "Chaikel," the Baal Shem Tov said, "how are things with you?"

Chaikel moaned, "Just look at me, Rabbi. Here I am, old and weak, and I have to drag heavy buckets of water in order to support myself."

The following day the Baal Shem Tov again asked Chaikel how he was faring. This time Chaikel answered, "Thank G-d, if at my age I can still *shlepp* water and support myself, I have no reason to complain."

The Baal Shem Tov then explained to his students that on Rosh Hashanah it was decreed that Chaikel be a water carrier. How Chaikel accepts that decree can vary from day to day.

This is also true with parents' reaction to a child with handicaps. Their perspective may be that this is a task or a challenge. It is possible that they may perceive it as a curse and feel shame on one day, or it may even be perceived as a blessing.

A blessing? In what way?

It is related that the *Chazon Ish* would stand up when parents with a Down's Syndrome child would pass by. He explained that every *neshamah* comes down to earth with a mission to accomplish, to perform sufficient *mitzvos* so that the *neshamah* can achieve its state of completion. If a *neshamah* comes into the world in the person of one whose limitations preclude diligent study of Torah or performance of all the *mitzvos*, this is because that *neshamah* has already neared a state of completion and requires just a bit more to do to reach its goal. This *neshamah* warrants being accorded special respect. The *Chazon Ish* saw beneath the surface, and parents who are capable of transcending superficial appearances and can have a more profound grasp of one's mission on earth may share in the *Chazon Ish's* insightfulness.

One cannot in the least fault distraught parents who have suffered such a disappointment, and who must contemplate a future comprised of various challenges and stresses. What particular needs will this child have? Will he be able to be mainstreamed or will he need special classes? If the former, will he require extra time and help that may not be readily available in a two-salaried family? If the latter, where will these be? Are there special classes that can also provide for Jewish education, and if all that is available is special classes for secular studies, how can the Jewish educational needs be met? What physical problems need to be anticipated? How will the siblings react? What about long-term considerations? What kind of place can this child have in the community as an adult?

As people who believe in Divine providence, parents should accept that it was the Divine will and by Divine wisdom that they were given this task, and they should look for ways to obtain the necessary help to manage a difficult situation. We would have to admit that this advanced degree of *emunah* (faith) does not always prevail, and that although parents may have felt that their primary purpose in having children was to fulfill the Divine will, their reaction of disappointment indicates that there may be very normal human strivings and feelings in relationship to having children over and above complying with the Divine will. Children can provide major challenges and we must avail ourselves of sources to reinforce our strength in coping with these challenges.

Torah-observant parents should realize that they have been entrusted with a *neshamah*, and that it is a sacred duty and responsibility to help that *neshamah* develop to its fullest.

The way the Jewish people came into being as a nation may serve as an example of the parental role. During the Egyptian captivity, the Israelites were in a "fetal" stage, as it were, and Moses was commissioned by G-d to "deliver" them and guide them in becoming "a kingdom of priests and a sacred nation" (*Exodus* 19:6). Moses realized the awesomeness of this task, and was rather reluctant to accept this responsibility (*Exodus* 3:11-4:13), but did so at the Divine insistence. From the very beginning, the Israelites behaved like some children do, criticizing their parents who were acting on their behalf. Moses continued to be a devoted parent for the next 40 years, absorbing their bickering, their discontent, and their outright defiance. He carried out his stewardship with the utmost devotion, to the point of repeatedly sacrificing himself for them. Yet, when Moses finally brought them to the point of success, he was not granted the opportunity to have the *nachas* of the rewards of his untiring efforts, to see them settle in the Promised Land, "Each person under his vine and under his fig tree" (*Micah* 4:4).

Bringing a child into the world is indeed a *mitzvah*, and let us never lose sight of this. One may certainly take great pleasure in performing any and every *mitzvah*, but the prime intent for doing the *mitzvah* is not the reward that it will bring, but the desire to fulfill the Divine will.

Let us return now to the typical child, and see what ego factors may be present in the parents. What kind of clothing does he wear? Those he really needs, or those bought to impress others? Why else would a toddler need designer clothes? What school will the child attend? That which is best for him, or perhaps one that the parents choose so that they can say that their child attends this school. Suppose the child appears manually dexterous but not academically oriented. Is he permitted to develop his manual skills, or must he become an academician whether or not this is realistic and appropriate for him?

Very often the needs of the child and those of the parent coincide, and there is then no pressing reason to identify a parental ego component, although this would no doubt be beneficial. However, the interests of the child and those of the parents may diverge, and if this should occur and the child's needs are set aside in favor of the parental needs, the groundwork has been laid for developmental problems. This may occur even early in the child's life.

Adults who come into therapy often reveal a great deal of anger because they feel they had been "used" to satisfy parental needs. Their feeling is that they did not ask to be born, and if two people choose to bring a child into this world, the least they could have done is to look out for the resulting child's best interest.

Many parents do make sacrifices for their children, and some children may be unappreciative of what parents have done for them. Children are indeed extensions of their parents. Yet, if they are seen *primarily* as extensions of the parents rather than as independent beings, even such sacrifice is not truly altruistic.

Given that children come into the world without having requested this privilege, and are subjected to many of the harsh realities of life, ranging from childhood diseases to the very real difficulties of growing up, it would seem logical that parents should be obligated to their children. There are certainly legitimate obligations that parents do have, and these are clearly defined in *halachah*. However, the reverse, i.e., the obligations of children towards parents, are not based solely on logic, but are rather a Torah requirement, and a fundamental one at that. In a Torah-observant family there should be total compliance with the *mitzvah* of respect for parents, and parents have a right to expect this. However, this can realistically be expected only when there is a consistence of Torah observance. But if parents are selective about which portions of Torah they wish to observe and which they feel may be dispensed with or modified, they can hardly expect their children to be any different. Parents who choose to dispense with any part of Torah are setting a precedent, and the child may very well choose to follow suit and dispense with other portions, such as with the commandment requiring parental respect.

The ideal situation for a child to come into the world is in a truly Torah-observant family, where all values are absolute and are dictated by the Torah. When the family's commitment to Torah is thorough and consistent, these values will permeate the entire home, and the child will experience not only the instinctual and the biological love of parents, but in addition the love that the family has for G-d and for Torah, and through them for him. Very early in life the child can sense that his parents consider him a gift from G-d, and as soon as his reason begins to develop and function, he can begin to understand that he is being raised for the predesignated goal for which he was brought into the world. The child's goal and the parents' goal are thus identical, and the parents are then in a position to make those decisions for and with the child that lead to achievement of that goal. When the parental goals and the child's goals are identical in all essential aspects, the incidence of conflict is greatly minimized, and even if the goals should diverge somewhat, they are likely to do so only in non-essential details.

One might ask: What about the fact that some Torah-observant families seem to have their fair share of parenting problems? Does this not disprove this theory?

Firstly, what we have postulated is that a Torah ambience in the home provides values and a philosophy of life which can serve as the background for application of effective parenting techniques. Both are essential for an optimum result. Mere application of techniques, even good techniques, in an environment where there are no clear goals or standards is somewhat akin to buying a radio with high-fidelity reception in the hope that it will improve the content of the programs. The failure of well-thought-out parenting techniques is often due to the absence of essential goals and direction within the home, and when the latter are present, then good parenting techniques can be very effective. But, by the same token, providing a conducive background does not in itself obviate the need for effective parenting techniques.

Secondly, G-d indeed assures us of His blessing for children in *Deuteronomy* 7:13. However, in 7:12, *Rashi* points out that this is contingent upon observing those *mitzvos* that people tend to trivialize, transgressions which are rationalized, such as *lashon hara*, questionable business practices, infringing upon the truth, and a host of others which some individuals may consider as acceptable and with which they may take liberties.

Let us be frank. Is it not possible that an observant parent returns from *shul* on Shabbos morning, and the talk at the Shabbos table may include gossip about some people, perhaps someone he met at *shul*? The children were taught that *lashon hara* is a grievous sin, yet they hear their parents transgressing this sin, which the Talmud equates to adultery, murder, and idolatry. The parents'

Torah observance thus becomes tainted, and may not command their children's respect.

The Talmud teaches that *derech eretz*, ethical and decent behavior, is a prerequisite for Torah. On Judgment Day a person will be asked, "Did you relate to G-d with appropriate respect?" and "Did you relate to other people with appropriate respect?" Both are given equal importance. Children who grow up in a household where *all* of Torah teachings are cherished and held sacred, where there is true love and reverence for both G-d and man, are much more likely to respond to the parenting techniques that Torah advocates.

The parent-child relationship can then be such that there would not be a need to depend on the coming of Elijah to "return the hearts of parents to their children and the hearts of children to their parents" (*Malachi* 3:24).

Chapter Two

Where to Begin

*P*arents who are concerned about how to best raise their children understandably ask, "What should I do?" Or, "How should I react to my child under particular circumstances?" When parents pose this question, it is only logical to try to answer the question with "Do thus and so." Unfortunately, too often even sound advice may fail to bring about the desired results.

The "How To" approach to parenting assumes that parenting is primarily a matter of "know-how." If only we knew the tricks of the trade we could raise healthy and well-adjusted children. But is a good parent really the one with the bigger bag of tricks? There is no doubt that having a larger repertoire of parenting strategies is helpful and allows a parent to be more flexible and therefore more effective. But to limit parenting to the accumulation of strategies and moves is to make a serious and costly error; namely, placing the entire emphasis and focus on the malleability of the child. This may be an incorrect emphasis.

It is unclear at exactly what stage in life children begin to absorb, and at what point they can be affected by parental training. There is a great deal of evidence that infants are highly impressionable, and it has been hypothesized that even in intra-uterine life the fetus can be affected emotionally as well as physically. Rabbi Samson Raphael Hirsch stated that training of a child should begin 20 years prior to his birth. What Rabbi Hirsch means is that the Talmudic principle, "Correct yourself and then correct others" (*Bava Metzia* 107b), applies to parenting as well to other relationships. *Healthy parenting should begin not with the focus on the child, but rather with the focus on oneself.*

This is a principle which is too often disregarded, as a recent incident demonstrated. I had attended a tribute luncheon for volunteers of an agency whose goal was to help elderly or sick "shut-ins," i.e., people who were widowed, who lived alone, and who — because of various physical limitations — were unable to get about. The volunteers were of all ages, from adolescence upward. They would go to these people's homes and take them to the supermarket for shopping, accompany them to their doctors' appointments, take them for a drive or a walk in the park, or perhaps just sit with them a bit and talk with them or play a game. The theme of this tribute event was "Doing Good Versus Feeling Good."

I was deeply moved by this group's activities, and it occurred to me that the population I encounter in my daily work, which involves treating alcoholics and drug addicts, are essentially victims of an attitude resulting from the incessant pursuit of "feeling good" as a goal in life, and when they do not achieve this desired goal in any other way, they turn to chemicals. I felt that if we could get people to change their priorities and make "doing good" their ultimate goal, we might actually prevent the development of these destructive addictions.

The very next day I met with a group of parents of youngsters who were in treatment for alcoholism and drug addiction, and being full of enthusiasm from my recent encounter with this volunteer group, I dwelt rather heavily on what I felt might be a key to attaining sobriety and to the prevention of addiction: adopting a philosophy of life where "doing good" was the ultimate purpose of living, rather than just trying to "feel good."

The following morning a staff therapist told me, "You really made a point with the parents last night. I overheard them talking among themselves, and one of them said, 'The doctor is right. We have to get our kids to start volunteering.' "

It was evident that the parents had not gotten the message at all. If the parents' goal in life remains pursuit of pleasure and getting as much fun out of life as reality will permit, then their children will follow suit, and may turn to alcohol or drugs for this pleasure. My point was not to get the *children* to volunteer, but for the *parents* to reevaluate their own goals and their own priorities. If the parents would establish for themselves a primary goal in life of "doing good" rather than just "feeling good," there is a greater likelihood that the children would emulate them. It is questionable whether children will do what their parents *say*, but it is far more likely that children do what they see their parents *do*.

There is a principle in Torah that the lives and actions of the patriarchs and matriarchs were meant to serve as a beacon to guide us in our lives. It is of interest that three of the matriarchs — Sarah, Rebecca, and Rachel — were childless for many years. The Midrash states that this was so because G-d wanted to hear their fervent prayers (*Yevamos* 64a). It is absurd to attribute to G-d the petty desire to be importuned. What the Midrash means is that there are levels of character development and spirituality which can be attained only through fervent prayer, and since the children that the matriarchs were to bring into the world were to become the fathers of the Jewish nation, who had to be of the highest degree of spirituality, their childbearing was delayed until they had reached the zenith of spirituality through their intense prayers.[1] It was the child of Sarah and Abraham, born to them after many decades of fervent prayers, who was willing to yield his life for the will of G-d.

While we are not entrusted with so awesome a responsibility of raising children to be like Isaac and Jacob, the message is nevertheless relevant. Our children will reflect what we are, and self-development is a prerequisite for optimum child development.

---

1. The matriarch Leah had elevated herself spiritually through intense prayers, as the Midrash relates, because she had assumed that she was destined to be the wife of Esau, and she tearfully prayed that she be spared this relationship (*Bava Basra* 123a).

It is not easy to make changes in oneself, and by the time we reach the age of being parents, we have already established many habits that are difficult to change and character traits that have been firmly ingrained into our personalities. Our children, however, are young and malleable, and we may therefore think that we can more easily mold them as we would like them to be, regardless of what we ourselves may be. While it is certainly true that children are indeed more flexible, the shaping of their personalities will result more from what we are and what we do rather than from what we say.

A distraught mother once asked a child psychologist what she could do to subdue her son's unrestrained behavior. She said that he was a terror at home, although when they went visiting, his behavior was much better. "I can't understand why he behaves one way at home and another way away from home." The psychologist responded, "Madam, don't you?"

Children are exquisitely sensitive and observant, and it is a serious mistake to think that we can put one over on them. If parents distort the truth, children are aware of this and may follow suit. If parents procrastinate or shirk their responsibilities, they should not be surprised when the children do so. If parents refuse to admit to having made mistakes and instead rationalize their behavior, they can be sure that their children will do likewise. If parents return from their offices and say, "Phew, what a day! Just got to have a drink," or if they frequently turn to valium or similar tranquilizers for relief of tension, they should understand that their children are getting the message that one relieves discomfort by means of chemicals. This provides fertile grounds for development of chemical use by children when they feel in any way distressed.

Osmosis is a powerful force, and attitudes of self-esteem, self-confidence, and trust are absorbed from the atmosphere within the home. Children of parents who have a healthy self-esteem are likely to feel positive about themselves. Children of parents who have feelings of inadequacy and inferiority are more likely to be anxious and insecure. They may adopt some of the parents' feelings of inferiority, or any of the various methods their parents have used to escape from these feelings of unworthiness, or any defenses other than those employed by the parents.

In addition to intrapsychic factors in each individual parent, the relationship between parents also serves as a model for the child's relationship with others. When parents set aside their own comfort and preference in deference to the spouse, children learn how to be accommodating. Parents who sincerely respect one another and treat each other with dignity are providing the raw materials for the development of constructive character traits within the child. As a whole, children are likely to adopt values that are espoused by the parents.

While this principle is generally valid, it would nevertheless be a mistake for parents to be overly self-critical when their children do not behave properly. It has happened that parents who are diligent may have offspring who are indolent, and parents who never touched a chemical may have an addicted child. In general, however, children are strongly influenced by parental behavior, and the principle is therefore sound. The most effective way of eliminating the probability of undesirable traits in children is for parents not to have them.

In the computer age we have come to believe that we can feed data into a machine, push a button, and obtain a printout. Even automobile mechanics can hook the engine up to a computer and get a printout of what is wrong. We may think that if we feed all the information into a computer, we can get a printout about how to manage our children or to raise them most effectively. This cannot be done with children. While we will present some suggestions in this book, you will not get the equivalent of a printout.

There is room for some specific suggestions, and the title of this chapter is therefore "Where to *begin*." While we may recommend some ways in which to relate to children, the beginning should be with oneself, because even constructive recommendations can be effective only if they emanate from healthy parental attitudes. Rejecting this approach and jumping to manipulation of children is most often of little value.

Chapter Three

Who Is This Little Person?

*I*n the Talmud there is a lively discussion whether an unborn fetus is considered an independent being or a part of the mother's body. However, there is no question that once he is delivered he is very much an independent being. Parents, for emotional reasons of their own, may consider the child to be an extension of themselves, but in the child's mind there is no doubt whatever that he is an independent being. Even if we concede to the psychological theory that the newborn infant does not yet grasp reality boundaries and does not know where he ends and where his mother begins, this is at best a transitory state, and he very soon comes to the realization that he is an independent, albeit not self-sufficient entity.

It is extremely important for parents to be aware of the sensitivity of children. Long before they can communicate verbally, children are exquisite receptors of body language and of attitudes in their surroundings, even if they have no way of translating these concepts into words.

Bear in mind that although during his lifetime the newborn will produce many trillions of cells in bone, liver, skin, muscle, blood, and other tissues, never, but never, will he produce even one additional brain cell. The newborn infant has the same 14½-billion brain cells as the mature adult. In contrast to the adult, these cells are not engaged with a massive amount of data, and are readily available to focus on whatever is at hand. Hence the infant can detect minute changes that would slip by a mature adult. When in the company of an infant, remember, everything registers on him. In the nuclear family, the *most* sensitive person is the infant. This is a crucial point to remember.

This little person is an entity all his own. He does indeed have genetic material from both parents, but this is a situation where $1+1=X$, a totally unknown quantity, whose nature will not be evident for some time. He is a person of immense potential, and is indeed very malleable. However, parents should not mistake malleability for controllability. Parents certainly can exert a great deal of influence and can provide factors which can help direct the child's growth and development, but they do not have absolute control.

At the center of parenting is the ability to be *empathic*. Empathy refers to the ability to see things from another person's perspective and to temporarily suspend one's own standpoint.

Why is empathy so critical in good parenting? It may be helpful to demonstrate this by use of an extreme example. The problem with abusive parents is often that they are unable to be empathic. They may see a crying baby as being disobedient, as if he is ungrateful and intentionally trying to upset them. We can see this tendency even in competent parents when they are extremely exhausted or overly stressed. Under such circumstances there is a failure of empathy and a tendency to personalize the child's conduct (actions); i.e., the parents may feel as if he is misbehaving on purpose.

Empathy is a thought process that requires making an inference. The mother looking at the crying baby has to make an inference, to guess why her child is inconsolable. Research has shown that competent mothers are good at guessing, and they command a repertoire of guesses based on their knowledge of babies in general and this baby in particular. The mother may change the baby's diaper, and if this does not help, she may assume that the last feeding was not sufficient. Based on her knowledge of the baby's personality and her past history with the baby, the mother will be able to generate a number of other interventions and explanations, one of which may be that the baby is tired and is crying himself to sleep. Because the mother is "empathic," i.e., tries to see things from the infant's point of view, she does not make the drastic mistake of the abusive parent, and is able to soothe her baby and take care of him in a reasonable fashion. The father of a large family mentioned to me that with their 10th child, he and his wife had to alternate nights holding the baby for the whole first year of her life. She was extremely cranky and would not settle down like their other children had. This busy mother and father were able to give this child what she needed without undue resentment because they were able to "read" the child's needs. Their empathy provided the foundation for competent parenting. The little girl eventually outgrew her crankiness and is today a lovely, sensitive child.

Not all children are equally easy to raise. Some children are more difficult, more taxing, and more demanding. Their style of interacting with the world is less balanced, more easily prone to disruptions, and they are less easily quieted. This is what we mean when we talk about individual differences in temperament; i.e., precisely such stylistic differences, all of which are within the broad spectrum that comprises "normalcy." Some babies can sleep through an earthquake, whereas others wake up at the slightest sound. For some, waiting for their bottle is relatively easy, while others seem to experience hunger with such intensity that there is barely time to warm up the formula. The more demanding children are sometimes referred to as "difficult" children.

Referring to a child as "difficult" puts the weight solely on the child. This label also fails to reflect that raising this "difficult" child is a two-way street. The problem of "difficulty" is not totally inherent within the child. The parent who is able to rise to this occasion can complement the child so that together they can form a functional duo. It is the match of parent and child that is important, and if the parent cannot empathize with the child, they form a dysfunctional duo.

Of course, the question of the nature of the child and the task posed to the parent becomes more intense when a child is born with health problems, developmental abnormalities, or later in life exhibits conditions that are out of the ordinary.

Empathy is more than a simple strategy, and refers to a state of mind that allows for competent parenting. In the previous chapter we discussed the difference between ego involvement versus self-investment. Investing oneself into the child requires the ability to be empathic. Having the right understanding of the child by putting ourselves into his shoes allows us to temporarily suspend our own needs. Lack of empathy may result in seeing children as an extension of ourselves; i.e., what I like, they must like; if I am hungry, they are hungry, or in treating them primarily as a means to fulfill our own needs.

Some psychologists used to consider infants as empty slates upon which parents and experience would engrave their marks. This is not true. An infant is by no means an empty slate, but a little person with thoughts, feelings, and perceptions. Empathic parents understand this, and try to put themselves in the child's position, to see things through his eyes.

Empathy does not mean that parents must give children everything they want. Parents may have to refuse children, but they should nevertheless try to understand them.

Let us now focus on the responsibilities of parents towards their child. Clearly, they are to provide him with the means to survive, and the necessary training and education to make an optimum adjustment to reality. Parents must understand that reality is what it is, and not necessarily what they would like it to be. Reality has many undesirable things, with which the child must be helped to cope. An ideal world would not have diphtheria, whooping cough, lockjaw, polio, and measles, but since the real world does have these, parents have the responsibility to immunize their child against these diseases. The immunization may be painful, with the sharp prick of the needle followed by two days of tenderness and fever, but this discomfort must be borne if the child is to be spared from crippling diseases.

Immunization represents a prototype of what will confront parents in the child's growth. A correct assessment of reality necessitates adequate preparation for coping with some of the harshness of reality. Because of their intense love for the child, parents may try to spare him from various distresses and discomforts, but such kindnesses may backfire. If parents fail to provide the requisite training for the actualities of life because they wish to protect the child from all distress, the results can be every bit as grave as if they forgo immunization because they wish to spare him the painful injection and the 48 hours of reaction to the vaccine.

Obviously, exposure to difficult situations and fostering the courage and the strength to deal with them must come at the appropriate time. Demanding something from the child at a stage where he is physically and/or emotionally incapable of delivering is a serious error and can undermine the child's faith in himself, as he fails at what is expected of him. By the same token, overprotection precludes development of coping skills.

As a child grows and begins to change from the totally self-centered infant to a youngster who must interact with others, situations arise which the young child does not yet know how to handle. For example, the child has candy or toys, and his infantile tendency is to keep them for himself. If he is to become a social being, he must learn how to give and share. Or perhaps someone else has something which the child desires. The young child does not know right from wrong, and he may try to take it away from another child. This is incompatible with living in society. The parents must begin to teach the child basic social skills.

To adults, taking things away from someone else is wrong, and it is conceivable that parents may scold the child, "Don't take Moshe's things away from him!" This reprimand would be appropriate if the child had already learned that this is wrong, but in the early stages the child is merely following the infantile acquisitive urge. The parents may scold him for refusing to share with friends and siblings, because they consider this as selfish. But how is the child to know that such selfishness is wrong?

Sharing one's belongings with others and not taking things away from others are not inborn traits. To the contrary, they are the direct opposite of the innate selfish and acquisitive drives. The child must be trained to modify these drives, to respect others' belongings, and to give of one's things to others. We may use this as a prototype for various other traits which parents must help the child develop.

We have already established that simply telling a child, "You must share," is likely to be futile, and reprimanding him for not sharing or for taking things from others when he does not yet know this is wrong can cause him to feel he is bad, although he may not understand why. When the child is rebuked and does not comprehend why, he may develop *shame*, feeling that he is inherently bad. How, then, should parents teach a child about sharing?

As we have noted earlier, parents teach most effectively by example. If a collector from a charitable institution is turned away empty-handed, or if he is given a few dollars grudgingly and after he leaves, one parent says to the other, "I can't stand these *schnorrers*, living like parasites off my hard-earned money. I don't like them imposing upon me," they might as well forget about teaching the child how to share. If, however, the collector is invited into the house, and offered a cup of coffee or a cold drink and given the donation with a smile in recognition of the importance of his fundraising, a significant message has been conveyed.

Performing the *mitzvos* of *gemillus chassadim* (acts of kindness) including *tzedakah* (charity) and *hachnassas orchim* (hospitality), and doing so with the joy that one has the opportunity to fulfill the Divine will, establishes a value system that the child is likely to incorporate. Let us remember the exquisite sensitivity of the young child who is not apt to be deceived by words and will detect the underlying feeling. A positive attitude towards these *mitzvos* on the part of the parents will carry over to the child. If we resent the charity collector, the child will detect it, and if parents then urge the child to share, he will be receiving a conflicting message. Such messages are not only confusing to the child, but they also undermine his trust in the parents. If the child receives a double message, one overt and the other covert, and determines that what the parents say is different than what they think and feel, the child cannot develop the basic trust that is essential not only for all aspects of successful parenting, but also for virtually all subsequent interpersonal relationships.

Infants begin to learn trust when parents respond to their cry for food or for relief from the discomfort of a wet diaper. These rudiments of trust need to be nurtured as the child grows. There will be plenty of time to teach him the appropriate limitations of trust, and that one must not be naive and credulous, but unless trust is carefully cultivated, it will be stunted, and an inadequate sense of trust may manifest itself years later in various interpersonal relationships, such as inability to love, distrust of superiors, and lack of respect for authority.

The little person must be taught values, and parents should consider this as vital a role as their providing food and shelter. Assuming that the parents have these values, there are ways of transmitting them other than didactically. Fulfilling the *mitzvos* that incorporate these values is one way.

I remember, as a very small child, hearing my father relate stories about our great Torah personalities, whose lives serve as the ideals which one should seek to emulate, and to aspire to their character traits, even if we cannot fully achieve them. I do not recall a Shabbos meal at which there were not several guests, often itinerant rabbis who solicited for charities. Their being at our home was a lesson, and the stories my father related at the Shabbos table reinforced these principles.

For example, my father would tell of the extraordinary selflessness of some of our great personalities. He told of one *tzaddik* who gave money to a poverty-stricken family, then returned later to make a second donation, explaining: "When I saw the poverty in the home, my heart ached, especially for the children who were so scantily clad and appeared underfed. When I gave my first donation, it was to relieve my pain at their suffering. I later realized that I had not given the money to fulfill the Divine *mitzvah* of *tzedakah*, but rather to assuage my own discomfort. I therefore went back and gave more, this time to fulfill the *mitzvah*." I distinctly recall hearing this and many other similar stories when I was five, and although I cannot recall hearing them at age two, I am sure that I did. My parents thus conveyed one of their most cherished values, not only by their manifest conduct, but also by the potent medium of stories which reinforced these values. Sincere practice of values and the embellishment of these through stories is a powerful training technique.

There are various charming allegories, such as those of the Maggid of Dubno and folk tales that are both amusing and inspiring.

For example, there is a story that I often heard at bedtime in my childhood. There was a stonecutter who earned his livelihood by hewing out rocks from the mountain. This was backbreaking, as well as spirit-breaking work, and he would often bewail his fate. "Why was I destined to be so lowly and humble? Why are some other people so wealthy and mighty, while I break my bones every day from dawn to dusk to put bread on my table?"

One day, as he was engaged in this reverie, he heard a loud tumult in the distance. He climbed to the top of the mountain, and from afar could see a parade. The king was passing by, and on either side of the road, there were throngs of people shouting, "Bravo," and throwing flowers at the royal coach.

"How wonderful it must be to be great and powerful," the stonecutter said. "I wish that I could be king."

The stonecutter did not know that this happened to be his moment of grace, when his wishes would be granted. He suddenly found himself transformed. He was no longer a stonecutter. He was the king, sitting in the royal coach drawn by white horses, and receiving the acclaim of the crowd. "How wonderful it is to be the mightiest in all the land!"

After a bit, he began to feel uncomfortable. The bright sun was shining down on him, making him sweat and squirm in his royal robes. "What is this?" he said. "If I am the mightiest in the land, then nothing should be able to affect me. If the sun can humble me, then the sun is mightier than I. But I wish to be the mightiest of all! I wish to be the sun."

Immediately, he was transformed into the sun. He felt his mighty, unparalleled force of energy. He could give light and warmth to everything in the world. He could provide warmth when he so wished or devastating fires when he was angry. "I am indeed the mightiest of all," he said.

But suddenly he found himself very frustrated. A great cloud had moved beneath him and obstructed his rays. "Here, here!" he said. "If I am the mightiest, then nothing should be able to hinder me. If a cloud can frustrate the sun, then the cloud is mightier, yet I wish to be the mightiest. I wish to be a cloud!"

As a great, heavy cloud, he felt very powerful, dumping torrents of rain wherever he wished, and particularly when he blocked the mighty sun. But his joy was short lived, for suddenly, he was swooped away by a sharp gust of wind.

"Aha!" he cried. "The wind is even mightier than a cloud! Then I shall be the wind."

Transformed into the wind, he roared over oceans, churning immense waves. He blew over forests, toppling tall trees as if they were toothpicks. "Now I am truly the mightiest," he said.

But suddenly, he felt himself stymied. He had come up against a tall mountain, and blow as he might, he could not get past. "So," he said, "a mountain is mightier than the wind! Then I wish to be a mountain."

As a tall mountain, he stood majestically, his peak reaching above the cloud. He was indeed formidable. Neither wind nor sun could affect him. Now he was indeed the mightiest.

All at once he felt a sharp pain. What was this? A stone-cutter, with a sharp pickax, was tearing pieces out of him. "How can this be?" he asked. "If someone can dismember me, then he must be even mightier than I. *I wish to be that man.*" His wish was granted, and he was transformed into the mightiest of all: a stonecutter.

It can be pointed out to the child that some people think that others are better off and happier than they are, and they therefore wish to be something else. But the fact is that being something else will not be more satisfying than what someone already is, and that while one should try to improve things for oneself, being some-thing different is not necessarily going to make one happy. A similar message can be conveyed by the charming story of Itzik Reb Yekale's.

In Cracow, there stands a synagogue known as "The Synagogue of Itzik the son of Reb Yekale." The story goes that Itzik was a peas-ant who had a recurring dream. Again and again he dreamed that under a particular bridge in Prague there lay buried a huge treasure, which would belong to anyone who unearthed it. At first Itzik dismissed the dream as an absurdity, but after numerous repetitions he began to take it more seriously. Yet the whole thing was so preposterous. How could Itzik, who did not have two copper coins to rub together, get to Prague? But the obsession gave him no rest, and although his wife told him to get the crazy idea out of his head, he decided once and for all that he must go to Prague and find the treasure. So, one day, he took some meager provisions and set out for Prague.

When Itzik was fortunate enough to hitch a ride on a passing wagon, he rode. Otherwise, he hiked.

After many weeks, Itzik arrived at Prague, and sought out the bridge he had envisioned in his dream. But alas, there were always police patrolling the area, and there was no way he could begin to dig.

Day after day, he loitered around the bridge, hoping that perhaps there would be a break in the patrol, and he would be able to dig for the treasure. Finally one of the police patrols approached him. "Why are you constantly loitering around this area day after day?" the policeman asked. "What is it that you want here?"

Itzik saw no other way than to simply tell the truth. He related his dream to the policeman, and also the weeks of travail until he came to Prague from his humble village near Cracow.

The policeman howled with laughter. "You fool!" he said. "And because of a silly dream you came all the way here? Well, I have had a recurring dream, too. I have been dreaming that in a tiny village near Cracow, there is a little hut that belongs to a peasant named Itzik the son of Reb Yekale, and that under the floor of that hut there lays buried an immense treasure."

The story goes that Itzik immediately returned home from Prague, and upon digging up the earthen floor of his hut, discovered an immense treasure. The Synagogue of Itzik the son of Reb Yekale's was built with part of this fortune.

Many people look for wealth elsewhere. They search for wealth of all kings, but especially for the greatest wealth of all: happiness. They think that it is to be found elsewhere, and they expend enormous energies to search it out. Little do they know that the happiness they seek lies right within themselves. No need to travel long distances or to work in foreign territories. It is there at one's fingertips, right within one's self. One only has to believe this and to look within.

Here, too, the message is that happiness lies within oneself, and that it is a mistake to look for it elsewhere.

Earlier we referred to the great Talmudic sage Rabbi Akiva, and children can be told how he was inspired at the age of 40 to begin to study Torah by his observations of a hole in a rock that had been formed by the constant drop of water from above. "If something as hard as a rock can be impressed by water, then certainly my heart can be impressed by Torah." Thus, although Rabbi Akiva was virtually illiterate at age 40, he began the study of the *aleph-beis,* eventually becoming the leading scholar of his time.

Children can be strengthened in their faith as they hear how blessings of our great *tzaddikim* were fulfilled. There is the story of the Gaon of Vilna.

One time the Gaon was sitting in the *sukkah* engrossed in his study of Torah when a man walked in to greet him on the festival. The Gaon was so absorbed that he was unaware of the man's presence. After waiting some time and still not being acknowledged, the man left, and on a subsequent occasion asked the Gaon what he had done that caused the Gaon to ignore him.

The Gaon was deeply affected. "Ignore you? My dear friend, why would I wish to ignore you?" And the Gaon apologized profusely, explaining that he had not been aware of the man's presence because of his preoccupation with his study. "Please forgive me," the Gaon said, "and I bless you to live 100 years."

The man did indeed live to be 100. When he was 98, he fell ill but refused the services of a doctor. "I know I will recover," he said, "because the Gaon promised me 100 years, and I know I shall not fall short by even a single day." He died on his 100th birthday.

As with learning to share, so it is with many other character traits that parents wish to cultivate in the child: tolerance, self-restraint, patience, cooperation, forgiveness, respect, etc. The parents must first exemplify these traits *in their own behavior,* then find ways whereby to reinforce it in the child. All the techniques for reinforcement can be effective only if there is something to reinforce; i.e., the parents' own attitudes. All the reinforcement techniques are of little value if the child does not see them operative in the parents. Parents who lose control of their anger cannot expect their teaching the child not to go into a rage when provoked to be effective.

There is a beautiful tradition of displaying a *Shir LaMaalos*, the 121st psalm, near a newborn infant's crib, so that as the infant's eyes begin to focus, he immediately sees the letters of the Torah. First impressions are indeed important, but they must be followed up if they are to have any influence. Parents who wish the child to develop Torah values should begin cultivating them right from the start.

I am amazed at the children's rhymes which prevail in the secular world. The content of some of them is simply insipid and foolish, while others contain overtly negative values. These are a far cry from the traditional lullaby which generations of Jewish mothers and grandmothers sang to infants, "*Rozhinkes mit Mandlen*." These verses taught that although raisins and almonds are sweet and precious, Torah is by far superior, and therefore little Yankele or Estherel will learn much Torah and grow up to be good, pious Jews.

As children grow up, the secular juvenile literature is nothing less than alarming: little children lost in the woods, captured by a mean witch who intends to eat them, and they escape by pushing her into the oven; a wolf who locks up a grandmother and threatens to eat a little girl, who is saved at the last minute by a passing woodsman who hacks the wolf to bits with his ax; a wicked stepmother who is envious of her pretty stepdaughter and poisons her. What do parents who read these gruesome tales to little tots expect their children to dream about?

There are now many fine juvenile books in Judaica shops that promote desirable character traits, and these can be used to entertain children or lull them to sleep. As mentioned, there are volumes of anecdotes about our great Torah personalities, and appropriate stories can be used at bedtime or related at the Shabbos table. At the risk of annoying redundance, I must state that all of these are effective when they are supportive of the parental attitudes. Rabbi Samson Raphael Hirsch was eminently correct when he said that child training should begin 20 years before the birth of the child.

The Torah states that Eve was punished for her sin with the distresses of labor pains and of raising children (*Genesis* 3:16). Yet it is possible to minimize this suffering, and just as it is halachically permissible to use medications and other techniques to minimize labor pains, so it is permissible to seek techniques to minimize the distress of raising children. While it may not be feasible to totally eliminate the latter distress, the suggestions in this book may provide some relief. However, while the suffering of immunization is largely borne by the infant, the inconveniences inherent in child rearing are shared by both parent and child. The suggestions in this book will hopefully yield long-term benefits, but will require at least some short-term inconveniences.

Section II

Jewish Children: Fundamentals Of Curriculum

Chapter Four

Education Towards Midos and Mitzvos

*A*s was indicated earlier, the birth of a child represents a dual gift. The Torah family brings the child into the world in fulfillment of the *mitzvah* to procreate, and accepts the child as G-d's gift to them. A person receiving a gift from the king would be highly honored if the king presented him with a gift, regardless of what the gift is. If it is a fine jewel, there would be the additional joy of being in possession of something so beautiful and valuable. If it was an object of lesser beauty and value, one would still be honored to be a recipient of a gift from the king. If we truly believe our children to be Divine gifts, then we should value them as such.

The Torah attitude toward children goes even beyond this. The first child born was Cain, whose parents were Adam and Eve. The

Torah states that Eve named the child Cain because this name is derived from the Hebrew word *kanisi*, "I acquired," and Eve's words were, "I acquired a child with G-d" (*Genesis* 4:1). Ramban explains that following their sin, Adam and Eve realized that they were mortal and that their lives on earth were limited. In giving birth to a child, Eve said, "I have acquired a child from G-d, to replace me and continue to serve Him when I am no longer living." According to this, a child is not only a gift from G-d to man, but is also a gift from man to G-d.

A child is thus extremely unique, being both a gift from G-d and a gift to G-d. This was eloquently expressed by Hannah, who named her child Samuel, "because I have asked him (or borrowed him) of G-d" (*I Samuel* 1:20), and later added, "I have lent him to G-d" (ibid. v. 28). The parents' duty is thus to love and care for the child as a gift from G-d, and to raise him so that his life will be a gift to G-d. This perspective requires a different set of rules for parenting than that which prevails in the secular world.

Perhaps we cannot aspire to the high level of spirituality of Hannah, who, after being childless for so many years and being so desperate to gratify her maternal instincts, nevertheless took the child to the Sanctuary at a very tender age, and dedicated him to the service of G-d. No doubt the separation from her beloved child must have been extremely difficult, but her personal needs did not enter into the equation. No one would have blamed her had she kept her only child at home, if not forever, at least until he matured. But had she done so, Judaism would have been deprived of one of its greatest prophets.

Even if we cannot equal the spirituality of Hannah, it should serve as an inspiration for us. The more we emphasize the goal of the child in this world in terms other than of how much *nachas* he will provide for us, the more like Samuel will the child be. But then, if we are to consider the goal of the child's life as being the fulfillment of the Divine will, that must be the goal of the parents' lives as well.

I wonder how often parents have consciously thought, "What qualities do I wish to develop in my child?" I have no doubt whatever that parents wish to develop the finest qualities in their children, and while I do not question this in the least, I nevertheless ask: How much *conscious* thought have they given to this? What are these finest qualities, and how should one go about developing them? Perhaps it is something we just take for granted.

There is a precedent for my concern about this. Rabbi Moshe Chaim Luzatto in the introduction to his monumental work, *Path of the Just*, points out that there is universal agreement on the primacy of belief in G-d, love of G-d, reverence for G-d, and all the desirable character attributes, but that precisely because everyone is so convinced of the importance of these, it rarely occurs to people that these concepts have to be analyzed and understood. What does it mean to love G-d? What is reverence for G-d? What are the desirable character attributes, and how does one go about developing them? Since all these are hardly innate and require development, how are they to be developed if one does not give them proper thought and planning?

We may take the same approach toward the character development of our children. Just what are the traits that we wish them to acquire and how should we go about helping our children acquire them? We will have little difficulty in rattling off a list of desirable and undesirable character traits, but can we simply assume that our children will spontaneously develop the former and avoid the latter? Can we sit back and rely on the environment to shape our children's characters? Is this something we can entrust to the school?

We may come up with different answers to these questions, but we will not come up with any answers unless we think about them. I suspect that too often these vital subjects receive far too little attention.

The Torah tells us that we are to cleave unto G-d (*Deuteronomy* 30:20) and that this should be the ultimate goal of every Jew. The Talmud and the ethical writings state that for a finite mortal to identify with the infinite G-d would actually be impossible, and is made possible only by the vehicle which G-d Himself provided, which is that a person must emulate the Divine attributes to be merciful, loving, patient, forgiving, truthful, etc.

Unity with G-d is possible because each person has a *neshamah*, a soul which is part of G-d Himself. The separation from G-d occurs only because the *neshamah* is contained within a physical body, whose cravings and strivings are antithetical to the Divine attributes. The physical body is selfish, and in pursuit of its desires may cause a person to act with lust, greed, envy, and hostility. It is these characteristics that comprise a barrier which prevents the unity between man and G-d.

A person must therefore strive to overcome these physical tendencies, to eliminate the barrier that precludes identifying with G-d, and his *neshamah* will then, by its very essence, be attracted to its Divine source. The Scriptures state that the human *neshamah* is like the flame of a candle (*Proverbs* 20:27), and our ethicists explain this simile to mean that just as when we hold a candle near a large flame, the flame of the candle is attracted to the greater flame, so is the *neshamah* attracted to its Divine source, and seeks to be absorbed within it, something which could be achieved if the barrier between it and the source was eliminated.

For the Torah Jew, enabling the *neshamah* to reunite with G-d's should be the goal in life for oneself and for one's children. Each child given to us is a *neshamah*, contained within a physical body. The young child lacks the capacity to understand and appreciate the ultimate goal, just as he lacks the capacity to understand what are the essential nutrients and necessary provisions for maintaining physical health. It is therefore the parents' responsibility to provide the young child with the means that will enable him to reach the ultimate goal.

If one were pressed to answer philosophical questions about the purpose of life, the Torah Jew would undoubtedly essentially come to these conclusions. As Luzatto says, it is not that we do not believe, but that we take too much for granted, and do not consciously think, hence we may fail to adopt the methodology that makes possible the achievement of our goals for ourselves and for our children.

Loving parents tenderly care for the child: feed him, clothe him, bathe him, caress him, and make certain that he receives the necessary health care — all things that will provide for an optimum of physical and emotional well-being. And yes, they provide the education including the requisite Torah education for the child. But how often do we as parents consciously think, "Am I doing the utmost to enable my child to achieve the optimum in spirituality? What should

I be doing to help the child reach this ultimate goal, of allowing his *neshamah* to unite with G-d?"

The beautiful prayer with which we start each day is, "My G-d, the *neshamah* You have placed within me is pure." This statement serves to alert us that we must live the day in such a manner that the purity of the *neshamah* not be negatively affected by our behavior. As parents, we should think of our children in the same way. Each child is a *neshamah*, and it is our responsibility to cultivate that *neshamah* properly and to make certain that it retains its purity.

Parents often daydream about what they would like their children to achieve: wealth, honor, fame. They may exert themselves to help realize these dreams for their children, and when the child is yet an infant, the parents may begin to put away money for his higher education two decades in the future. This can be justified if it is seen as contributing toward the ultimate goal, but would we not be less than truthful if we did not admit that the thought of our children's true ultimate goal does not enter our minds and our daydreams quite as often?

Luzatto was so right. He advocates repeatedly reviewing his book, because our absorption in our daily tasks of living costs us to lose sight of our ultimate goal. Torah-observant Jews who are inspired by spiritual goals may indeed study *mussar* and re-read *Path of the Just* occasionally. But even those who do so may be thinking primarily how to further their own spiritual growth, rather than that of their children as well. Perhaps we should study *Path of the Just* again, this time with the focus of applying its teachings in a manner that will enable our children to achieve their ultimate goal in life.

A healthy self-esteem is an essential pre-condition for spiritual growth and character development. The elimination of the barriers between the *neshamah* and its source is not at all a simple task. To the contrary, it is a major challenge, and the child must have the self-confidence that he can achieve it. Many of the suggestions about quality parenting that are mentioned in this book relate to self-esteem elevation, but let us first examine this concept a bit more closely.

In order for a child to reach a goal, any goal, he must feel that he is capable of doing so. If a child lacks confidence in himself, he will not attempt to master any situation or strive for any goals. "What's the use?" he may say, and will resign himself to an existence where he is carried along by the tide, whichever way that may take him.

For a proper understanding of self-esteem, we should note the words of the great ethicist, Rabbi Yeruchem Levovitz. "Woe to the person who does not recognize his defects, because he does not know what he needs to correct. But far worse off is the person who does not recognize his capabilities and talents, who is not even aware of the tools he has with which to effect any changes in himself."

Because all the great ethical works emphasize humility and self-effacement as the fundamental character trait that a person should possess, it is important to note the words of the ethicist Rabbi Leib Chasman. "A person who does not recognize his capabilities and strengths is not a humble person, but rather a fool. A humble person is one who is fully aware of his capabilities and strengths, and knows that these are Divine gifts to him that he must utilize in reaching the true goal in his life. The more one is aware of these capabilities and strengths, the more humble he becomes as he realizes how relatively little he has accomplished with these Divine gifts."

From the statements of these two ethicists, we see that self-esteem, properly defined (I elaborated on this theme in *Let Us Make Man*, CIS 1989), is not the vanity that is condemned in all Torah literature. To the contrary, self-esteem consists of an awareness of one's potential and abilities, and it is this awareness that empowers a person to conduct the struggle involved in reaching one's goal. The Torah states that "Man was created to toil" (*Job* 5:7), and the commentaries explain that this refers to the enormous efforts one must expend to overcome the lures of the *yetzer hara* (evil inclination) to indulge in physical gratifications. Development of the character traits that Torah requires presents a formidable struggle, and success in this struggle depends on man's confidence that one can triumph. The goal of life cannot be achieved by coasting along, and from the very earliest years in life a child should be helped to build the self-confidence that will encourage him to make the necessary effort. There are many hurdles to overcome en route to both intermediate goals and the ultimate goal, and each challenge will require confidence in oneself. It has been aptly said, "Give a child self-esteem and you have given him everything. If you fail to give him self-esteem, you have given him nothing."

In *Life's Too Short* (St. Martin's Press 1995) I pointed out some sources and contributing factors for low self-esteem. Suffice it here to say that many children begin life with unwarranted feelings of inadequacy and inferiority, and that parents should be aware that they must do everything possible to enhance self-esteem and assiduously avoid anything which may depress the child's self-esteem. Throughout the chapters in this book you will note that in discussing parent-child relationships great emphasis is placed on acting toward children in a manner that is most conducive to self-esteem enhancement.

For example, we will note how caring parents may try to help a child solve his problem, but in spite of their good intentions, they may actually be depriving the child of an opportunity to enhance his self-esteem.

Notti is an 11-year-old boy who comes home spewing anger at his teacher. "I'm never going back into that class again. You know what Mr. Phillips did? I raised my hand and answered a question, and he said that was the dumbest answer he ever heard in his life. All the kids laughed, and at recess they called me 'the dumb kid.'"

His mother and father may react with righteous indignation. "He said that to you and humiliated you in front of the class? I'll talk to the principal about that tomorrow morning. We're not going to have teachers like that in our school. We'll see to it that he is kicked out."

Notti may be gratified because his parents have come to his rescue. Assuming that the teacher did indeed make a foolish comment, the parents' promise to have him fired does nothing for Notti's long-term welfare. Are the parents going to intervene 20 years later when Notti's supervisor at work mistreats their son? Notti has not gained in self-confidence by his parents taking up the cudgel in his behalf. (This of course does not preclude the parent discussing the incompetence of the teacher with the principal. However, this is not Notti's concern.)

Suppose, however, that his father responded to Notti's complaint with, "Boy, you sure got yourself a humdinger of a teacher this year."

"Yeah, he's a real dope. He's done that to other kids too."

"Makes you angry to have a teacher like that."

"He's terrible. None of the kids like him."

"Well, there are a lot of good teachers in the school, and a few bad ones. Things haven't changed much since I was in school."

"What did you do if you had a bad teacher?"

"There was nothing I could do. I tried to learn the best I could, and waited it out until next semester."

"Yeah, I guess I'll have to do that too. I don't think that the other kids take him seriously. He's done that to them too."

His father did not provide a solution, and Notti came to a realization on his own that he can withstand the ineptitude of a teacher and even the jibes of his peers.

We often hear that if you love your children, that is really all that counts. It is certainly axiomatic that parental love is crucial for a child's healthy personality development, and perhaps comprises the lion's share of self-esteem development. But even love may not be enough. At the very least, we must analyze and understand what it is to truly love a child. Caressing and kissing a child are certainly important positive emotional inputs, but love does not stop there. Love requires preparing the child for life, and this may sometimes require harsh discipline. Love may require being extremely sensitive to the child's needs, which may not be readily apparent. Love may demand a great deal of parental restraint, so that a child's provocation of parental anger should be responded to constructively.

Parenting thus turns out to be, at the very least, a full-time job. Even at times when we are not engaged in a direct relationship with our children, we may have to give some forethought as to how we will relate to various eventualities.

Just as a child tends to emulate parental character traits, so it is with self-esteem. Parents who feel secure and are self-confident are likely to pass these feelings on to their children. Parents who are insecure and anxious may transmit these feelings to their children.

For example, the downsizing in industry that has resulted in many layoffs has been a source of anxiety to many families. The father may consider himself to be in a vulnerable position, which may result in much anxiety. Parents may think that allowing the children to share in this will provoke unease in them, and that it is best to shield them from this. However, the efforts at concealment may be futile, because children do pick up the vibes of anxiety and insecurity in their parents.

Loss of a job can indeed be devastating, yet it is a fact of life. Let's take the focus off the children and turn to the parents. How should parents cope with this stress?

Parents who can come around to realizing that somehow people have adjusted to such stresses, and that life has gone on albeit with some difficulties, who feel more secure in their own skills that they will find something, and who have a faith that G-d will not abandon them, will react with far less anxiety. At an appropriate time, when the subject is in the news or when some comment opens the door for a remark, the father may say, "That could happen to anyone. No one has a guarantee these days. But I'm no slouch. If anything were to happen to my job, I'll eventually get another or do something else. Hashem cares for all of us, and we will never go without food on the table."

It is thus paramount that we turn our attention to ourselves and improve our own self-esteem. In *Life's Too Short* I indicated how a person may discover that he is lacking self-esteem, and presented some ideas on how to improve self-esteem. This is important for ourselves, and will pay rich dividends in our fostering self-esteem in our children.

Chapter Five

Self-Esteem —
What Is It Really

W e all have a notion about what self-esteem is, but notions may be vague and may even be incorrect, so let us try and define the term a bit more accurately.

Although I am inclined to explain this concept in positive terms rather than negative ones, I feel that in this case a good way to avoid a conceptual error is by stating what self-esteem is *not*. Some people may have the idea that self-esteem means "feeling good." In western civilization, where so much emphasis is placed on feeling good and so many people believe that the ideal goal in life is to achieve a constant good feeling, self-esteem may be equated with success in this endeavor. If one has not "made it" in life, one is deprived of the basic ingredient of self-esteem.

Of course, if it were true that to have self-esteem means to feel good, I suppose we would have to put at the top of the self-esteem pyramid the heroin or cocaine addict who feel euphoric, and that at least for the duration of the chemical effect, he is experiencing self-esteem at a very high level. Inasmuch as this is patently absurd, we will have to look for other definitions of self-esteem. Merely to substitute a non-destructive way of feeling good for the narcotic euphoria is not enough. We will probably agree that whereas the vacationer resting comfortably is feeling good in a non-destructive way, he really has not thereby achieved self-esteem.

Let us divide the term into its component parts. "Self" refers to a sense of one's being a unique individual, and the feeling of uniqueness is not only acceptable, but is actually mandatory according to the Talmudic dictum "Every single person is *obligated* to say 'the world was created for me, and the Torah was given to me' " (*Sanhedrin* 37a). Note the wording of the passage, "Every single person," which indicates an awareness of one's singularity and uniqueness, and "is obligated;" thus it is mandatory, not merely recommended as desirable. The Torah clearly wishes that we have a sense of self.

The Torah places importance on a person's name. The *kabbalistic* writings state that parents are Divinely inspired to choose a name for their child, a name which in some marvelous way relates to his *neshamah*. One's name is more than a "handle" by which a person can be identified. One's name is unique, just as each *neshamah* is unique.

The word "esteem" is derived from the Latin word which means "to value or to appraise." *Self-esteem, then, is that the "Self" is being evaluated or appraised.*

Evaluating or appraising something presupposes a set of standards. We measure the value of something by how closely it approaches the standard or the ideal. On what basis, and by what standards, do we esteem or evaluate the self?

It becomes clear that "feeling good" is not the standard any of us would accept. We are not ready to accord the highest evaluation to gluttons who indulge themselves and feel good, and the lowest evaluations to our great *tzaddikim* who were constantly brokenhearted because they felt they were derelict in their service of G-d.

The standards we should apply are Torah standards, which differ sharply from secular standards. Ask any secular person to list the wealthiest people in the world, and he will undoubtedly reply with the names of the most affluent people listed in *Fortune* magazine. The Torah says, however, that a wealthy person is one who is satisfied with whatever he has (*Ethics of the Fathers* 4:1). To the secular person, the mightiest person is either the physically strongest or the one controlling the greatest military force. In the Torah, it is the one who can be master over his urges (ibid.), and so it is with all other values.

To give our children self-esteem, then, we must provide both elements. We must recognize them for their uniqueness and individuality (not, "Why can't you be like. . .?"), and we must provide them with appropriate standards toward which they should strive.

In setting standards we must be careful not to set expectations so high that one despairs of trying or feels grossly inadequate when they are beyond one's reach. Parents must indicate that it is not the absolute level that is important, but the effort one invests. As one ethicist put it, we will not be judged by where we were on the ladder of spirituality, but by whether we were ascending or descending it.

For example, we may relate that the Chofetz Chaim's trust in G-d was so complete and profound, that he only permitted his store to remain open until he had earned enough for that particular day, whereupon he spent the rest of the day in the study of Torah. When he closed the store and had the customers shop at other vendors, he lived according to the principle of the manna, which teaches that G-d will provide for our needs each day.

This is indeed an aspiring thought for our children, but we may expect them to think, if not to ask, why do their parents not ascribe to this? Why does Daddy spend the lion's share of his day at the office? We may be able to explain that the economic needs of modern life are much more complex than in the days of the *shtetl* of the Chofetz Chaim. But we would also be wise to tell our children that the reason we relate this story is not only to provide them with the finest in Torah perspectives, but also that we may hear it ourselves, to remind ourselves to increase the time we devote to prayer and Torah study.

All one is expected to do is to try. Luzatto in Chapter 26 of the *Path of the Just* points out that the attainment of spirituality is both a labor and a gift. It is a labor because a person is expected to work for it, and a gift because G-d grants it as a gift to those who have tried sincerely to get it. In other words, there are things that are not attainable by our own efforts, yet we must try for them, and not feel defeated because we have not yet reached them.

How do we convey this to our children? We can relate this to them, but let us again recall that we teach best by example. Let our children see that we are forever trying, that we continue to try throughout our lives, and that we do not condemn ourselves if we have not achieved our goal. We just try harder.

A child must also understand that making a mistake is no reason to lose self-esteem. The Talmud has numerous homilies such as, "A person does not grasp a Torah concept well unless he errs in it and is corrected" (*Gittin* 43a), or "A place which is occupied by a *baal teshuvah* (repentant) cannot be reached by an absolute *tzaddik*" (*Berachos* 34b). *Teshuvah* means returning, and we may think of it as a rocket on a trajectory to a distant planet, which has a corrective mechanism built in so that if it veers from its assigned path, it will be readjusted and *returned* to its correct path so that it should arrive at the intended destination. This is the *return* concept of *teshuvah*, and we must convey this to our children.

At this point you will probably ask how we are to impress children with this concept of *teshuvah*; actually, by now you know the answer: (1) by talking to them about the positive aspects of *teshuvah* as it is discussed in our ethical works; (2) by citing from the rich repository of the lives of our great Torah personalities, who spent their entire lives in *teshuvah*; and (3) by setting an example as we put to constructive use the not-infrequent mistakes we make in our own lives.

I often receive phone calls at my unlisted phone at home from people who are essentially asking for free psychiatric advice. Occasionally I even receive collect calls, which I never refuse for fear that the person calling may be in a state of desperation and is at a pay phone without money for the call.

One night, after a very exhausting day, I received such a collect call, and the problem was not at all an emergency. After answering the caller's question, I soundly thrashed him for the *chutzpah* of making me pay for a question that was not of an emergency nature, and angrily I hung up the phone.

Only later did I recall that the operator had asked for me personally, but did not ask me to accept the charges. I had misinterpreted a person-to-person call as being a collect call, and I had unjustly chastised the caller.

I shared this with my children, and pointed out that due to my hasty misjudgment, I had offended someone, and since I did not know the identity of the caller, I did not have the opportunity to apologize. I was feeling guilty because I had jumped to an erroneous conclusion, and I emphasized how careful we must be to deliberate before we speak or act, especially when we may be offending others. I believe that sharing this personal experience was more impressive than a lecture on the virtue of tolerance.

Although we are instructed in emulate G-d, there are some ways in which we should not emulate Him. The chassidic master, the Shpoler Zeide once turned to G-d, "Master of the Universe!" he said. "How do You expect people not to sin? You have put temptation right before their very eyes, but You have concealed the torments of hell in esoteric books. The scales are simply tipped toward sin. Now, if You had put the torment of hell right before peoples' eyes and had hidden temptation in the books, I assure You, no one would ever sin."

We expect our children to do that which is right and avoid that which is wrong. Do we provide them with enough opportunity and incentive to encourage our children to do right and avoid wrong, or are we to pattern ourselves after G-d, Who has placed mankind in so difficult a position, albeit for its ultimate benefit?

As parents, we should look for ways whereby we can facilitate our children doing good and avoiding wrong. Each good they do would increase their self-esteem and strengthen their resolve to do more good.

Chapter Six

The Trap Of
Low Self-Esteem

ow self-esteem among children is quite common, and the awareness that one's child has low self-esteem is not grounds for panic. This appears to be a phase which many, if not most, or even all children go through, and they can emerge from it triumphantly. They may need considerable parental help in doing so, and it is therefore important for parents to be alert to signs of low self-esteem and to develop methods to help the child raise his self-esteem. Poor performance in school may be the result of a child's lack of self-confidence, so that he gives up on a problem without even making an attempt at solving it. Angry outbursts or defiance of parents can be the child's way of asserting himself. Jealousy of a sibling may reflect the belief that he does not feel himself loved, perhaps because he feels undeserving of being loved. Excessive daydreaming may be an escape into fantasy because of the feeling that one cannot achieve much in reality. All of these may be manifestations of a poor self-concept.

Children, like adults, are naturally gregarious. When a child withdraws from peers, it is probably for the same reasons that adults withdraw from their peers: a feeling that one is not desirable company, that one does not belong, and that one is likely to be rejected. The parent may pose the question, "Why aren't you out there playing with your friends?" Rather than being just a question that requires an answer, the parent should be aware that the child's withdrawing from friends is very likely due to a self-esteem problem. Parental sensitivity to this can result in a child's overcoming it.

Some of the more common reasons for such withdrawal are: (1) I'm a winner/loser. (2) Nobody understands me. (3) I'm going to fail/succeed:

1. I'm a winner/loser.

Not infrequently the child may be concerned that by playing with his friends he might be the loser, and in order to avoid the pain of losing, he withdraws from participation with them. This raises two questions: (a) Why does the child anticipate losing? (b) Why is losing so painful that it must be absolutely avoided?

Let us begin with the latter question. Granted, winning is certainly far more pleasant than losing, but obviously games are played everywhere, and since there is invariably an equal or greater number of losers as winners, contestants enter the contest hoping that they will win, but knowing that they might lose. They are not frightened off by the prospect of losing. Why is this child so sensitive to losing that he cannot risk it?

The increased sensitivity to losing may be for the same reason that the child anticipates losing; namely, feelings of incompetence and inferiority, so that losing is a foregone conclusion. We will investigate this feeling shortly. But there is another important factor that is also operative.

One can argue reasonably that winning is not the point of the game; it is playing well that counts. This is a logical position, but inasmuch as a child often reflects parental attitudes, we must ask, do the parents ascribe to this philosophy themselves? If not, it is unrealistic to expect it of the child.

The Torah value is indeed that it is the process rather than the conclusion that counts. All a person can do is the best he can do under given circumstances. All G-d asks of us is to give everything we do our best shot and pray for success. *A person cannot control outcome.* This is clearly stated in *Ethics of the Fathers* (2:21), "Completion of the task is not within your domain, but you are not absolved from doing your share."

We are so profoundly influenced by what goes on in the commercial world that we sometimes adopt values that may have a legitimate place in commerce but are not appropriate for matters of a moral-ethical nature. In commerce, good or bad is determined by the bottom line. A profitable venture is good, and a losing venture is bad. How one operated the business is immaterial. A business venture that was started with the best economic guidelines and operated with maximum efficiency and integrity but which nevertheless failed is a bad business venture. One that was entered into recklessly in violation of every sound economic principle, yet ended up with a windfall profit, is a good venture, and the entrepreneur is an economic hero. Our culture is result oriented, and a venture that does not produce a successful result is seen as a failed venture. So it is with business, and perhaps it cannot be otherwise, because all that matters in business is profit and loss.

It is much different with moral-ethical issues, where the reverse applies. Whether an act is good or bad is dependent upon the virtue and sincerity with which it is performed. A surgeon who performs a totally unnecessary operation out of avarice, solely for the purpose of getting a fee, and happens to accidentally discover a small cancerous growth which had been unsuspected, and by removing it saves the patient's life, is nevertheless an unscrupulous doctor. On the other hand, a surgeon who agonizes whether or not to perform an operation, and after much deliberation and consultation performs the operation solely for the patient's benefit, yet the patient dies, is nevertheless a highly ethical surgeon. Only G-d can know the outcome of anything. All a person can do is act with sincere motivation and integrity.

This difference between Torah and secular attitudes is stated in the prayer of gratitude recited upon completion of a volume of the Talmud. "Those who toil in Torah receive a reward for their efforts, whereas those who do not toil in Torah do not receive a reward for their efforts." This elicited a comment from the Chofetz Chaim who asked, "Do not all workers receive compensation for their efforts?"

The Chofetz Chaim explained, "Workers receive compensation for those efforts that lead to a product. Thus, a tailor is paid for his labor that will result in a garment. If one were to know that regardless of how much time and effort the tailor puts in, no garment will ever be produced, one would certainly not pay the tailor for his labor. No one is compensated for pure effort, only for those efforts that contribute, in one way or another, to a usable product.

"Torah is different. The effort of studying Torah is rewarded even if there will never be an ultimate product. For example, there are some *halachos* that the Talmud states 'never were and never will be applied in reality.' Why then study them? Because the study of Torah is in itself of value (*Sanhedrin* 71a). It is the effort rather than the result that counts."

I know of children of abusive and neglecting parents who nevertheless grew up to be fine, upright citizens of the community. I also know of children of caring parents, who gave their children the best upbringing they could, and yet the children turned out to be antisocial. Which are the good parents and which are the bad? We should not judge by outcome. Neglectful parents are bad parents, and caring, diligent parents are good. The fact that the results were the reverse of what we would have expected does not change the evaluation of the behavior.

If parents truly adopt these ethical-moral guidelines in their own lives, and judge acts by their character rather than by their outcome, they may thereby convey to their children that it is the way the game is played, and not the winning that is of primary importance. But if parents blame themselves when things do not turn out as desired in spite of their best efforts, they can hardly tell the child that it is the play that counts rather than the victory, and that as long as he did his best he should be proud of it. Why should he give greater value to the process rather than to the results if the father and mother do not sincerely believe that?

Suppose that the father has been trying to acquire an account for his firm, but the contract ended up going to a competitor. I don't expect the father to be ecstatic with joy over this, but what he should say is: "I did the best I could. You win some and you lose some. I put my best effort forth, and I have nothing to regret." The child then gets the message that you can live with a loss. But if the father continues to mope over losing a lucrative contract, and goes through a postmortem to detect what he did wrong that resulted in the contract going to a competitor, or perhaps blames this on others who did not do their share to acquire the contract, then the message the child receives is that one cannot accept defeat gracefully.

When the child loses a game, whether it is at checkers or being on a losing team in baseball, a parent should be able to sincerely say, "I'm proud of your effort. You gave it your best shot." But these will be empty words if they do not reflect how the parents feel when they face a defeat of any sort.

2. Nobody understands me.

Children need to be understood. Children wish to be understood. It is a most serious mistake to fail to consider the exquisite sensitivities which children have. It is of the greatest importance that children be made to feel that their parents empathize with them and that they are trying to understand them.

Children look up to their parents as infallible. In practice, tiny tots are impotent and parents are all powerful. Little children equate the parents' physical stature and power with their being right. To the small child, "Might is right."

Let me digress a moment to point out that many juvenile traits may linger on for years, well into adult life. This was impressed upon me very forcefully when during my father's final illness, I took him to the doctor for chemotherapy. In his weakened condition he leaned upon me, and this was a most painful feeling for me. During my childhood, I had leaned on him, and although a half century had passed and the current reality was totally different, my unconscious mind had not respected the progress of time. My juvenile emotions had persisted, and there was something terribly absurd about my father's leaning on me.

If so many years later, one still can have the feeling, "I am little, my father is big," just imagine how powerful this feeling must be during childhood, when the reality is indeed such, that the child is little and the father is big.

But let us get back to the child who conceptualizes his parents as powerful. Parents may not be aware that this is how the child perceives them. When the child fails in something, he may feel totally alone. He thinks that no one can understand him, certainly not his parents, because they have never failed at anything. It is interesting to observe the facial expression of a small child when the parents share having had a similar experience. "I know what you feel like. I remember when our team lost. I was the last one at bat in the ninth inning with two out and two men on base, and I struck out. I felt terrible. I not only felt that I had failed, but that I had let the whole team down." Invariably the child's eyes widen, and he is likely to grin. "You did? What did the team do to you? Did they ever let you play again?"

"Oh, sure they did. I wasn't the first person in the world to strike out. They knew I wanted to get on base and that I had tried my best. We were all disappointed, but we got over it."

How much this means to a child is evident by the way the child pursues the issue. "But didn't the kids make fun of you? Weren't they mad at you?" And an hour later the child may come back saying, "Tell me again about how you struck out."

Empathy. A magic word that is as important at age 6 as at age 65.

Again a digression. Early in my professional life I was prescribed a new medication for hay fever. It was not known at that time that this medication can cause depression in some people, but I became profoundly dejected, experiencing the whole gamut of depressive symptoms that I had observed in my depressed patients. When the medication was identified as the culprit and eliminated, the depression disappeared. As distressful as it was, I am extremely grateful that I had experienced these feelings, because I have since been able to empathize with patients who manifest these symptoms. I understand their pain and desperation.

The feeling of aloneness, "No one understands me," can be devastating, no less in childhood than in adult life. One of the major reasons for the efficacy of various kinds of group therapy is that people discover that they are not alone in the way they feel. Children, too, need to feel that they are understood, and they need to know this even more than adults, because the tremendous gap in age and size between children and their parents makes them feel qualitatively different, and they think that their parents cannot possibly understand them.

Children are easily hurt, and since many children lack restraint, they may frequently inflict pain on other children. A child may make himself leader of the group and seek to exercise his authority by ostracizing one of the children, for no particular reason other than to show he is boss (rather reminiscent of what "mature" adults do). That ostracized child who doesn't want to go out and face the hostility of the group might just be yours. This child is hurting, hurting badly.

The worst thing you can possibly do is to trivialize the incident. This is as important to him as those slights you have suffered are important to you.

What to do? Empathy, the magic word.

First, of course, you should try to establish what happened. "Don't you want to be out with your friends?"

"No."

"Why not?"

" 'Cause."

"Anything happen between you and your friends?"

"Nope." (The child's pride is not going to let him tell you he's been ostracized.)

Here is your opportunity to empathize. Unless you were raised in a bubble, you should be able to search your memory for some incident that can serve as a bridge between you and the child, so that he can see that you understand.

For example, "Well, when I was your age, I used to enjoy playing with my friends. There was this one kid, Sammy, who thought he was king of the mountain. For some reason Sammy decided one day to kick me out of the group."

"Why? What did you do?"

"I don't really remember doing anything. Sammy was a kid who liked to show he was boss. He didn't beat me up, but he just began making fun of me. He called me names, and the other kids who wanted to be on Sammy's good side followed suit. I came home and cried. Zaidy asked me what was wrong, and I told him."

"What did Zaidy do? Did he yell at Sammy or call Sammy's father?"

"Oh, no. That would have been the worst thing. That would have meant that I was a weakling who needed to be protected. Zaidy just explained to me that Sammy must feel awfully little about himself if he has to show off to everyone how big and powerful he is. He told me that I had not done anything wrong and I had no reason to feel ashamed. He said that in a few days the kids will forget about it, and Sammy would probably pick on somebody else, which was true. He told me just to go about my business, and act as if nothing had happened, that if the kids still stayed away from me to just say hello to them, and if they called me names, just make believe I didn't hear them. That would be the worst thing for them, to know that they weren't getting to me.

"That week the new airport opened, and Zaidy took me down to watch the planes take off. That helped me forget a little bit about Sammy.

"Zaidy was right. I went on my own way, and after a few days the kids began including me. Two months later I had a birthday party. I think I was nine, and I invited Sammy and the kids, and we all had a great time.

"There's nothing exciting about going to the airport today, but maybe you and I could go for an ice-cream soda after dinner tonight. Okay?"

A bit of ingenuity should allow you to accommodate to such situations. Picking up the cudgel for the child and scolding his friends or talking to the other children's parents is the wrong thing to do. Your obligation as a parent is to train the child to stand up to adversity.

While sipping the ice-cream soda you might tell the child about how the Talmud has the highest praise for someone who is *maavir al midosav,* willing to overlook an insult without retaliating, and that it refers to such people as those who truly love G-d (*Yoma* 23a).

You then tell the child about how some of our great Torah

personalities dealt with people who insulted them. Perhaps you may tell them of the great Rabbi Zundel of Salant, who once traveled in a coach with several other people. Rabbi Zundel used to dress like every ordinary person, not in rabbinic garb. Some people in the coach were very rude to him and mocked him. When they arrived at the destination and saw that there was a reception committee of rabbis and community leaders waiting to greet Rabbi Zundel, they realized they had insulted a great man. With their heads hung down in shame, they came to ask forgiveness from Rabbi Zundel.

Rabbi Zundel smiled and said to them that he had no hard feelings against them, and gently pointed out to them that just because he did not appear to them to be a scholar gave them no right to be rude to him. Rabbi Zundel made them promise that henceforth they would treat every person with respect, regardless of who he may be.

You may then point out to the child, "See? By accepting an insult and not reacting, you are like the great *tzaddik* Rabbi Zundel."

At the Shabbos table you may again discuss the virtues of overlooking a personal slight, and tell another story about one of our great Torah personalities who was *maavir al midosav*. There are an abundance of such stories in the biographies of our great personalities. You may then say to the people at the table, "This week our Chaim was like our great *tzaddikim*." The whole episode can thus be converted into a positive experience.

Such an incident can provide an opportunity for teaching that being a *maavir al midosav* does not mean becoming a doormat. These same personalities that overlooked personal insults were very assertive and demonstrated great strength and courage if anyone showed a disrespect for Torah. They could be fierce warriors in the battle for truth and justice, and their taking personal insults in stride was by no means a sign of weakness. Again, anecdotes of how our great Torah leaders fought vigorously to uphold *halachah*, tradition, and respect for Torah can be found in their biographies.

The child can thus be taught the virtue of overlooking personal slights while maintaining a sense of strength and pride. But as pointed out, all these teachings and impressive stories can only serve as supports to reinforce parental traits. Parents must practice these ethical principles in their own lives in order for their children to adopt them. Children who see that parents defer when there is a question of one's personal honor, yet are staunch advocates for Torah principles and are not hesitant to assert themselves when necessary, can develop these traits within themselves.

3. I'm going to fail/succeed.

Let us now address the first question we had raised. Why does a child anticipate losing? Granted there are always winners and losers, but this should provide a 50-50 chance. Yet some children are convinced they will lose. Why?

In most of my writings, I have focused on the problem of low self-esteem, of people having unwarranted feelings of unworthiness, inadequacy, and inferiority. I have exploited the keen insights of cartoonist Charles Schulz in my books, *When Do the Good Things Start?* and *I Didn't Ask to Be in This Family*, whereby he illustrates the defeatist attitude of Charlie Brown, the defensive vanity and arrogance of Lucy, and the escapist fantasies of Snoopy, all ways in which a person either manifests feelings of inferiority or tries to defend against them.

It seems that low self-esteem is almost a universal problem; i.e., everybody has it to some degree, but in some people it is more intense. We can readily understand why children who are raised in problem-ridden homes might develop low self-esteem, but why is it so often seen in people who did not suffer deprivation or abuse in their childhood?

Part of the problem might be due simply to being human. All other forms of life achieve a state of self-sufficiency relatively early in their life span. Little bear cubs are running around on their first day of life, and within a very short time learn how to find food and survive on their own. This is not so with human beings, who could not survive without the care of adults, and this dependency continues for a very long time. Even when a child reaches a stage of physical growth where he could technically survive on his own, he is in fact dependent on his parents for survival at least into his adolescence. Given today's sophisticated culture and requirement of various degrees of education for self-sufficiency, the period of dependence on adults extends well into adult life. Being dependent does not foster positive self-esteem.

Furthermore, a small child feels totally dwarfed in a world inhabited by adults, and his actual helplessness is magnified by his seeing himself as diminutive in a world of giants.

Several enterprising psychologists once designed an experimental house, whose dimensions were four times those of a normal house. I.e., the ceilings were 40-feet high, the tables and chairs were three times regular height, etc. This house was proportionately for adults what a normal house is for little children. They then had perfectly healthy, stable adults move into this house, and within three days they began to manifest neurotic symptoms. Each time they wished to reach a doorknob, they had to stretch on their tiptoes, and sitting down on a chair was an ordeal, requiring much effort to climb up.

As adults we take the comforts of our home for granted, giving little thought that what may be convenient for us may be a major ordeal for a small child. Children live in a reverse Lilliput — very little creatures among a race of giants. The anxiety this can cause is evident in the report of the spies Moses sent to Canaan: "There we saw giants, and we felt like we were grasshoppers" (*Numbers* 13:33). This huge, oversized world can be very threatening to a small child who feels lost in its immensity. The anxiety this generates might be completely unbearable if it were not for parents, who provide some security and a sense of being protected. Parents are the link that makes life tolerable during infancy. Thus, over and above the basic needs for survival which parents provide, they are like a lifeline to a person adrift in a stormy sea. He must hold on to the lifeline at all costs, because to lose hold means certain death. So it is with a small child, who cannot risk losing the security of the parents, because they stand between him and an overwhelming Gargantuan world.

When a child is punished for something and, as may often happen, cannot understand what he did that was wrong, or even if he does, why the punishment is so severe, he may not conclude, "My parents don't know what they're doing," because to do so would undermine his trust in his parents as his protectors and jeopardize his sense of security. He must therefore maintain that his parents are right and just, and the only conclusion that would explain his being punished is, "I am bad." It is not "I did something bad," but "I *am* bad."

There is a fine line between the feelings of guilt and shame. Guilt, correctly defined, refers to a feeling for having done something wrong.

Shame, on the other hand, is a feeling for being defective in some way. Although this may appear to be a subtle distinction, there is actually a major difference between the two. To put it simply, guilt is the feeling of "I made a mistake." Shame is the feeling of "I am a mistake."

Guilt, like physical pain, can be healthy and constructive. If there were no physical pain, a person might place his hand on an electric hot-plate and sustain a dangerous burn without being aware of it, and there are indeed diseases where this actually occurs. Without pain, a person would have no warning that his appendix is about to rupture or that his heart muscle does not have adequate oxygen. Pain is thus essential for physical health.

Healthy guilt, much like physical pain, is necessary to maintain spiritual health. The distress of guilt upon doing something wrong is a major deterrent from doing wrong. Sociopaths, who have no sense of guilt, do all kinds of terrible things without the slightest pangs of conscience, and appear to be unable to learn not to do wrong. Guilt is what keeps us decent. Furthermore, if we have done something wrong, guilt is what nags us until we rectify the wrong we have done.

Shame, on the other hand, as defined above, does not relate to any specific acts, but rather to a self-concept. "I am bad. I am defective. I am a noxious person." These feelings may occur even in absence of any wrong deeds. Shame is toxic because there is little that one can do to get rid of it. There is no making amends or rectifying a wrong deed, since shame is not related to any deeds. The only way shame can be eliminated is if a person comes to the realization that he was in error about his self-concept, and this is no small task.

Many children are shame ridden. Parents may unwittingly convey the concept, "You are bad," instead of, "What you did was wrong." An expletive in a moment of anger, "You are a rotten kid," may have far-reaching consequences.

It is also possible that a young child may not understand why it is necessary for the parents to give more attention to a younger sibling, or to an older sibling who may have a health problem. The logical reasons which are so easily understandable to an adult are not necessarily grasped by the child, who may conclude, "They love him/her more than they do me." Not having any reason to which to attribute what he sees as a less-favored status, he concludes that he is in some way not lovable. This can be a source of toxic shame, which is not due to any delinquency on the part of the parents.

It is surprising how many adults recall feeling shame as children. A successful surgeon, who grew up in a caring, affluent home, reflected, "I remember that at age nine, I felt that all the other children were better than I was. That feeling has stayed with me throughout my life. When I walk into a room full of people, I feel I don't belong." He could give no reason for having developed such feelings.

While little children may lack the capacity to understand everything that goes on in the world, we must also admit that there is much that occurs in the adult world that doesn't make much sense at all. Even parents may sometimes do things that are not of the highest order. The young child, however, cannot risk thinking, "My parents do not know that what they are doing is wrong," because as pointed out earlier, he must maintain the image of parental perfection to subdue his anxiety. He therefore concludes, "My parents are right. The fact that I don't understand this is because I lack the capacity to understand and to make good judgments," and repetition of this kind of thinking results in a person growing up with a lack of trust in his ability to make correct judgments. People like this are indecisive, and are always dependent on others to make decisions for them.

You may think that such sophisticated thought processes cannot occur in a 3-year-old, but let me assure you that they do. Children of 2 and 3 may already have a negative self-image. The challenge to parents is thus much greater than if the child were starting from a zero position and has to be helped to reach +10. The child may actually be beginning from a -5 position in self-esteem, and has to first be raised from there to zero, and then proceed on to greater positivity.

Children who are shame ridden may perceive themselves as losers and, when defeat is a foregone conclusion, see no reason to even try to compete. In my book, *When Do the Good Things Start* (St. Martin's Press 1995), I utilized the psychological insights and wit of cartoonist Charles Schulz, creator of the Peanuts comic strip. Charlie Brown is a child who consistently loses, primarily because he believes he will lose. When told that a horseshoe pit was installed at the playground, Charlie Brown sadly remarks, "Just one more thing to lose at." Charlie Brown hopes for good weather to permit a ball game, and when it rains he concludes, "I can't even hope good."

One young girl with fine artistic talents repeatedly tore up her drawings as not being good enough, and refused to join an art class because all the other students would draw better than she. A young man confided how he had failed to learn in the yeshivah because he was reluctant to reveal to the *rebbi* that he did not understand a portion of the Talmud, since that would reveal to others that he was stupid. He confirmed the teachings of the sages, "A person who feels shame cannot learn" (*Ethics of the Fathers* 2:6).

Parents understandably wish to know, "What can we do to help our child develop a positive self-image?" There are a number of recommendations. By far the most effective method is for the parents to have a positive self-image themselves. Self-esteem is contagious. Parents who are self confident and secure will transmit this feeling to their children. Parents who are insecure and lack self-confidence will transmit that attitude to their children.

It is never too late to work on one's own self-image. If you have any doubt about whether you harbor such feelings, see if you do not identify with some of the behavior of either Charlie Brown or Lucy. These are two classic examples of negative self-image problems, the one manifesting it overtly, and the other defending against it with an "I am perfect" attitude. Self image distortions are probably responsible for many, if not most, of the problems people may encounter in life. I dealt with this in my books *Let Us Make Man* (CIS Publications 1986) and *Life's Too Short* (St. Martin's Press 1995).

Let us look now at some suggestions for elevating a child's self-esteem, or at least to avoid depressing him.

Chapter Seven

Elevating a Child's Self-Esteem

The Chassidic master, Rabbi Dovid of Lelov, used to say that he learned the essence of *ahavas Yisrael,* love of a fellow Jew, by over-hearing a tavern conversation.

Two men were well along in their cups when one said, "Ivan, I love you. I really love you."

"No, you don't, Stepan," the other said. "You don't love me at all."

The drunken Stepan began crying and protesting, "Don't say that, Ivan. I love you with all my heart. I swear it."

"If you really love me," Ivan said, "then tell me, Stepan, can you feel my needs? Do you know what distresses me, what I am lacking?"

The Rabbi of Lelov said, "I learned then and there that to truly love another person you must feel his needs and know what it is that is causing him distress."

There is no question that we love our children. We will sacrifice our very lives for them. But do we meet the criteria of Rabbi Dovid of Lelov? Do we know what is bothering them? Do we really know their needs and feel what it is they are lacking?

In a previous chapter we encountered a child who very much wanted to play with his friends but had withdrawn for fear of having been hurt by them or for fear of losing. This is but one of many manifestations of a child's distress. There are sundry others, too numerous to list. But let's look at just a few.

"How come Yoni gets everything and I never get anything?" Or, "How come Yoni always gets to go places, and I never do?"

These statements may be completely false, but this is the way the child sees them, and to him they are as real as if they were true. Even if the child himself may know that these statements are not factual, he is using them as his way of expressing something that is bothering him.

Of course, it may happen that Yoni is a favorite child. The reason the Torah tells us about Yaakov and Yosef is so that we should realize that it can happen to anyone. Yoni may be a charismatic child who lights up the room with his presence, whereas Shmuli lacks this particular trait.

But let us proceed on the assumption that Yoni is not favored, that Shmuli just sees it that way. You tell Shmuli, "That's just not true. You have been places that Yoni never went to, just as he has been to places that you have not. We try to give each of you what you need."

You have made a statement of fact, but fact was never the issue, and the statement is not only of no value, but is actually counterproductive. What Shmuli concludes is, "They haven't heard me. They don't understand what is bothering me." As the Rabbi of Lelov said, our love for our children should make us sensitive to what is bothering them.

Acknowledge the feeling. Your immediate response may be accompanied by a hug and kiss, and you may say something like, "Sometimes we have feelings that are not true, but are very real to us. It is like in a dream, when you see things very clearly that are not there, but during the dream they sure look very real. Daddy and Mommy love all our children equally." You may not have solved the problem, but you have acknowledged the feeling, and while Shmuli may not be completely reassured, he has reason to hope that by being aware of how he feels you may do something about it.

There is a high probability that the statement, "You love him more than you do me," has its roots in the child's feelings that he is less lovable. In other words, this is an expression of a low self-esteem problem. The long-term solution for the problem, as well as for other low self-esteem manifestations that children may have, is to look for ways to elevate the child's self-esteem. This is not a simple task and cannot be accomplished overnight. But with the proper patience and perseverance, it can be done.

Praise is a very effective method of raising self-esteem, but it is important to realize that flattery is not the same as praise. Children need positive strokes, but false praise is of questionable value and may even defeat the purpose. In contrast to adults, who have accommodated to the falsity that prevails in society, children are much more sensitive, and can detect when something is not true. Empty compliments may leave the child with the feeling that he cannot believe anything the parents say about him.

When my grandchild was seven, he began taking violin lessons, and after his fourth lesson he wanted to audition for me. Needless to say, his performance was a bit less than that of a virtuoso, but I was able to recognize the melody, even with all the sharps and flats that were uncalled for. My first impulse was to compliment him, "That was beautiful!" But I caught myself in time, realizing that this would be a lie, because it was not beautiful. Instead, I said, "I know that tune. Play it again, and I'll sing it along with you." We did so twice, and we had a duet which pleased him to no end, as his facial expression revealed. I had complimented him on his performance without lying to him.

Posting a child's drawing or a test with good grades on the refrigerator door is helpful, as is a chart with gold stars to acknowledge good behavior. Each child needs to be evaluated as to what is to be expected of him, and his performances should be duly acknowledged. For example, for a four-year-old, the chart may contain: "Said *Modeh Ani,*" "Brushed my teeth," "Put on my *tzitzis.*" And as the child grows, appropriate items should be added.

It is important to maintain a state of alertness for those things which one can legitimately praise. We are certainly sufficiently alert to detect when the child does wrong and discipline him, and we need to be equally alert to detect things that a child does that are proper and commend him for it. Too often we take good behavior for granted, singling out only bad behavior for discipline.

There is an amusing anecdote about the Rabbi of Lelov who once returned home very late and explained, "I passed by a house and heard much shouting. I went to the window and saw that a man was shouting to his elderly father, 'You are a parasite! All you do is eat and sleep. You do nothing around the house to help and you constantly criticize me. I swear, if I were not a G-d-fearing person, I would kill you.'

"When I heard that I was in the presence of a G-d-fearing person, I could not tear myself away. I just had to go in and talk with him."

Even in a case of a son who was so grossly rude to his elderly father, the Rabbi of Lelov could find a redeeming feature. We could certainly detect many things in our children's behavior that we can point out as commendable and praise them for it. As noted earlier, praise must be genuine. The child must be able to feel that his parents are truly pleased with what it is they are praising him for. We again come back to the importance of the parents being sincere about this in other aspects of their lives.

The Chassidic master Rabbi Elimelech of Lizensk used to pray, "May it be Thy will that we see the virtue of other people and not their faults." This is not too common a practice. Most people are more generous with criticism than with praise. When the child hears the parents talking about other people's faults and foibles (which incidentally is *lashon hara*) and not about their virtues, he is more likely to consider his parents' praise of him as artificial rather than as honest and sincere.

Many of the interactions that can affect self-esteem are not dramatic or traumatic events, but rather things to which we ascribe little significance. For example, the child asks you something while you are absorbed reading an article, and with your eyes on the paper or at best halfway on the paper, you respond to the child's question, "Um, yeah, I guess it's okay." No big deal, is it?

But think about it a moment. The child's question, perhaps whether he may go over to a friend's house, may be trivial to you, but it is important to him. Suppose you wanted to ask your employer something that was of importance to you, and he gave your question scant attention, mumbling some kind of answer while he was absorbed doing something else. How would you feel? Would that give you the feeling that your employer is really concerned about you and your cares? That is how the child feels when you act similarly.

You are not required to put the paper or the magazine aside, but you might say, "Honey, I'm in the middle of reading this, and I want to hear what you have to say. I'll be through with this in just a few moments, and then I can listen to you." When you finish the article or come to a break, you can then listen to his question attentively, and perhaps even ask what he plans to do at the friend's house. The child should have reason to feel that his needs are considered important.

Do you know the names of all your child's teachers? These people are very important to him. They are his authorities. In addition to knowing their names, you should care about how the child feels about his teachers. Also, you should know the names of at least his closest friends. It is a sign of his significance to you when you show concern about the people with whom he associates.

While there are a few rules that are without any exceptions, here is one that is absolute. Never, but never, humiliate a child. Discipline does not require his being shamed. A child should not be humiliated in the presence of his friends or even his own sisters or brothers. When reprimand or punishment is necessary, call the child aside, and in privacy carry out the required discipline. Although the child may resent the reprimand, he will appreciate your concern for his self-respect. On the other hand, if you reprimand him in the presence of others, the pain of being humiliated may be so intense that it obscures the message of the reprimand, and the discipline is of little value.

The Talmud is unusually harsh in denouncing someone who humiliates another person. "If someone embarrasses another person publicly, even though he may be in possession of Torah and good deeds, he forfeits his portion in the World to Come" (*Ethics of the Fathers* 3:15). The Talmud is very careful with its words, yet here it metes out a sentence more severe than on a person who has committed major Scriptural transgressions who does not lose his portion in the eternal world. There is no reason to believe that embarrassing one's own child is any less of an offense. Discipline him when necessary? Of course! That is a parent's obligation. Degrade him and crush him by humiliating him? Never.

The respect one should have for a child's sensitivities can be appreciated from the following incident. In his later years, although walking was very difficult for him, the Steipler Gaon insisted on going to a distant *shul* one Shabbos. He later explained:

"Some time ago I saw a young boy put a *Gemara* (volume of the Talmud) on the bookshelf upside down. I called him over and reprimanded him for not showing proper respect for holy books. The boy showed me that this volume had been bound incorrectly, and that he had indeed put it right side up.

"I apologized to the child, but then it occurred to me that according to *halachah* a minor is not competent to grant forgiveness. But today was his *bar mitzvah,* and he is now a competent adult, and this was the first opportunity I had to ask for forgiveness."

The Steipler had not publicly embarrassed the boy, but nevertheless sought his forgiveness. Furthermore, he kept track of the incident, and did not allow it to escape his mind until the boy became of age. Finally, instead of waiting until Sunday, when he could have avoided a long, arduous walk, he walked the distance on Shabbos because he felt it was not proper to delay the least in obtaining forgiveness.

This is why stories about the life experiences of our Torah personalities are significant. There is so much we can learn from them.

Over and above avoiding depressing the child's self-esteem, taking care not to humiliate him teaches him to avoid doing this to others, a trait which will be extremely valuable to him in his interpersonal relationships as he matures.

I said that this rule has no exception. But what about when the child has done something which requires setting an example for the other children? Failure to discipline the child in the presence of his siblings may leave them with the impression that what he has done is not wrong. It is accepted that an offense committed in public requires a public reprimand. How does one achieve this without humiliating the child?

This is an example of why quality parenting requires a concerted effort, and cannot be left to knee-jerk reactions. Such a situation requires a bit of strategy, since it appears that one is dealing with two irreconcilable goals.

You may call the child aside and say, "You know that I never scold you in front of others, but the other children saw what you did, and I can't let this go by without pointing out to them that it was wrong, or else they will think it's okay to act this way. Now you and I are going back into that room, and we will tell the kids why what you did was wrong. In fact, it would even be better if you said it to them instead of me, because when a person can admit his mistakes, that makes him a great person. Now, let's go."

If the child makes any effort at admitting he was wrong, this should be properly acknowledged. "Now look, kids, what Yitzchak did was wrong. We are human, and we all make mistakes. I have made my mistakes, and you may make yours. No person is perfect. But some people can never admit they were wrong. It takes a lot of courage and character to do that, and Yitzchak has shown us that he has that courage and character."

If time permits, you can elaborate a bit on the importance of promptly admitting a mistake and not trying to defend it. You might point out how the Talmud says that King Saul had only one sin but was not forgiven for it, whereas King David had two sins and was forgiven. King Saul tried to defend his mistake (*I Samuel* 15:13-21), whereas when David was told by the prophet that he had sinned, he promptly admitted it (*II Samuel* 12:13).

You might also tell them one of the stories about our great Torah personalities who did not hesitate to publicly admit their mistakes. In my book, *Generation to Generation* (CIS Publications), I relate a story of a *dayan* (magistrate), who accused someone of misappropriating money, and when he later discovered his error, he made a public declaration in *shul* of his mistake and asked the person's forgiveness. This is an impressive story which I heard as a child and never forgot, and neither will your children. A child can gain stature when it is pointed out to him that he is emulating our great Torah personalities. If time does not permit such elaboration, this may be done at greater leisure at the Shabbos table.

This tactic will have combined both the reprimand for the misdeed and appropriate praise for the child for admitting his mistake. In the event the child is stubborn and refuses to do so, you must nevertheless carry out the reprimand in front of the other children, but you will have prepared him for it, and if he chooses to let you go ahead on your own, he at least will understand that you had given him the opportunity to redeem himself. Furthermore, the other children will appreciate that you are trying to preserve his dignity.

But you may say, "Look, I am busy and I have a million other things to do. I can't take time out for such a *megillah* every time one of the children does something wrong."

If this is the case, you had better recheck your priorities. Failure to take some measure to protect the child's self-esteem is a dereliction in parental responsibility: giving your child the best opportunity to redeem himself and grow up psychologically healthy.

It is paradoxical that if I were to ask you just what is so pressing that you cannot take the few minutes time to provide wholesome discipline, you might tell me that you have to run off to work or to a business meeting, or to get something done in the house. The goal of these efforts, of course, is to provide in one way or another for the family. It is important to realize that taking these few minutes to provide necessary reprimand in a setting that will preserve a child's self-esteem is every bit as vital to the children's welfare as whatever you will be doing for them at work or in the home.

As with other traits, preserving a person's dignity when reprimanding him or disagreeing with him must be demonstrated by the parents in their own lives. Unfortunately, many parents are not too careful how they disagree with one another, and they exchange some sharp words and even insults in the presence of their children. This is extremely poor judgment, as it diminishes the children's respect for their parents.

Husbands and wives should exercise respect for one another even when not in the children's presence, but should be meticulously cautious not to be disrespectful to one another when the children are present. Because of the traditional position of the husband and father as the head of the household, the Talmud places great emphasis in according the wife the utmost respect. "A husband should love his wife as he does himself, but should respect her even more than he respects himself" (*Yevamos* 62b).

Because of the greater emotional sensitivity of a woman, the Talmud cautions the husband to be extremely careful not to move her to tears (*Bava Metzia* 59b). We have noted that self-esteem is contagious: Children "catch it" from their parents. If children see their parents relating with mutual respect and dignity, they will not only develop this trait in relating to others, but this will also raise their own self-esteem.

Chapter Eight

More About Self-Esteem

Grownups like to feel important. So do children.

One way to help a child feel important is to provide him with a judicious amount of privacy and to respect it. Every child should have a corner in the house, even if it is only a drawer, which is exclusively his. If it is feasible for this place to have a lock with a key which the child can keep, so much the better.

It is important for parents and siblings to respect a child's privacy. Parents do not like children to rummage through their things or to enter a closed room without knocking. These same considerations should be shown to children. Their territory is their own, and parents should knock on a child's door before entering and ask his permission to look into his drawer if necessary. These may be small acts, but by acknowledging the child's individuality, they contribute to his self-esteem.

Sometimes we may scold a child or mete out a punishment only to later discover that we had been misinformed and that the child was not at fault. It is imperative that the parent apologize to the child. An attitude of "I am the father. I don't have to apologize for my actions" is totally wrong and indicates to a child that his feelings are of no account.

Don't compare a child to other children, especially siblings. "Why can't you be like Zalman? He always listens and never sasses back." If G-d would have wanted you to have two Zalmans, He would have given you identical twins. (As a matter of fact, even identical twins can differ greatly in behavior.) Shimon is not Zalman and is not supposed to be. If you wish to point out to Shimon where his behavior needs improvement, leave Zalman out of it.

There are many decisions which parents must make in their small children's behalf because the latter are not sufficiently mature to make them. However, every opportunity should be exploited to let children make decisions of their own when these are not detrimental to them.

A mother and father took their child with them to a restaurant. After taking the parents' orders, the waitress asked the child, "What would you like to have?" and the child answered, "Two hot dogs with lots of mustard and a coke." The mother smiled knowingly and said, "You can bring him roast beef and mashed potatoes." When the waitress returned with two hot dogs, mustard, and a coke, the mother was horrified. The child smiled and said, "Look, Mommy, she thinks I'm real!"

Children who are never given the opportunity to make decisions for themselves may see themselves only as appendages of the parent and develop no sense of self.

When things are bothering you, let children know why you may be in a bad mood. Children often think that they are to blame for everything that goes wrong. It may be a great relief for a child to hear, "Mommy's upset because she found out that a friend of hers is very sick." It is appropriate to tell the child, "We may be grumpy because of some things that have happened, and we may even shout at you when you don't deserve it." It is helpful for the child not to incriminate himself, and it does not hurt for him to discover that his parents are human.

Self-esteem is increased by a sense of trust; i.e., when a child feels that he is being trusted. Parents should be on the lookout for things that they know the child can be trusted with, and when the child successfully executes this trust, this should be acknowledged and praised. As the child matures and the things that he can be trusted with increase in significance and complexity, his self-esteem is enhanced.

Setting up situations in which the parent knows the child can perform adequately has a precedent in Torah. The Talmud says, "Because G-d wished to benefit Israel, He gave them abundant mitzvos" (Makkos 23b). In what way is this a benefit? One of the commentaries explains that some of the things which were decreed as mitzvos would have been observed had they not been so designated; for example, the prohibition against consuming insects. But when Jews avoid eating insects, they thereby fulfill a mitzvah, and the nature of fulfilling one mitzvah is that it facilitates the observance of the next mitzvah. Hence, the abundance of mitzvos is a benefit. Similarly, allowing your child to prove himself trustworthy in a simple task provides him with the courage and self-confidence that fosters an ever greater capacity for successful performance of more difficult tasks.

Earlier we mentioned that "to esteem" means "to appraise," and that presupposes some standard; i.e., how closely does the item or act approach the ideal. The ideal for the Torah family that should serve as the standard of value is mitzvos and middos. Again, the emphasis is not on the completion of the mitzvah or the middah, but on the effort made to attain it. Sometimes there is partial achievement, sometimes total achievement, and sometimes there is no achievement. Yet, even the latter has value. The Talmud says, "If a person wished to do a mitzvah but circumstances beyond his control precluded his doing so, the Torah considers it as though he had actually performed it" (Berachos 6a).

Middos is the fabric of which character is fashioned. Proper middos will provide a child with the ability to adapt to life's circumstances in the healthiest way. No one can foresee all the possible challenges a child will encounter in the future, and there is no way one can give specific guidelines for coping with the great variety of challenges in life. One can only give the child proper principles to use in coping with life. Indeed, it is much the same as our approach in this book. We cannot possibly provide techniques for dealing with every eventuality which may occur in parenting, but if we can establish optimum principles of parenting, these can be used to apply to a vast variety of situations.

The human being stands as an intermediate between, perhaps better, as a composite of two opposites, animals and angels. Angels are pure spirit, and there is nothing to deter them from carrying out the Divine will. Animals are pure body, pure impulse, and there is nothing internal to deter them from acting on impulse. The human being is a composite, having an animal body with an abundance of impulses, but also having a spirit which can exert mastery over these impulses. Mastery over one's animalistic impulses is essentially the goal of *middos*. The newborn infant is pure impulse, and the development of *middos* is a gradual process, one that will continue throughout a person's entire lifetime.

Development of *middos* does not occur as an uninterrupted ascent. Usually there are advances and regressions, and the latter must be viewed as learning experiences and converted into such. Each regression is an opportunity for advancement.

Let me cite an example from my practice. A 15-year-old youngster who was being treated for alcohol and drug abuse was defiant with the staff and one day abruptly left the treatment center. Two days later he returned, reporting that he had been drinking while he was out, but had come to the realization that it did nothing for him, and that he was just as unhappy after drinking, in fact more so, whereupon he decided to return. This acting out might well have been considered sufficient grounds for discharge. Instead of discharging him, we pointed out to him that he had now discovered for himself what we had been telling him for the past month; namely, that whatever his problems may be, drinking is not the solution. While this episode was in one way unfortunate, it could be seen as an important lesson, and we hoped that he would capitalize on it to utilize the treatment program for his own betterment. This approach indeed proved to be very efficacious.

Children's self-esteem should come not only from their successes, not only from the efforts they make and from partial achievements, but also from mistakes and failures. Parents can help their children convert the latter into valuable learning experiences. It helps, of course, if children can see how parents convert their own mistakes into learning experiences.

The Talmud states that a person does not acquire full grasp of a *halachah* until he makes a mistake regarding it (*Gittin* 43a). This is in contrast to the aphorism that "Experience is a hard teacher but fools will learn no other way." The Talmud's position is that fools are those who do *not* learn from experience, and that it is the wise who learn from experience, i.e., mistakes.

Ari brings home a test paper with a failing grade, and is moping, probably expecting a dressing down from his parents.

"Looks like you're angry at yourself for getting a low grade."

"Dumb teacher. He didn't even warn us we were going to have a test."

"The low grade was because you were unprepared? Well, all you have to do is study well enough so that if you are given an unexpected quiz, you"ll always be prepared."

"But then I won't have enough time to play with the kids."

"Playing with the kids is certainly having fun, and you should have your share of fun. But if you take just a few extra minutes to study, you can avoid the misery of a low grade. Actually, the low grade you received will help you to do what's necessary for a better grade next time around."

Parents should respect the child's individuality and uniqueness. Children vary greatly in innate talents, and while there is some flexibility subject to training and education, there are limits which cannot be successfully transcended. Education and training that are in accordance with the child's natural tendencies will bear far greater fruit than those that are not within the child's indigenous composition. Each child's unique potential should be noted, and a child should not be coerced to suppress his innate inclinations in favor of parental desires. For example, I know of young people with innate mechanical skills who wished to pursue careers that would allow them to work with motors and engines, something that they would have enjoyed doing, but were forced by their parents into "more respectable" occupations, which resulted in unnecessary frustration.

Both the Vilna Gaon and Rabbi Samson Raphael Hirsch interpreted the verse in *Proverbs*: "Train a child according to his way;

even when he grows old he will not deviate from it" (22:6) to mean that the inherent way of a child, the basic traits with which he was born, will persist into his adult life. Parents may try to coerce the child to suppress his natural talents, and while they may succeed in intimidating him into compliance with their wishes, he will eventually return to his natural bent when he is free of parental domination. Therefore, these great Torah scholars say, one should cultivate the child's natural interests and develop them to the fullest. Traits that can be either negative or positive should be channeled positively, as we have noted in the Midrash about Moses, but attempts to totally eradicate traits are futile. The child should be helped to develop and mature within his innate qualities.

When the child's natural traits are acknowledged and developed, this constitutes an acceptance of the child as he is. Parental insistence of a child being what they wish him to be instead of what he is, is in fact a rejection of the child, and there is no doubt that the child senses this, resulting in an erosion of his self-esteem. The classic example of this is the insistence of parents that the child who is obviously left-handed should be trained to use his right hand. This is not only a foolish endeavor, but also seeks to alter the child's physiology and can result in both emotional and neurological problems.

This should not be misinterpreted to mean that an indolent child should be allowed to linger in bed until late in the day because it is his natural tendency. Rather, parents should try to understand the reason for the child's indolence, because then it may be amenable to correction.

It is a common occurrence that little children resent being put to bed, and will use all kinds of manipulations to extend their period of being awake. On the other hand, many adults cannot wait for the moment that they can retire. Why? It is because the young child is stimulated by the things he can do, whether playing with toys or satisfying his curiosity of the world about him, whereas adults have lost this enthusiasm and are rather disgruntled with the drabness of the world, and when nighttime approaches they are eager to escape from the boredom into sleep. An adult who usually retires at a certain hour will find himself quite alert if there is some exciting experience to watch or in which he can participate.

Indolence in a child is indicative of a lack of interest in life, and should be an indication that parents are missing a cue. The same child that cannot be dragged out of bed with a tractor will be up at the crack of dawn to leave with his friends on a camping trip. The parents of an indolent child should therefore be alert to find what it is that does interest and stimulate the child, and increase such content in the child's daily life.

What about the child that obviously dislikes school, and the parents have a daily battle with getting him up in time to make the school bus? The answer is obvious. For this child, school is boring, and the parents are faced with the challenge of making education more exciting and interesting. This is a formidable task, particularly since much of what transpires in school is out of the parents' hands. Nevertheless, it is important to realize what the cause of the child's indolence is for two reasons. Firstly, it may be possible for parents to devise some ingenious methods of making the schoolwork interesting. Secondly, if this is not feasible, acknowledging it and helping the child realize that there are things in life that are obligatory even if they are not very exciting, and that we must overcome our resistances in order to do them is preparing the child for the realities of life.

It should be recognized that the child's indolence is therefore usually not the fault of the child, but rather of the "system," i.e., the school and parents combined, who have not succeeded in making education exciting. Children are very much like adults, who may stay awake when a lecture is stimulating, but fall asleep when it is boring. To blame the child for being indolent is like the father who chastised his daughter, "You must become a *bas talmid chacham* (daughter of a Torah scholar)." The reprimand in this case should be directed at the father rather than towards the daughter. Chastising the child for something that is not his fault can severely depress his self-esteem. Acknowledging the fact that the system has not succeeded in making education interesting and impressing upon the child that this is one of the tasks we must do even when we are less than enthusiastic will avoid an assault on the child's self-esteem and may enable him to cope with the problem more satisfactorily.

Section III

Jewish Parents: Fundamentals Of Parenting

Chapter Nine

Parents Are Teachers

*W*hile the essence and the responsibilities of parenting are familiar to us, Luzatto says in his introduction to the *Path of the Just* that it is precisely the things which we take for granted that require special attention. It is the most familiar principles that should be refreshed and clarified, and to which we should consciously rededicate ourselves, lest they lose their vitality and become items of lifeless rote. Parenting is far too important to be allowed to regress to rote performance.

When we came into being as a nation at Sinai and accepted Torah as the reason for our nationhood, G-d asked, "Who are your guarantors that you will preserve the Torah?" and our ancestors responded, "Our children are our guarantors" (*Tanchuma, Vayigash* 2). It is thus the responsibility of parents to transmit Torah, the *raison d'etre* for our existence, to their children. The role of a parent is thus that of a teacher.

The Talmudic statement, "Whoever teaches the child of another person Torah is considered as though he bore him" (*Sanhedrin* 19b), indicates the close identity of the role of parent and teacher. Although we eventually turn our children over to a professional teacher for formal education, parents are the primary teachers, and this is a function which they never outgrow. The professional teacher augments the parental role, but the parents never divest themselves of this responsibility.

For all intents and purposes, Torah is not something which one acquires on his own. *Ethics of the Fathers* begins with the statement that Moses received the Torah from G-d and transmitted it to Joshua, who in turn transmitted it to his successors in an endless chain which has continued to this very day. Torah is thus something which is transmitted from generation to generation.

Transmission of Torah requires more than didactic instruction. The latter may be compared to a seed, whose optimal growth into a plant will occur only if it is planted in soil that has been adequately prepared, and it is the parents who prepare the child for Torah. The Talmud relates that the mother of the great sage Rabbi Joshua placed his carriage outside the *Beis Hamedrash*, so that he would absorb the words of Torah in his infancy (*Jerusalem Talmud Yevamos* 1:6). She certainly knew that the infant could not understand what he heard, but she wished the sensitive mind of the infant to be impressed with the sound of Torah study. But perhaps it is not so much this early exposure which resulted in the child becoming the greatest scholar of his generation, as it was his mother's attitude, which emphasized the primacy of Torah. The infant may have indeed absorbed the sound of Torah from the scholars, but he acquired the love of Torah from his mother.

Not all parents are in a position to transmit the scholarly content of Torah to their children, any more than all parents can transmit scientific data. Furthermore, the parental preoccupation with earning a livelihood and running a household does not allow them sufficient time to be formal teachers, and it is for this reason that there is a need for professional teachers. Yet, parents, like professional teachers, will succeed in this role only to the degree that they get to know and understand the child/student and how to reach him. The Solomonic instruction, "Train the child according to his way"

(*Proverbs* 22:6), presupposes that the parents/teacher knows the particular way of the child/student and that he is teaching accordingly. If one does not know the way of the child, one must make an effort to get to know it. We cannot assume that the child's way is our way, or that all children can be approached in any one way.

We are living in an age of mass production. No longer does an artisan invest his efforts in fashioning a product. Rather, various workers provide different parts which are then assembled into a whole. This is a practice which has proven itself profitable for industry, and has allowed for greater production of automobiles and various mechanical apparatuses.

Unfortunately, we are often impressed by the dramatic success of technology in industry, and we have consequently adapted the "mass production" method to education. But alas! We have often produced students who are essentially "mechanical apparatuses." The erosion of the more intense teacher/student relationship which was sacrificed for the efficiency of mass production education has given the parental teaching function even greater importance.

In Israel, I once had a suit made for me by an old-world tailor. I was quite satisfied with the suit at the last fitting, but the tailor shook his head sadly, and told me that I must return for yet another fitting. When I returned he said, "I could not sleep all night. I did not like the way the suit fit you, and I kept thinking, 'What must I do so that the suit fits properly?' " This kind of investment is not feasible with an "off the rack" garment, and is possible only with an artisan whose pride makes him emotionally involved in his product. It is this kind of dedication and thought that teachers should ideally have for their students. Unfortunately, modern students are most often "off the rack" products, and while this is a fact of life in formal education, it should never occur in parental training.

The importance of Torah education and the degree of dedication required of a teacher is evident in the Talmudic law that if a student is sent into exile to a city of refuge for the accidental killing of a person, his teacher must accompany him (*Makkos* 10a). It is no more conceivable to deprive a person of his Torah instruction than of food and water. Certainly the parental responsibility of transmitting Torah to a child surpasses even that of a formal teacher.

The methods and techniques of approaching each child in "his way" will vary with each child. While some of the "how to" books are helpful, there is no way in which packaged instructions can suffice. Each child's personality is as unique as his fingerprints. Each child's mind is a lock which requires a specific key and there is no skeleton or master key that will work for all. G-d gives the parents the means to understand their children, but just as everything that G-d gives us exists in potential and we must make it operational, so it is with the understanding and teaching of our children. Like the tailor, we may have to be awake nights not only to provide a child with his feedings in infancy, but also to think about what it is that we must do to achieve the "perfect fitting" for each child.

What parents should eventually arrive at in relating to their children and in transmitting Torah values to them is essentially a *formula*; i.e., the right combination of ingredients. The components for each child may be the same, but it is the unique blend of the ingredients in quantity and quality which will maximize for the child his emotional strengths and allow him to use his intellectual capacities to their optimum. Let us look at some of these.

Chapter Ten

Blending the Ingredients

*P*arents begin their teaching roles upon the birth of an infant, a tiny being that has a unique genetic composition which is in a state of "raw material." The infant at birth is essentially pure desire, knowing of no rules, no discipline, essentially nothing other than whether he is comfortable or uncomfortable. The parents must help and develop the raw material into the spiritual person he is to become, one who is superior to lower forms of life not only in intellect, but in being a master over his physical inclinations rather than being enslaved by them.

The prototype for this is the transformation of a population which only knew of a slave mentality into one which would be a "kingdom of priests and a holy nation" (*Exodus* 19:6). A seven-week interval elapsed between the deliverance from slavery to the acceptance of the Torah, and we have perpetuated that period of near-miraculous transformation by the *mitzvah* of the counting of the *omer* in the seven weeks between Passover and Shavuos. Following each day's counting, we recite a prayer wherein we say that by virtue of this *mitzvah* we wish to rectify a defect of particular character trait.

The *kabbalah* speaks of seven *middos* (traits), two of which are primary: *chesed* (kindness, mercy) and *gevurah* (harshness and strictness). There are five derivative traits: *tiferes* (splendor), *netzach* (triumph), *hod* (glory), *yesod* (fundamentals), and *malchus* (sovereignty). These traits do not always exist as a pure culture. There may be *chesed shebechesed*, kindness in its purest form, or *chesed shebegevurah*, kindness which is contained within strictness, or *chesed shebemalchus*, kindness which is contained within sovereignty. There may thus be seven variations of each of the seven traits, for a total of 49 combinations, or one for each day of the seven weeks. By rectifying one of these combined traits each day, the necessary character transformation was achieved in the seven weeks between the Exodus and the giving of the Torah at Sinai. So rapid a transformation could be accomplished only under the leadership of Moses, and for us, character development requires a greater amount of time. Nevertheless, the pattern established by Moses still applies: defining the traits and gradually working toward their perfection.

Chesed and *gevurah* may at first appear to be irreconcilable opposites, because kindness and strictness seem to be at opposite poles. Just a bit of reflection, however, will indicate that this is not so.

Devoted mothers take their infants to the doctor for immunization, and allow the doctor to cause the child pain with an injection, which is often followed by 48 hours of pain and fever. This is nevertheless an indication of the mother's love for the child, as she wishes to protect him from life-threatening diseases. The *gevurah* or harshness which is manifest is in fact a true kindness or *chesed*. While giving a child the candy he desires is *chesed shebechesed*, a kindness which both mother and child recognize as such, the immunization is *gevurah shebechesed*, strictness which is in fact a kindness. The same pattern holds true for all the traits, the majority of which are alloys.

All the *middos* are inherent in the newborn infant, and it is the parents' task to help the child direct them into proper channels. This is accomplished primarily by parental role-modeling, and can be augmented by verbal teaching.

On several occasions I have referred to the Shabbos table as being a forum where parents can discuss happenings of the week and relate stories of our great personalities. The Shabbos table presents a unique teaching opportunity which should not be overlooked. It is rather rare to have the entire family together in a setting which is conducive to discussions. During the week, everyone is occupied doing his own thing. The father may be working late at the office, and the mother may have a meeting. The children may be busy doing their homework, taking music lessons, or are at friends' homes. Shabbos may be the only occasion when all activities are restricted, and the family can share time together. This is an invaluable opportunity and should be utilized to the maximum.

The weekly portion of the Torah can be used to teach *middos* (character development). There are many fine books and audiotapes that elaborate on the weekly portion of the Torah. Children should be encouraged to say a few words about what they have studied in Torah during the week, and virtually everything in Torah can be expanded to refer to *middos*.

Even young children can absorb much from the Torah discussions at the Shabbos table. I distinctly remember that at age six or seven I heard my father explain why we cover our eyes when we say the *Shema*. He said that when we refer to G-d in the *Shema* as "*Hashem*," we are referring to the attribute of *chesed*, whereby the kindness, mercy, and compassion of G-d are immediately apparent to us. When we say, "*Elokeinu*," we are referring to the attribute of G-d when He appears to be acting toward us with strictness, firmness, and even harshness. When we say, "*Hashem Elokeinu Hashem Echad*," we are not only declaring the unity of G-d, but we are also asserting that both the manifest kindness (*Hashem*) and the manifest harshness (*Elokeinu*) are both *Hashem Echad*, one and the same, all kindness. Everything that G-d does is kindness, even though we may not always see it as such. We may perceive

"*Elokeinu*" as conducting Himself in a way that may not appear to us at all to be kindness.

We thus have a conflict between something we accept as a principle of faith; namely, that everything that G-d does is *chesed*, and our human perception, that there are things He does which we see as being *gevurah*. In the *Shema* we testify that it is our belief that is correct, and that our human perception is fallible. To reinforce this, we symbolically cover our eyes, to indicate that we will set aside that which we perceive to be harshness, in deference to our *emunah* (faith), in the absolute kindness of G-d, and that what appears to us as *gevurah* is really *gevurah shebechesed*.

I recall my father quoting the *Zohar*, who states that the episode of Joseph and his brothers contains the secret of the *Shema*. My father explained this passage in the *Zohar* by pointing out that the patriarch Jacob mourned incessantly over the disappearance of his beloved son, and complained to G-d about his suffering. The *Midrash* states that G-d said, "Here I am arranging things so that his son will become ruler over the mightiest empire in the world, yet he complains." My father said that the loss of Joseph appeared to Jacob to be an unmitigated catastrophe, yet years later he discovered that it was all for the good. That good can sometimes be delivered via an unpleasant vehicle is the message of the *Shema*.

I heard this explanation at the Shabbos table when I was six years old, and for the next 60 years I have been reciting the *Shema* daily, putting my hand in front of my eyes to remind me that my human perception is fallible. As I grew older and encountered various difficult experiences in life, which may not have been made any less difficult by this — when a tooth hurts, it hurts — but accepting some of the unpleasantness of life with serenity has been made somewhat easier. Furthermore, time has indeed demonstrated that many things that appeared to be disadvantageous at the time they occurred were subsequently proven to have been blessings in disguise.

But such teachings, important as they may be, are of value only if they augment what parents manifest in their behavior. How do they adapt to adversity? Parents are not expected to react joyfully to adversity, but neither should they fall into despair. Life is not without unpleasant experiences, and how parents react to these becomes an example from which children can learn. When parents' reaction to adversity is tempered by faith and trust in the Divine wisdom and judgment, then the teachings of the Talmud that "Everything that G-d does is for the ultimate good" can be more effective.

My father used to relate a story of a man who asked the Maggid of Mezeritch how the Talmud can require a person to express gratitude to G-d for the bad as well as the good, and the Maggid referred him to his disciple, Rabbi Zusia. When the man posed the question, Rabbi Zusia shrugged his shoulders and said, "I couldn't possibly know the answer to this question, because nothing bad has ever happened to me." Observing Rabbi Zusia's tattered clothes and his frail condition, the man had the answer to his question. We may not be able to achieve the degree of faith and trust of Rabbi Zusia, but such stories do help create a perspective that *chesed* and *gevurah* are compatible.

Chesed and *gevurah* appear to be polar opposites, yet are reconcilable when we realize that *gevurah* is but an outer garment with which *chesed* is sometimes covered.

There are many other pairs of opposites in life, and the correct path in life requires obtaining a proper balance between the two. Rambam preaches, "The mean of virtue," contending that all extremes are inappropriate, and that for each set of opposites there is a mean which is healthy and proper. The mean is not necessarily a midpoint, because there are pairs of traits where the mean is closer to one pole than the other.

Children can quite easily grasp that there are extreme conditions which are incompatible with life, such as extreme heat and extreme cold, and that life can exist only when the two are in proper balance. Similarly, both intense light and intense darkness are not conducive to life. We cannot function in absolute darkness, nor can we bear to look at the brightness of the midday sun. As children mature, they learn more about the balance of nature, and that there are conflicting forces that keep each other in check.

Children are prone to extremes. They are either euphoric when they get what they want or they wail tearfully when their wishes are denied. Children must be taught to appreciate the grays of reality. They will hear much about evil: floods, earthquakes, fires, killings, death, destruction, and they will want to know why a kind, benevolent G-d allows so many terrible things to happen. They will ask relevant questions, some of which adults may tend to avoid because they generate too much anxiety in them. "Come to think of it, why does G-d permit such terrible things to happen?" Children will hear about the Holocaust, and they will want to know why.

These questions should not be avoided. We should do extensive reading ourselves, for example, philosophical works such as Luzatto's *Ways of G-d,* and then try to make it understandable to young children to the best of our ability. Essentially, Luzatto states that G-d wished man to have free choice, and in order for there to be free choice, the amount of good and evil in the world must be equal. Any dominance of one over the other would distort the delicate balance which is necessary to permit a human being to make a truly free choice.

There is much kindness in the world, much love and friendship, much healing, and many constructive deeds. To maintain a balance, there must be an equivalent amount of evil, and man is then free to choose between the two.

We have to share with our children that there are some questions to which we have no adequate answers, such as: Why would G-d want man to have free choice? Why not just make the world full of goodness? What is the reason for creation in the first place?

These may seem to be profound philosophical questions that should be relegated to scholars who can wrestle with them. But make no mistake about it. Children do think and question. We may describe G-d to them as being pure Goodness and Kindness, and if they do not ask it in so many words, they may be thinking, "Then why did Zeidy die when he was so young and such a kind person?" Or why one of their little friends was stricken with a terrible disease, or why any of the other bad things happen. Their young minds might not be capable of digesting the Book of *Job,* but rest assured that they, like Job and the rest of us, are wondering why bad things happen to good people.

We must tell our children that there are some things which human beings are simply incapable of understanding, because intelligence is finite, whereas G-d's wisdom is infinite. If parents are comfortable in accepting these principles of faith themselves, children are likely to follow suit.

In discussing Torah at the Shabbos table there will be many opportunities to talk about *ahavah* (love of G-d) and *yirah* (fear of G-d). Here again we have two apparent opposites, because in our experience, love and fear toward the same person appear to be mutually exclusive. We should explain to our children that *yirah* also refers to a sense of awe, of being overcome by the infinity of G-d, to which we can relate in everyday experience, just as one feels his breath being taken away at the first sight of Niagara Falls or when peering down the Grand Canyon. The sheer vastness of these natural phenomena overwhelm a person. We should explain the concept of Divine punishment as being an act of consideration, whereby G-d wishes us to avoid what is harmful to us, although we may not understand in what ways transgressing His will is harmful. We may point out that a small child whose rubber ball has gone into the street may run after it because he is not aware of the danger of oncoming cars. If the parent spanks the child for running into the street, it is not because the parent is angry, but because he wishes to protect the child from injury. Similarly, we believe that violating the Torah is harmful to us, but if a person does not perceive this, he is similar to the child who is ignorant of the danger of running into the street, and may have to be "spanked" for his own good.

There are things we ask of G-d that he may deny us because they are not for our ultimate good, just as a mother may deny her child's wish for ice cream before a meal. In relationship to the superior wisdom of G-d, even mature adults may be very much like a child, who may be frustrated and resentful because he craves the ice cream and cannot understand why his mother is denying him this pleasure. We can teach our children that while G-d hears all our prayers, we are only *asking* for things, and are not giving Him commands. When the things we ask for are not to our advantage according to His infinite wisdom, He will not give them to us. These concepts can be understood even by young children, and can help them adjust better to the realities of life. However, they will be convincing only if the parents themselves genuinely believe them.

Guests who are invited to the Shabbos table should be told that the occasion is being utilized for family education. They are certainly welcome to participate and contribute to the discussion, but a guest should not be permitted to preempt the conversation with topics that are not of educational value for the children. Other matters the guests wish to discuss can wait for after the meal.

We are fortunate in having many anecdotes about Torah personalities that we can utilize to clarify things for children. Also, there are many interesting parables in Jewish literature that can illuminate more abstract concepts, and a collection of these can be found in the works of the great Maggid of Dubno. There are also charming stories that have been retold by Rabbi Sholom Schwadron as related in ArtScroll's *Maggid* series. The association of Shabbos discussions with the delicacies of the Shabbos table can result in a lasting impression on the minds of young children.

Chapter Eleven

Fathers and Mothers

ar too often, parenting is taken for granted, and insufficient attention is paid to the specific roles of the father and mother. Traditionalists may assume that the father is the breadwinner and the mother is the homemaker; i.e., the father provides the means whereby the mother prepares the meals and buys the children's clothes. This is too simplistic and fails to delineate the specific contributions of the father and mother in the child's spiritual upbringing and character development. With many families today having both parents employed, the assignment of who is to do what in the child's character development has become even more blurred. And, of course, in the case of a single parent family, the parent having primary responsibility for raising the children must know what functions he/she must perform.

If we turn to Torah and *halachah* for guidelines we will be well rewarded. *Halachah* states that whether a child is a Jew or not is determined by the identity of the mother, but whether a child is a *Kohen, Levi,* or *Yisrael* is determined by the identity of the father.

Philosophic writings are replete with discussions of "form" and "substance," and often these discussions of abstract concepts are of rather limited interest to anyone other than a philosopher. However, in regard to parenting these terms are applicable in a quite lucid way. "Substance" refers to that of which an item is made, and "form" is what the artisan makes of it. Gold, silver, and clay are different substances and each may be given the same form as one fashions a plate out of each. On the other hand, the same substance may be given different forms, as when one fashions silver into candlesticks, jewelry, or cutlery.

The "substance" of the child, whether he is Jewish or not, is determined by the mother. What *kind* of a Jew he will be is determined by the father. The essence of a child's Jewishness is derived from the mother. The "fine tuning" of his Jewishness is determined by the father.

Let us now turn to the Scriptures for further direction. It is customary to teach a child the words of Torah as soon as he is old enough to speak. Traditionally the first words a child is taught are "Moses commanded us Torah, which is an inheritance to the congregation of Jacob" (*Deuteronomy* 33:4), the *Shema,* and in many families also the verse of *Proverbs,* "Hear, my son, the educating words of your father, and do not forsake the teachings of your mother" (1:8); the latter verse is particularly enlightening.

Students of Torah know that each word is significant and each word has its own connotations and particular meaning. In the verse from *Proverbs,* the child is instructed to listen to the *mussar* of his father, and not to forsake the *Torah* of his mother. Scriptural words are not chosen at random. Solomon was very specific when he assigned *mussar* to the father, and *Torah* to the mother.

Rabbi Samson Raphael Hirsch states that the word *yassar,* "to discipline," is closely related to the word *yatzar,* "to fashion." Thus, although we may generally think of *mussar* as being chastisement or reprimand, it must be understood in the sense of "formation." While *mussar may* sometimes have a connotation of admonition, it is primarily the process whereby a father helps "fashion" the child and direct him to development of *middos*, channeling his traits in the proper direction.

According to Solomon, *Torah* is transmitted by the mother. This may come a surprise to many, since we generally assume Torah teaching to be the fraternal role. Perhaps we need a better understanding of *Torah*.

One of the *mussar* authorities quotes the statement of Rabbi Akiva, that the *klal* or all-inclusive rule of Torah is "Love your neighbor as yourself" (*Nedarim* 9:4). He states that every *prat* or detail must be subject to the *klal*. Hence, he says, every single *mitzvah* is part of the *klal* of *ahavas Yisrael*, of love for your neighbor. If one has performed a *mitzvah*, and has not thereby strengthened and improved his *ahavas Yisrael*, then the performance of the *mitzvah* is incomplete. We can further understand this by the teaching of the Baal Shem Tov, that *ahavas Hashem* is accessible only through *ahavas Yisrael*.

This is an overwhelmingly important and perhaps a somewhat revolutionary insight. It means that *ahavas Yisrael* cannot be achieved without performance of *mitzvos*, regardless of how much one might insist otherwise, and it also means that the performance of *mitzvos* which does not result in enhancement of *ahavas Yisrael* is defective.

How can performance of *mitzvos* enhance *ahavas Yisrael*? Rabbi Mendel of Rimanov points out that the reason the *manna* was given prior to Sinai was because the obstacles to *ahavas Yisrael* are generally greed, lust, and envy, all of which emanate from the desire to acquire that which is not one's own. The *manna* was collected and retained only in the amount needed per person for each day, and any excess rotted. The message of the *manna* was therefore that each person will get exactly what his needs are, no more and no less, hence there is no reason to desire what others have. This attitude is conducive to eliminating all the offenses that a person can commit against others.

This attitude can also be fostered by performance of other *mitzvos*. One may ask: How does putting on *tefillin* or taking the *lulav* and *esrog* contribute to *ahavas Yisrael*? All the *mitzvos* represent the conviction that we were placed in this world, not *primarily* but *solely* and *totally* to fulfill the will of G-d, and we reinforced this belief with performance of every *mitzvah.* While we may certainly enjoy life, gratification of our desires is not the reason for living. As we strengthen our conviction that life is for the fulfillment of the Divine will, the self-centered drives that present obstacles to *ahavas Yisrael* are eliminated.

Identifying Torah with *ahavas Yisrael* helps us understand why Solomon assigns the transmission of *Torah* to the mother. *Ahavas Yisrael* is essentially an emotional concept. The emotional makeup of a child is much more influenced by the mother than the father. It is primarily the mother who cares for the child in its infancy, feeds, bathes, and dresses him. In early life, there is generally much more physical contact with the mother than with the father.

Commenting on the verse in *Proverbs,* "A wise son gladdens a father, but a foolish son is the grief of his mother" (10:1), Rabbi Hirsch states:

> It is interesting that joy from a successful son is foretold here to the father, while sorrow from an unsuccessful son is linked with the mother. We believe this may be based on the following consideration: No matter how much a father does for his child, it cannot be compared to the sacrifices and privations of a mother. For her, months and years of suffering and renunciation set in from the very beginning of her child's existence. By the time the father directs his personal attention to the child's development, the mother has already devoted years of constant care to his physical, spiritual, and moral growth. It follows that if the child turns out to be well-brought up, and the parents are fortunate enough to find joy in a wise and successful son, the father has won a big prize — in return for a comparatively low stake. If, on the other hand, the child becomes an inept, foolish person, then who can fathom the grief of his mother? She is forced to admit that she has wasted years of anxious days and sleepless nights, that she has spent the best part of her physical strength and mental energy, and all this for what result? — a foolish son.

Rabbi Hirsch continues with a quote from *Proverbs,* "What, my son? And what, son of my womb? And what, son of my vows?" (31:2).

Thus begins a mother's admonition to her son, the king. A true mother has been preparing her thoughts for the spiritual future of her child while he was yet in her womb; her solemn vows accompany his entrance into the world. He is the son of her womb and the son of her vows. A mother's thoughts and emotions during the time that she bears and suckles her child are not without effect. The saying "to imbibe something with one's mother's milk" is no empty phrase. That is the time when the seed is planted for the child's qualities of character, for gentleness or violence, for modesty or sensuality, for a conduct of nobility or vulgarity. This seed is planted within her child by his mother's thoughts while he is still physically connected with her. After that it is his mother's example which shows his awakening soul the ideas that he should follow — truth, decency, purity, or their opposites! Showing her child the right way takes intelligence and firm resolve on the part of a mother, for the success of his future behavior depends on her teaching him the first requirement: to control his own will.

The father's teachings are of great importance, but just as the value of a finished product made by the finest craftsmen depends on the material he was given to work with—gold, silver, tin— the child produced by the father's education cannot be better than the substance provided by the mother; i.e., the basic traits of love, trust, consideration, reverence, and patience.

The uniqueness of the human being is that while he has a physical and essentially animal body that has many biological drives, he also has a spirit, a Divine component which enables him to be master of his bodily drives. Rabbi Hirsch states that the seed for this mastery is implanted by the mother as early as when the child is developing within her. Let us go back to Rabbi Hirsch:

And so, when this son of his mother's womb and his mother's vows has become a king, wishing to transmit wisdom to his people, he looks back upon the period of his earliest childhood, saying:

Yet was I a son to my father, tender and alone before my mother. Then he taught me and said to me: Let your heart hold fast my words, keep my commandments, and live; acquire wisdom, acquire understanding (*Proverbs* 4:3-5).

Note carefully that Solomon inserts the phrase "tender and alone before my mother," which appears to be not only superfluous but out of context. The verse would seem to run more smoothly if it read, "Yet was I a son to my father, who taught me ..." What Solomon is telling us is that the father's teaching would have fallen on deaf ears if the mother had not nurtured and prepared the child to be receptive to the father's words. It is she who gives him the tenderness and develops the soul for emergence of the *middos* requisite for *ahavas Yisrael*. It is she who makes him feel unique and plants the seeds for self-esteem, for only then can the father's transmission of Torah take root and result in wisdom and understanding.

There is certainly some overlapping of parental roles, and the above delineation is not meant to be restrictive. However, defining the roles of the father and mother gives us greater insight into the enormous responsibility of parenting, and that it is not something that can be relegated to rot. Much conscious effort must be invested in these vital processes.

Toward a Toolbox
for Jewish Parents

Chapter Twelve

Tools of Teaching

hile providing for all the child's physical and emotional needs is a prime responsibility of parents, teaching the child the values of his community and transmitting the treasures of his culture are uniquely human parental responsibilities. When we send children to educational institutions, whether elementary or advanced, we hope that the child's instructors will be well educated in the art of teaching, so that they may be able to bring out the best in the child and stimulate him not only to learn but to be desirous of learning. There are few people who are natural-born teachers with intuitive pedagogic skills. Most others have acquired or greatly improved these skills by diligent study, practice and training under master teachers.

There is no reason why the approach toward optimum parenting should be any different. While some rare people are gifted with excellent parenting skills and an intuitive sense of children, most of us need to work more or less diligently on becoming quality parents. With effort, patience, practice and a willingness to learn, most of us can improve our parenting skills. Most parents experience a second child as distinctively less anxiety provoking than a first. Much of what was cause for concern — a first fever spiking to 102 degrees — is taken in stride and seems less dramatic. This illustrates the effect of simple practice. The second time around is actually easier, all things considered. Yet there seems to be a rather prevalent assumption that all parents are intuitively endowed with parenting skills and do not require any additional learning or knowledge. This is surely not so. Most parents could benefit greatly from learning more optimal and effective approaches to parenting their children.

Teaching comes in many forms and shapes. The most skilled parent is the one who has a repertoire that encompasses many different teaching tools. The more tools, the larger the toolbox. The more tools, the more diverse the tasks that can be accomplished. A skilled worker can tackle more complex, intricate, challenging, and novel jobs with the necessary tools at his disposal. Better and quicker solutions are dependent upon a rich array of skills and tools that can be combined in a myriad of ways.

I recall being told that a pair of pliers is the most versatile tool a person can own. It can grasp and be used as a wrench, one can pound a nail with it, giving it the function of a hammer, and if the end of one handle is sufficiently thin, it can be used as a screwdriver. Yet, a skilled worker would hardly avail himself of the many possible applications of this single tool, and would have in his tool chest a wrench, a hammer, and a screwdriver, in addition to the pliers.

It is also meaningless to state that a hammer is a better tool than a screwdriver. Obviously, the value of any tool at any given time will depend on the function it is called upon to perform. Similarly, one cannot say that teaching via reward system is superior to teaching via explanation. One method may be preferable for one task, and the other for another. Part of the art of parenting is to match the tool to the situation and the child. A large toolbox gives parents flexibility in parenting and presents them with more choices of how to respond, how to intervene, what to say and do. This way we are more likely to reach the child and influence his development and guide his education. It is vital to understand this simple point. The best parenting technique is worthless if it does not reach the child. In a way, we need to customize our parenting to fit the child. As *Proverbs* reminds us: "Teach the child according to *his* way." Since children come in all shapes and sizes, we need to be prepared as parents to meet their needs at their level and according to their ways.

Doctrinaire approaches in psychotherapy have often been counterproductive. For example, a therapist who utilizes only a psychodynamic, psychoanalytic approach to all persons' problems will do some of them a disservice. An eclectic approach, tailoring the methodology to the particular needs of the patient, will provide the most effective results.

Teachers and therapists, while providing a service to students and clients, may not always have the latter's interest as their primary motivation. To some, teaching or counseling may just be the way of earning a livelihood, and it is conceivable that a personal interest may operate to the student's or client's detriment, as when a patient is held in treatment longer than necessary because the therapist wishes to continue charging a fee.

As a rule, parents are motivated by their children's best interest. However, this is not always pure and is not without exception. Personal interests of parents may consciously or unconsciously influence how they relate to their children. Parents are subject to the human frailty of self-interest, and rather than be frightened of the awareness that their management of their children may be tainted with their personal desires, parents would do well to recognize this as a possibility, and direct their attention to eliminating such influences so that they may be totally motivated by what is best for their children.

Let us now take a closer look at parental toolboxes.

Chapter Thirteen

Tool Kit #1: Environmental Engineering

here is much that we do in our homes that provides a setting for Torah teaching, and with a bit of creative thinking, we can enhance the message of an otherwise silent environment.

Our doors are marked by *mezuzos,* so that when we leave our homes to interact with the outside world and when we return home to relate to one another, we do so in the spirit of the *Shema,* which we discussed in an earlier chapter. Kissing the *mezuzah* as we leave and enter is indeed a wonderful practice, but too often it is merely a perfunctory gesture, devoid of much — if any — feeling and thought. I know of a man who would not perform the gesture of kissing the *mezuzah,* but as he entered the doorway, he would place his hand on the *mezuzah* and spend a few moments in silent meditation. This is no doubt superior to a habitual gesture.

The *mezuzah* represents the watchful presence of G-d as He protects the home. Would it not be foolish to install a burglar alarm to protect a home and then invite thieves into the house? How can we expect our homes to be protected by G-d if we invite destructive influences into the home, such as television channels that portray the worst of all possible human behaviors? Let alone that even a mature adult is not immune to the immoral impact of these programs, how can we expect our children to behave according to high moral standards when we expose them to such frank scenes of corruption? What can children who watch the sitcoms conclude other than that all children are precocious and that all parents are nothing more than bewildered and blundering incompetents. Providing a means for these television shows to enter our homes defeats the message of the *mezuzah.*

Parents who kiss the *mezuzah* religiously and allow a television to infiltrate their home remind me of the man who entered a purportedly kosher restaurant and asked the proprietor, "Is this restaurant really kosher?"

The proprietor responded, "How can you even ask such a question? Just look at whose pictures are hanging on the wall: the Baal HaTanya and the Chofetz Chaim."

The customer said, "If you were hanging on the wall and the Baal HaTanya and the Chofetz Chaim were here, I would have no question whatever. Given that they are on the wall and you are here, I have my doubts."

I think that if we spent more time thinking about the *mezuzah* and perfunctorily kissing the television set, our children would be far better influenced than if we perfunctorily kiss the *mezuzah* and spend too much time with the television.

I know of some families that have television sets and the parents claim that they are in total control of what the children watch. If we are indeed aware of the toxic content of some television shows, then this is a mistake. In psychology we speak of "stimulus control," an example of which is to avoid having ice cream in the freezer or other fattening foods in the house if one is dieting. Think of the things you wish your children not to do, and eliminate the stimuli that are related to these. Think of things you *do* wish the children to do, then have these stimuli prominent in the home.

Many Jewish homes are graced by the presence of sacred books: the Scriptures and a set of the Talmud. This is admirable indeed, but not nearly as effective as when children see their parents reading these sacred books. The Scriptures, the Talmud, and many great Torah works are now available in English, so that they are accessible to all. We indeed indicate that we love Torah by displaying these sacred books in our home, but the message is enhanced manifold if they are put to more than ornamental use.

There are now many items of Judaica available, and their presence in the home expresses an attitude toward Torah observance. There is a principle of beautifying performance of the *mitzvos.* An attractive *kiddush* cup, candlesticks for the *Shabbos* candles, container for the *esrog,* spice box for the *havdalah* service, Chanukah *menorah, seder* plate — all these convey our love for *mitzvos.* Putting up the *sukkah* and decorating it can be a *mitzvah* project in which the entire family participates. Family heirlooms, such as a *kiddush* cup used by a grandfather, may symbolize the continuity of tradition, and the love with which such items are cherished can help influence our children with the importance of the *mitzvos.*

It might be wise to take a stroll around the house and look at the layout, as to whether it is optimally conducive to family cohesiveness, to self-esteem development, and to transmission of values. For example, suppose there is not enough room in the kitchen for the family to eat together during the week, with the result that meals are eaten almost cafeteria-style. Remodeling the kitchen to provide space for an eating area may require sacrificing storage and counter space. Might the trade-off, i.e., bringing the family together for meals and snacks, not be worth the sacrifice? The children's awareness that very desirable space was sacrificed in order to bring the family together for meals may be sending an important message.

When a newborn child enters the house, it is traditional to affix a *Shir Lamaalos* (Psalm 121) near the infant's crib, so that the first object the child sees as his vision begins to focus is words of Torah.

Do we perpetuate this message, so that the first thing on arising and that the last thing on retiring is exposure to Torah?

We would like our children to develop habits of neatness and orderliness. Have we created enough space, easily accessible, for the children to put away their toys, coats, boots, and sweaters? Are the shelves for children's books at a level where they can easily reach them?

Both the attitudinal and physical environments created in the home by the parents should provide the appropriate background, the fertile ground, in which their goals can begin to take root.

Chapter Fourteen

Tool Kit #2: Observing and Imitating

here are some cultures where children are not taught directly, but observe how their parents do things and behave. The adults do not instruct their children, and do not even encourage questions. How then do these children learn?

Learning can occur in many different ways. Learning by observation is a very powerful teaching tool. Children tend to imitate parents from the earliest ages, and pick up many things that parents do not actually "teach" them.

We have a prototype in this in *Judges*, "Observe what I do, and do likewise" (7:17). The Talmud states that G-d rejects an offering that is acquired dishonestly. A king and his entourage were reentering the country, and the king told his servants to pay the customs tax on the items they bought. "What purpose is there in doing so, Your Majesty?" the servants asked. "The tax will ultimately go to you anyway." The king responded, "Yes, but I want my subjects to see that the king observes the law of the land, so that they will do likewise." Similarly, although everything belongs to G-d, He will not receive an offering that was acquired dishonestly, thereby setting an example that people should not accept anything that was acquired dishonestly (*Sukkah* 30a).

It is common to see a young child drape himself with a towel, take a *siddur,* and sway to and fro, imitating how his father prays wearing a *talis.* While this is cute, imitation may at times be embarrassing, but also enlightening, as when, in the presence of company, the little girl scolds her doll, and wagging her finger at it says in a stern voice, "And this time I really mean it."

A psychologist was consulted by parents who complained that their son was aggressive and belligerent, and would hit his younger siblings whenever there was a conflict. Further investigation revealed that the child was merely repeating the behavior that he observed when his parents punished the children or when his older siblings were frustrated with him. There is no question that how we resolve conflicts or how we react to adversity, or how we treat others, greatly influences how our children will react in similar situations.

Imitation occurs not only with behavior, but also with attitudes. When I lecture on the subject of self-esteem, someone in the audience invariably asks, "What can we do as parents to enhance self-esteem in our children?" My response is that self-esteem is contagious. Parents who feel self-confident and adequate convey this attitude to their children. Parents who feel anxious and insecure will convey these feelings to their children. Everything parents do, and even how parents think and feel, has an impact on their children.

While we wish to serve as models for our children, there is also some apprehension in this. We are all far from perfect, and we may feel guilty if our children adapt some of our undesirable traits. One father who had a violent temper, and rejected the recommendation that he get psychological help in controlling his anger, regretted his recalcitrance when his son was ejected from a yeshivah because of belligerent behavior. Parents must be aware that they are constantly under scrutiny, and that their behavior will likely be imitated by their children.

One Rebbe confided that he must watch his every move, because some of his *chassidim* watch him carefully and may imitate every thing he does. Parents should have an awareness that the way they talk and act is being observed by their children, who are likely to adopt similar behavior. If parents wish to eradicate certain behaviors in their children, they should examine their own behavior for similarities and eliminate them, and if they wish to establish or re-inforce certain behaviors in their children, they should make these part of their own behavior.

As with other feelings that we wish to deny, we may sometimes deny the impact of our behavior on our children. There is a story of an immigrant father with a heavy accent, who complained about his son's difficulty in speaking English properly. "Ah don know vere he get it; Ah don let im outa mine sight forr a minute!"

We can preach at length about *lashon hara* and *ahavas Yisrael*, but when we gossip on the phone or exchange information about others that serves no purpose other than gratifying our desire to gossip, we are telling our children that *lashon hara* and offending others is permissible. Parents may forget how omnipotent, grand, and all knowing their children assume them to be.

Modeling may occur in all stages of life. One time a very wealthy man told my father that he was placing his elderly mother in the home for the aged. My father believed that such institutions were intended for people who had no children to care for them, but that children have a responsibility to look after parents in their old age. My father said to the man, "Just be aware that your children are observing what you are doing. Inasmuch as there is often a waiting list for the home for the aged, you may perhaps wish to make your own reservation well in advance."

Let us be aware of the dangerous message conveyed by a parent who smokes. It is now common knowledge that smoking is hazardous to one's health. Each time parents light a cigarette, they are telling their children, "You may indulge in a pleasurable behavior even if it is harmful, and the discomfort involved in dis-continuing such behavior justifies your continuing it." Can they then really blame the child for using marijuana or cocaine? Furthermore, inasmuch as passive smoking has been proven to be harmful, smoking also conveys the message, "You do not have to be considerate of others if it interferes with your pleasure."

A young girl was consulting a psychologist because of compulsive perfectionism. For her, any mistake was a tragedy. If a drawing she did was not quite right, she crumpled the paper in frustration. As part of the treatment, the parents were put on the alert to highlight their own small mistakes, and to model problem-solving. Once when the mother burnt the bottom of her *challah*, she called her daughter's attention to this, and at the same time showed her that she could manage to salvage the Shabbos. Another time the father and the family all had a hearty laugh when he realized in the evening that he had worn two different colored socks all day long.

By the same token, parents can be positive models. Each time they give *tzedakah* cheerfully or perform a benevolent act, they are teaching the children to be considerate of others. When husband and wife discuss their disagreements in a civil manner and avoid vituperation and screaming, they teach their children how to resolve conflicts amicably. When they discipline their children with controlled firmness rather than with volatile anger they are teaching them how to react constructively to errant behavior. When they recite the *bentching* (blessing after the meal) slowly and with *kavannah* (concentration) they are teaching their children how to express gratitude to G-d. When they set aside all thoughts of business and celebrate the Shabbos with joy and peace of mind, they are not only teaching their children to observe Shabbos, but are also giving them a powerful and invaluable lesson in *bitachon* (trust in G-d) and how to avoid being terrorized by the vicissitudes of the marketplace. When they behave toward a Torah scholar with reverence, they are teaching their children to respect authority.

The potency of stories has already been mentioned, but it is worthwhile repeating. While parents serve as the most significant models for their children, the great Torah personalities in our rich heritage can also be used as models, and parents should develop a repertoire of appropriate stories of our *tzaddikim*. By the same token, we must realize that our children will be impressed by whom we choose as models for ourselves. We may relate to them how the Chofetz Chaim was self-effacing and how he sustained himself with the bare necessities of life, but if we take offense at every personal slight and strive to accumulate wealth and live in luxury, the stories about the Chofetz Chaim will have little impact.

The power of stories or a particular modeling can carry an individual through difficult times, and inspire hope where all seems lost. Stories and modeling can give a person a window to alternate ways of thinking or feeling about difficult periods in life. It is not unusual for adults in psychotherapy to recall how a story carried them through a period of adversity, or how their parents' trust in G-d during a period of sadness served as a pillar of strength for them in similar times.

What kind of models are we for our children in the face of adversity, disappointment, or fatigue? Do we catastrophize or do we model problem-solving? Are we able to take care of ourselves and give to ourselves when we need it? How often can we remain calm in the face of chaos and children fighting? Do we express joy and gratitude at the small things in life that cross our paths everyday?

Self-awareness is essential for parenting as well as for our own adjustment to life. If we have an honest picture of ourselves, we can then plan the kind of changes we like to make in ourselves as models for our children.

In summary, parents become teaching tools themselves. Although we should improve our *middos* primarily for our own selves, in order to become better persons, it is also a potent method to help teach our children the right way to live.

Chapter Fifteen

Tool Kit #3: Visions, Expectations and Meaning

W hen a child is born, the prayer that is recited when the father is called to the Torah is "May the parents raise her/him to Torah, to marriage, and to performance of good deeds." The promise and prayer for a bright future is said when the child has just entered the world.

The Scriptural verse to which we have referred earlier and which may serve as the basis of optimum parenting is "Train the child according to his way, so that when he grows older he will not deviate therefrom" (*Proverbs* 22:6). Like a perfect gem that reflects kaleidoscopic colors, this phrase provides a number of teachings.

The Hebrew word for "train," *chinuch*, is perhaps better translated as "prepare," for that is what *chinuch* really is: a preparation for life as a mature and responsible adult. The *chinuch* which begins in infancy must consider what the child will be as she/he grows older. Parents must already begin to think about the child's study of Torah, her/his behavior, and her/his marriage.

Of course, Jewish parents are sometimes thought to be overzealous about their children's future. There is a story of the mother who was very worried about her son's adaptation to college. Would he become discouraged if he does not make high grades? Is he likely to succumb to peer pressure and smoke marijuana? As she was contemplating all this, she heard him crying, so she went into the next room and changed his diaper.

While we may chuckle at this mother's premature worrying, we might nevertheless ask: When *should* parents begin to worry about such things? The answer is that preparation for the child's ultimate adjustment to the challenges of adult life should indeed begin when he is still in diapers. Use of drugs results from a lack of tolerance of any discomfort, and from pursuing "feeling good" at whatever cost. Parents who swallow tranquilizers when things do not go their way are setting an example that the child may later translate into drug use. Relief from normal stress via taking a chemical is the basis of addiction. A child must learn from observing his parents that a person can cope with stress and can tolerate tension and discomfort. While the child is still very young, the parents should behave in a manner that will prepare him and teach him how to cope when he is much older. Parents must think of and plan for the future long before the child can do so.

It is important to understand that children are not just miniature adults, differing only quantitatively in intelligence. Small children are in many ways *qualitatively* different than adults.

For example, a child may have no concept whatever of "future," and even a very limited concept of past. To the child everything is "now," in the present. Yesterday, a month ago, and a year ago, are all "yesterday," and "tomorrow" may be a meaningless word. Mature concepts of a remote past and a distant future develop very gradually, and at different times with different children. A promise to a child to do something in the summer or at some later date may seem perfectly reasonable to the parent, yet be totally meaningless to the child. It is not that the young child does not *consider* the future, but that he simply has no grasp of the concept of future at all. The present is his only reality.

We know that some adults may have been fixated at some point in their maturation, and may even retain some juvenile patterns of thought. In working with alcoholics, for example, it is clear that many of them are emotionally fixated at a juvenile stage; hence, a highly intelligent and even well-educated person may use alcohol destructively for his immediate gratification, giving no thought whatever to the harm it will eventually cause. In this respect, "future" may not exist even for a highly educated and sophisticated person. The same is true for a person who lights up a cigarette, with total disregard of the grave consequences which smoking may cause, because of a lack of consideration or grasp of the future.

Development of abstract concepts such as "past" and "future" is gradual, and children can be helped to develop these concepts, as they see them operative in their parents. The young child may be helped to develop rudimentary elements of the past and future by utilizing the unit of the "week." His juvenile mind may not be able to grasp next year, next summer, or two months from now, but he may be introduced to time abstractions by talking about "last Shabbos" and "next Shabbos," to which he may be able to relate. It is interesting that Torah literature refers to Shabbos as being the pivotal day of week, with Sunday through Tuesday belonging to the bygone Shabbos, and Wednesday through Friday to the oncoming Shabbos. While it may seem trivial, it may be beneficial to reflect perhaps at Tuesday night's dinner that "The kugel this past Shabbos was delicious, Mother. We're already looking forward to next Shabbos' kugel." Or, "Let's see. Last Shabbos we had Yoni as a guest. Whom would you like to invite for next Shabbos?" This is just one possible way of introducing the concepts of past and future to very young children.

As children gradually develop a concept of future and distinguish between "tomorrow" and some more remote time, it is important that they begin to learn to postpone gratification, and that the pleasure of "now" may have to be sacrificed for various reasons, often because of a greater good in the "future." Obviously, parental modeling is all important in making postponement of gratification acceptable.

Children may also not have a concept of death, and for them, separation and death may be synonymous. If Zeide died, they may fully expect him to come back next week, and on the other hand, if someone is gone for a week or so, they may think that he has died. Children ask questions about death, which should be answered as simply as possible without distortion, and even though they may not be able to grasp the finality of death at this point, they can retain the words and associate to them as they mature.

Parents should look for what may lie behind a child's question. Although a child's mind should not be overloaded, it is appropriate to consider what the child may really be asking, and respond accordingly. For example, "Mommy, could I have a cheeseburger?" "No, honey, cheeseburgers are not kosher. We don't eat cheeseburgers."

"Are they bad?"

What does this mean? Is the child asking whether they taste bad, or whether they are harmful to health?

"There are things we don't eat because *Hashem* said that we shouldn't, even if they may taste good." This is a prime lesson for the acceptance of a higher authority even when one does not understand the reason for a specific order.

There may well be a hidden wisdom in the father's taking his little son with him to the *mikveh* on Fridays. The child may begin to associate *mikveh* with a preparation for the sanctity of Shabbos, and when he later learns of the role of *mikveh* in marriage, he may grasp that the latter, too, is sacred, not to be profaned. This is a most vital concept in an era when the culture about us has given free reign to relationships, and has desecrated the physical bond of marriage.

Young children may be incapable of abstracting, and of making the leap from the particular to the general. Thus, if the child has taken away a toy from another child, and is reprimanded for it, he knows only that he may not take away a toy from *that* child, but does not extend this to taking things away from all other children. It is only with repetition and with maturation that the principle "taking others' belongings is wrong" emerges.

All values are principles; hence, all values are abstractions. As a child begins to grasp values, it is helpful to relate them to him. For example, when he returns the toy he can be told, "Giving the toy back to Yoni is a good thing to do." When the child has read off the *alef-beis* or a page in his elementary reader, the remark "You are becoming a really good student" helps shape a future expectation.

Parents can provide their children with an enthusiasm for life. As we have said, small children are alert and active, and it is often an ordeal to get them into bed at night. Many adults, on the other hand, cannot wait to retire. Why the difference? It is because children are curious, are constantly in the process of discovering new things, and sleep will interrupt the fascinating process of finding new things. Adults may be bored with a humdrum world which may have lost its glitter for them.

The Torah tells us to "Observe the *mitzvos* I instruct you *today*" (*Deuteronomy* 11:13), upon which Rashi comments, "Today," i.e., every day, we should consider the Torah and *mitzvos* as something fresh and new, to be learned and observed with the excitement of a novel experience. If, in the observance of Torah and *mitzvos*, parents exhibit this kind of interest, they will themselves find something new in the Torah each day, and will be able to transmit this attitude to their children.

A number of years ago, I was privileged to collect portions from our vast Torah literature and organize them into daily readings (*Living Each Day*, Mesorah Publications). Many people have reported that they repeatedly find new meanings in these Torah excerpts, and they actually anticipate reading them again to discover additional meanings. That is the magic of Torah, and this unique charm can provide children with the thrill of living as they grow older, saving them from the boredom of rote and habit.

Children need to know what their parents value and cherish, what they disapprove of, and what they abhor. This cannot simply occur in the abstract, but needs to be connected to the children's sense of themselves.

At a tender age children are taught to recite the *Shema*, which is a statement of *kabbalas ol malchus shamayim*, accepting upon oneself the yoke of Divine rule. While a young child cannot grasp this concept if it is explained to him verbally, he is capable of grasping the *feeling* contained in the *Shema* if the parents recite it in this way. Children can incorporate emotions long before their intellect has matured sufficiently to understand abstractions.

Teaching the child that non-kosher foods must be avoided and that certain acts cannot be done on Shabbos conveys the principle of Divine authority and teaches the child self-discipline, that there are behavioral restrictions which must be heeded even in absence of punishment.

One Passover, Rabbi Levi Yitzchok of Berditchev sent some of his *chassidim* to fetch him Turkish snuff and Turkish wool, the possession of which was forbidden by the Russian government because of the hostilities between Russia and Turkey, and possession of contraband was punishable by death. Nonetheless, people found the forbidden items and brought them to the *tzaddik,* who then ordered them to bring him a piece of bread from a Jewish home.

When the *chassidim* returned empty handed, Rabbi Levi Yitzchok lifted his eyes to heaven and said, "Master of the Universe! The Czar has forbidden possession of Turkish goods under penalty of death, and he has a huge army and police force that may shoot any transgressor on sight. Yet, people do have these forbidden items. You, Almighty G-d, do not have police who shoot violators of Your laws, but because You said that there should be no *chametz* in the house on Passover, there is not a morsel of bread in any Jewish home. Do You not have devoted children?"

The true identity of the Jewish child is that he is a child not only of his parents, but along with his parents, is a child to G-d. Accepting the authority of *Hashem* is not only an all-important lesson in self-discipline, but also helps establish one's identity: a child of G-d.

To summarize, our visions for our children and our expectations of them are in themselves powerful teaching tools, but are such only if we, as parents, have a clear picture of the values and goals we desire for our children. This means that we need to be aware of our values and how Torah is actually translated into our lives. For example, in a kosher home, children learn from infancy that *kashrus* is an important value, and that they are expected to adhere to kosher laws. We also talk of *ahavas Yisrael* as being an important value. However, some parents who would shudder at the thought of shellfish in their pots may tolerate violence, name-calling, and other forms of abuse in the house, whether among parents or among siblings. It may not be realistic to expect that there is never any fighting in the home and that siblings are always crazy about each other, but parents must elevate expectations of civility, kindness, and problem solving to a top-priority position. Words like "sharing, caring, turn-taking, helping, handling things, being honest, cooperating, being friendly, brave, and considerate" need to become everyday words in parents' vocabulary. Children learn the important concepts of Torah if we make them come alive in our daily lives and in mundane activities.

Children need to know what is expected of them and what we envision for them. By communicating with them and by insisting on Torah-inspired ways of relating to others, by pointing out lofty examples from our great personalities, and above all, by substantiating these values in our daily lives and showing our children that these values matter to us personally, we can make our vision for their future one which they will adopt and introject.

Chapter Sixteen

Tool Kit #4: Responses, Consequences and Feedback

*I*n his classic experiment, the psychologist Harry Harlow impressively demonstrated the crucial importance of parental responsiveness. Harlow took some infant monkeys and put them in cages with various mannequins, from which they could receive their nutrition, but which could not, of course, respond to them. He took movies of these monkeys and compared them to monkeys nurtured by their mothers. The movies show how the mannequin-nurtured monkeys withdraw and isolate themselves, how they refuse to relate to other monkeys, how they manifest fear rather than typical monkey curiosity when a new object is put into the cage, and how they refuse to mate when they mature. This dramatic experiment reinforces the impression gained from observation of children raised in orphanages, who received relatively little response from their caretakers, and who developed typical childhood depressive syndromes.

Just as children who are lead depleted will peel paint off the wall and eat it to get the necessary mineral, so will children do anything necessary to get parental responses. If they cannot get a positive response, they will evoke a negative response. As unpleasant as an angry and screaming parent may be, it is preferable to a quiet, withdrawn parent. A child who misbehaves may be saying, "Hit me and scold me, but for heaven's sake, acknowledge my existence."

While response per se is important, *how* we respond is also important. It is well known that behavior that is rewarded is reinforced, whereas behavior that is punished is eradicated. Parents who do not show the child much attention, but become very concerned and caring when the child is sick, should not be surprised if the child becomes a hypochondriac, having learned that the way to get attention is to be sick. Furthermore, although punishment eliminates negative behavior, the punishment itself may become a reward if it is the only response that the child can elicit from a passive or overly busy parent.

Parents often take children's proper behavior for granted, and react only when the child misbehaves. The desire for parental attention may thus result in the child's acting in such a way that he knows will elicit a parental response.

The child may pop a candy into his mouth without saying a *brachah,* and the parent may respond with "Take that candy out of your mouth and say a *brachah* first." However, when the child does say a *brachah,* it often goes unnoticed. A hearty parental response of "*Omain*!," followed by a comment such as, "How wonderful to always be mindful of thanking *Hashem* for what we have," is both conducive to encouraging *brachos* as well as building self-esteem.

Whereas we often draw analogies between human parents and G-d as our Father, there is one important distinction. We are at every moment of our lives totally dependent upon G-d, and one of the functions of our frequent prayer and recitation of blessings for everything of which we partake is to keep us aware of our dependency upon Him, a dependency which we never outgrow. This is in contrast to the human parent-child relationship, where the goal is for the child to become self-sufficient and independent of the parent.

Thus, while as children of G-d, we should ask Him for everything, we should encourage our children to do for themselves when this is age and situation appropriate. As children reach stages in life where it is appropriate that they do things for themselves, this should be encouraged.

Some parents who have a wish to be needed may feel threatened by a child's manifestations of self-sufficiency, and may actually thwart it. In the days when it was perfectly safe for a 12-year-old to travel by bus, there was a mother who refused to allow her son to come for his therapy appointments alone, restricting the sessions to those times when she was able to escort him. There are things that parents must do for their children to provide for the *child's* needs, but when parents do things for the child primarily for their *own* needs, this may lead to pathological dependence or defiant, reckless independence. Inasmuch as we may not be objective to our own behavior and motivations, it is always helpful to get some guidance from an outsider who can be objective as to whether the way we are providing for our children is productive or counterproductive.

There are additional differences between the man-G-d and child-parent relationship. We believe that G-d knows our thoughts, and silent, meditative prayer can be effective. Infants may well have similar convictions, since a mother may feed a hungry child or change a wet diaper even before he has made his displeasure known, and the child may develop the idea that "people know what I need and want, and take care of it for me." Children eventually outgrow this, and learn that they must ask for things, and that parents do not know their thoughts. Every once in a while, a child may fixate at this primitive stage, and believe that he can control things by his thoughts. This concept of "magical thinking" can be the source of much anxiety. Just think of what might happen if everything we wished for would come true! This can be extremely frightening. It can thus be very reassuring to tell a child, "You must tell me what you want. We are not mind readers."

Children need positive strokes to validate and reinforce their good actions. But we should note that positive strokes must be true, and not be false flattery. The latter does not reinforce anything, and may leave the child with the feeling that his parents' statements are not reliable.

While proper praise is essential, it too must be applied with sensitivity and caution. We may be accustomed to compliment the child for doing a good deed with "You are a real *tzaddik*!" That may be helpful, but it may also backfire. Although the child did as he was told, he may have done so grudgingly and with resentment, and may have been very angry with his parents for making him do it. He does not at all feel like a *tzaddik*, and may have no way of dealing with this undeserved praise. It is therefore better to *praise the deed and not the person*, e.g., "We're proud of what you did." When the child helps with the dishes, a proper comment is "Thank you for doing the dishes. It was a real help." That is a true and non-controversial statement. However, "You are a real angel" may be a problematic statement.

As elsewhere, Torah provides us with guidelines. Firstly, "Do not praise a person lavishly to his face" (*Rashi, Genesis* 7:1). Secondly, even when praising G-d, praise only His deeds, as the psalmist says, "Give thanks to G-d. . .make known His deeds to the nations" (*Psalms* 105:1). The only adjectives we are permitted to say about G-d are the three enumerated in the Torah, "Great, mighty, and awesome," but since we can know nothing about the essence of G-d, we may not add praises, other than to relate His wondrous deeds, which are known to us.

What we may learn from this is that we should relate only to a person's actions, which are known to us, and not to the person's character, which is unknown to us. Therefore, praise what a child *has done*, but do not tell him what he *is*. The latter is an inference he must draw for himself.

Children need to learn to respect truth, and there is probably nothing that ranks in importance with integration of truth in a child's character.

The Talmud says that a person should not give a child an *esrog* and *lulav* to make a *brachah* the first day of *Sukkos*, because where-as the child can acquire a property, he does not have the legal capacity to transfer property; hence, once he acquires the *esrog-lulav*, he cannot return it for anyone else's use. The question arises: Why not just give it to the child without the intention for it to become his possession? Let him make the *brachah* "as if" it were his. The answer is that "as if" is not *chinuch*. A child should be trained with the reality of truth. Going through the motions with "make believe" is not *chinuch*.

Children will learn respect for truth when they see the parents value truth and practice it. This is equally true of every other trait.

Modern research indicates that there may be prenatal influences on an unborn infant. This is no news to students of the Talmud, who read the story of Rabbi Yochanan's mother who was seized by an inordinate craving for food on Yom Kippur when she was expecting him. When she was reminded that it was Yom Kippur, she suppressed her desire for food, and "This," the Talmud says, "was why the child became the great Rabbi Yochanan" (*Yuma* 82b). Certainly the parental responses and modeling when a child is able to observe these are of even greater impact.

Children learn to avoid destructive behavior by experiencing negative consequences. No one needs to teach a child who has touched an electric hotplate to avoid doing so again. When inappropriate behaviors are immediately followed by negative consequences, the impression is quickly integrated. This is equally true of parental disapproval.

For example, infants do not know that bugs are disgusting, and are not beyond putting them in their mouths. The mother's shudder and intense expression of "*Feh*! *Fui*!" is most effective in conveying the abhorrence of bugs, and few children fail to integrate this repulsive attitude. *If parents would respond with similar revulsion to all other undesirable behavior, it is very likely that children would avoid these as well.*

Let us be perfectly honest with ourselves. The disapproval toward a child's lying or even taking something that does not belong to him may indeed elicit a reprimand from the parent, but the latter may not carry the same gut reaction of "*Feh*! *Fui*!" as when a child puts a bug in his mouth. Children can easily distinguish a gut "*Feh*! *Fui*!" from a lecture in proper ethics but which lacks the intensity and quality of the gut response.

Parents should be extremely careful about how they communicate things to their children. One man told me how he came to develop a resentment toward *meshulachim* (representatives of institutions who collect charity funds). When he was a child, one *meshulach* needed a place to stay overnight, and his parents gave the *meshulach* the child's bed, having the child sleep on the floor. Why was this not a positive lesson in hospitality? Because what the parents should have done was sacrifice their *own* room rather than the child's. This would have taught the child how *they* value the *mitzvah* of hospitality to travelers.

One of the thirteen principles of Torah is that of reward and punishment: *Mitzvos* are rewarded and sins are punished. Yet, for all its importance, this principle is de-emphasized, since we are instructed, "Do not be like servants who serve their master for compensation, but rather be like servants who serve their master without anticipation of compensation" (*Ethics of the Fathers* 1:3). While reward and punishment is a fact, it should not serve as the prime motivating force.

We can easily understand this by noting that with small children we may provide a reward for what they do for their own welfare. I.e., they receive a dime, a candy, or a trinket for each time they brush their teeth, wash their hands, etc. How ridiculous this would be if this were done for a mature adult! A grown-up understands that brushing his teeth and washing his hands is for his own welfare, and to reward him for such behavior would be the height of insult. Similarly, doing *mitzvos* for the reward they will bring is a juvenile concept. A mature person should realize that G-d is all perfect and does not need our *mitzvos.* Torah and *mitzvos* were given to us for *our* betterment, and we should not be seeking external rewards. This is what is meant by "The reward for a *mitzvah* is the *mitzvah* itself" (*Ethics of the Fathers* 4:2).

The importance of hygienic habits can be appreciated by a child at a relatively early age, whereas the good that is inherent in *mitzvos* and the harm that is inherent in sin is not immediately evident; hence, there is a need for the concept of reward and punishment even for adults. As a person grows spiritually, one should come to understand the teachings found in *Ethics of the Fathers* and realize that *mitzvos* are their own reward.

Children can be taught this abstract concept when they are beyond the age of gold stars for brushing their teeth.

"Tell me, Dovid, how would you feel if Mommy put a gold star on your chart each time you brush your teeth, the way she does for Itzi?"

"That would be silly. That's baby stuff, Daddy."

"Well, that's how it is with the things Hashem tells us to do. We might not always understand how His *mitzvos* make us healthier, but they are there for our benefit, not for His. *Mitzvos* are to make us into better people. Some *mitzvos* may be hard to do and may even be unpleasant, like having to wake up when it is still dark in order to go to *Selichos* (additional early morning services prior to and during the Ten Days of Repentance), but we should understand that this is for our own good. Sometimes when we are sick, we may have to take a medicine that has an unpleasant taste to make us well. When we make you swallow medicine that you don't like, it's because we love you and we want you to get better. This is also true of those *mitzvos* that may be difficult. We do them to become better people in many ways."

The truly mature adult understands this, and will experience a pleasant sensation in the knowledge that by doing a *mitzvah,* one is improving himself, but a child may also be able to grasp the rudiments of this concept even though he cannot yet fully formulate it.

There are messages in feedback. Feedback is not so much a reward as it is much-needed information to keep us on track. The positive message of approval is "What you did is good," and the negative message of disapproval is "What you did is not good." However, we may think of feedback in parenting as analogous to the built-in corrections in a missile that return it to its proper trajectory when it deviates from the prescribed course. In contrast to the inanimate missile, a child feels and thinks, and can utilize the feedback not only to stay on course, but to figure out just who he is and what he is for. One value in comparing feedback to the computerized mechanism of a missile is that the computer corrects the deviation immediately, and this should certainly be applied to parental approval or disapproval, which should immediately follow the child's actions without delay. The often-heard threat, "Just wait until your father comes home," is not only anxiety provoking, but also essentially worthless as a corrective measure for whatever wrong the child may have done.

Even such simple things as teeth-brushing and hand-washing can contribute to identity formation. There is a beautiful account in the Midrash that when the great sage Hillel left the academy, his students asked him where he was going. "Why, to do a *mitzvah*," Hillel said.

"What kind of *mitzvah*?" the students asked.

"To wash myself in the bath house," Hillel responded.

"What kind of *mitzvah* is that?" the students asked.

Hillel answered, "Does not the government engage someone to wash and polish the statues of the king that are displayed in public places? Now I, who was created in the image of G-d, am I not duty-bound to see that that image is cleansed and polished?" (*Vayikra Rabbah* 34:3).

While personal hygiene is important for health reasons, it can also contribute to self-esteem. The child needs to be made aware of this, but the child's awareness can only come from parental awareness of this principle. Too often we take our children's good behavior for granted, and react only to their misbehavior. Let us remember the Torah teaching that G-d rewards us for doing what we are supposed to do. Let us be more alert to "catch" our children doing good, and reward them for it, even if only with a smile or a brief compliment.

There is no more powerful source for development of healthy self-esteem than true accomplishments, validated efforts, and a job well done. A practical point is to make a goal for ourselves to "catch" each child at least three times a day doing something good: listening, helping, sharing, solving problems, waiting, keeping his cool, playing nicely, being friendly, etc., and letting him know that we noticed and appreciated his behavior. For a three-year-old this may be something like bringing a diaper to Mommy for the new baby, and for a 17-year-old it may be having studied well for an exam or bringing in the groceries from the family car.

The power of positive feedback is frequently underappreciated, and some parents may feel that the child's behavior does not warrant positive feedback. "Why should I compliment him for taking out the garbage when it's his job anyway?" But of all parental techniques, there is none that has so many beneficial side effects as positive feedback. Positivity gives both parents and children a more joyous perspective on life.

The reason we teach our children Torah values is that given by Moses: "I have set before you life and death, the blessing and the curse, and you shall choose life, so that you may live, you and your children" (*Deuteronomy* 30:19). Torah is a blessing of life, and deviation from Torah is the reverse. Our children should be helped to understand that the reason we wish them to have Torah values is not only because that is what our ancestors did or because it is right. These reasons might not be able to withstand the impact of the secular environment in which we live. A reason that they may readily accept is the one given by Moses, because Torah life is a blessing.

When Moses speaks of doing good and avoiding evil, he does so at the end of the Torah, after he has laboriously enumerated all the positive commandments and the prohibitions. He also pointed out to the Israelites how they suffered harm when they disobeyed the Divine commandments. To have just told the Israelites to "be good" would have been meaningless, because they had no concept of what constitutes "good."

Parents may tell their children to "be good," assuming that the child knows what "being good" means. This is taking too much for granted. A child will learn what "good" is by seeing what is rewarded, what is encouraged, and what the parents do themselves.

Let us look more closely at Moses' precise words: "So that you may live, *you* and your children." Moses emphasizes that only if *you* see Torah life as a blessing, only then will your children adopt it as such. In spite of the various stresses and challenges in life, children must see that their parents can find happiness in Torah.

Performance of *mitzvos*, whether listening to *shofar* or giving *tzedakah*, should be done with joy. Children are most sensitive, and the joy associated with *mitzvos* endows the latter with a flavor that makes them attractive to children. The psalmist says, "I rejoice over Your words as one who has found a great treasure" (*Psalms* 119:162). If the parents' attitude on performing a *mitzvah* would approach that of winning a huge sum of money, the children's love for *mitzvos* would be assured.

Chapter Seventeen

Tool Kit #5: Transmitting and Instructing

Whereas instruction in the classroom is primarily didactic, parents should find additional ways of transmitting knowledge. In fact, formal didactic teaching in the home should play a relatively minor role. Instruction is only one of the ways in which we transmit important information. As Jewish parents we are faced with a formidable task: We need to transmit to our children the heritage of Mount Sinai. This includes knowledge and practice of *mitzvos* and *minhagim*, the mastery of Hebrew, knowledge of our history and a connection with Eretz Yisrael.

It is important for parents to also assume the role of teachers and not to relegate this task to the school. There are many opportunities in the home to teach children. This may not take the form of formal lessons, and often happens in the context of other activities.

The Shabbos table is a model setting for transmitting and instructing in the home. On Shabbos we should enjoy the high point of the week. On Shabbos the whole family gathers together, and the gift of rest from our labors allows us to focus on what is really important. A truly touching image is the return of the "peddler" father who has labored all week and been exposed to the scorn of the world at large. On Shabbos he turns into a king and the wife into a queen.

When a father and mother truly hold court on Shabbos, the children can both learn and display their learning. Many schools give the children questions for the *parshah* of the week to bring home. Even little ones have pictures to help them tell a story. The tradition of saying a *d'var Torah* sets the example for the children of the value of learning and transmitting Torah knowledge. When the Shabbos table becomes an overall forum for sharing Torah and *Yiddishkeit*, the children are exposed to a full menu of forms of Jewish learning. The reading of a story, the telling of an event that the mother is grateful for, the pointing out of yet another interpretation of a part of the *parshah*, the admiration of a picture of Noah's ark that the youngest made in preschool, all these weave into a tapestry of Jewish learning and transmitting that can unite the family in spite of all its diversity.

On the way to *shul* many opportunities present themselves for teaching. Importantly, this may be teaching on a topic initiated by the children. The art is to transfer what is so clear on Shabbos to the hustle and bustle of the weekdays. When *Havdalah* is said, the Shabbos should linger on and suffuse our week.

Didactic teaching need not always be direct, and may be even more effective when it is indirect. There is a Jewish proverb, "I may be saying it to you, my daughter, but I am intending it for my daughter-in-law." Thus, a mother-in-law who is afraid that her daughter-in-law will be offended by a reprimand directs it toward her daughter, although the latter may not be deserving of it, in the hope that her daughter will not be offended and that the daughter-in-law will get the message. Things can be said in a manner that the child will apply them to himself, without their being overtly directed toward him. Reprimand by a story or allegory is also effective, as can be seen in the Scriptures (*II Samuel* 12:1-10). There is no dearth of happenings in the world, both positive and negative, and these can serve as examples for discussing good and evil, right and wrong.

It is unfortunate that western civilization has adopted the attitude of everyone "doing one's own thing" to the point where a family may consist of a number of people who live in the same house but are rarely all together at any one time and place. The Torah-observant family at least has the Shabbos meal, at which all family members are present. This provides a unique opportunity for discussion of concepts of value. Certainly each weekly Torah portion and the many commentaries thereupon are resources for ideas, and there may also be happenings of the week that can be a point of focus.

A valuable practice is for each member of the family to cite "What was the best thing that happened this week?" Even if someone feels that the whole week was a "down week," one can nevertheless point out what was the best among whatever happened. A person may block out a positive event, and others may call it to his attention.

While family discussions are extremely important, they do not take the place of one-to-one dialogue. Even in large families, parents should find some time to spend with each child separately. Parents may have a very busy schedule and claim that they just cannot find time to spend with each child individually. When asked why their schedule is so busy, they will say that it takes all their time to earn a decent livelihood for their large family. Let us remember, however, that attending to a child's emotional needs is every bit as important as providing for his physical needs, and that depriving a child of individual attention because one must work harder to earn for him is not a wise trade-off.

Furthermore, one-to-one dialogues need not be lengthy. Some children have a short attention span, and many children believe that adults talk too much anyway. An expression of interest in what is going on in the child's life, in school and with friends, opens the door for communication. Parents should have a genuine interest in what is going on with a child's life, and if the child knows that he can come to the parent with a problem and that the parent will have time for him, that is sufficient.

The Talmud says that there can be no meaningful communication with people when they are in the throes of an intense emotional state (*Ethics of the Fathers* 4:23). This holds true for children as well. When children are very angry or hurt, it is best to delay any discussions. Let them know that you wish to understand their problem, and that as soon as they feel a bit more settled, you will be glad to hear them out and try to help them with their problem.

Teaching consists of the transmission of knowledge from someone who knows more to someone who knows less. However, the statement, "Here, let me show you how to do it," may result in a demeaning attitude.

One might say, but do we not go to school to learn from those who know more, and certainly young children should know that their parents are wiser than they are. What is wrong with recognizing this to be a fact?

There is nothing wrong with it, as long as one does not restrict the learning process to children. It is demeaning only if children see themselves as the only ones who need to learn, and view the parents as omniscient.

In Torah literature, a scholar is generally not referred to as a *chacham*, a wise man, but rather as a *talmid chacham*, a *student* of the wise. Every person should be a perpetual student. When parents attend *shiurim* (Torah lessons) and particularly when they verbalize, "I learned something new today," this helps a child to be more receptive to learning.

Opportunities for transmitting and modeling abound. One mother ran into the kitchen a bit too late to save the vegetables that had burned. In a tone of deep disappointment, she said, "I'll have to scrape the pot to get rid of this burned stuff and start all over again." Her 9-year-old daughter, who was doing homework in the kitchen, said, "That's what our teacher said about *teshuvah*. When we make a mistake, we have to start all over again."

The child brilliantly applied the concept of *teshuvah* to the mother's culinary mishap. Mistakes are certain to occur, both to children and adults. Acknowledging a mistake and accepting that one must start over again, this time exercising greater caution that the mistake does not recur, is an excellent way to teach the concept of *teshuvah*.

Children are highly susceptible to peer pressure, even more so than adults. Desire to conform is a major factor in the widespread use of alcohol and drugs among adolescents, and it is important that children learn that they must not succumb to peer pressure. This requires the courage of standing up for one's convictions in defiance of prevailing attitudes. Parents who always conform to what others do even when they believe it to be wrong are transmitting a message of conformity to their children. Parents who have the courage to resist peer pressure are conveying the value of courage to their children.

The importance of this can be conveyed by pointing out that the very first paragraph of the *Shulchan Aruch* sets the tone for our daily behavior by stating that one should not allow mocking or ridicule to keep one from doing what is appropriate.

Children need to learn how to accept responsibility for their actions and particularly not to place blame on others. Early in childhood we can observe this virtually innate tendency: "He did it! She did it! It wasn't me!"

It might be well to share with children that the tendency to blame is a universal trait, present in everyone, but something we must learn to overcome. The universality of this trait is pointed out by Rabbi Chaim Shmuelevitz. The Torah tells us how desperate the matriarch, Rachel, was for a child, and when she did not conceive she said to Jacob, "If I do not have children I might as well be dead!" (*Genesis* 30:1). We can understand how disappointed she was that she had not borne a child to Jacob, and how overjoyed she must have been on the birth of her first son. Yet Rachel said, "G-d has removed my shame," which Rashi interprets to be, "Now if something is broken in the house, I will be able to blame it on the child, and Jacob will not be angry with me" (ibid. 30:23).

Think of it! The saintly matriarch Rachel, to whom having a child was equivalent to life itself — yet what does she see in this long-awaited, unique gift from heaven? Someone to blame! "That," Rabbi Shmuelevitz says, "shows us how deep seated in the human personality is the need to blame (*Sichos Mussar* 5732:6).

We might let children know that we understand their need to blame others being an almost reflex reaction, yet like many other inborn traits, it is something we must overcome.

As with praise, criticism should relate to the act and not to the person. Spilling milk on the table should elicit a response, "Here is a sponge. Please clean it up," and not "You are so clumsy." Reaction to a lie should be along the line of "That was a lie, and I will not tolerate lies," and not "You are a liar." Abusive terms, "stupid, bad, selfish," that apply to the person rather than to the act should never be used.

We expect children to gradually become masters over their desires and impulses; i.e., to act *responsibly*. Responsibility is an extremely important trait and develops very gradually throughout maturity.

To be in control of one's impulses and drives, one must know what they are. One can hardly be in control of an unknown force. Of course, a person can make believe that certain impulses and drives simply do not exist in him, hence there is no need to worry about controlling them. Unfortunately, this is what constitutes *repression*, and denying the existence of something does not make it go away.

The Talmud relates that when Moses went up to heaven to receive the Torah, the angels objected to its being given to sinful mortals, arguing that the sanctity of the Torah warrants its being given to the heavenly host. Moses rebutted the angels' argument, contending, among other things, that the *mitzvos*, "You shall not kill, you shall not steal, you shall not commit adultery, you shall not covet possessions of others," are not relevant to angels, who have no hate, no envy, no greed, and no lust. Angels thus have no need for the Torah, and it is precisely because humans have these various drives and impulses that they are in need of Torah.

There is thus no denying the fact that the human being, who is a composite of an animal body and a Divine spirit, has all the biological drives of an animal. Some of these are so repulsive that we wish to disown them, but Moses' response to the angels indicates that there are 365 desires which operate within every human being: the 365 negative *mitzvos* or prohibitions of the Torah.

At some point it is well to apprise children of this, that we understand that they may have strong feelings which may be negative. However, it is precisely because we have these negative feelings that we were given the Torah, the observance of which should refine us and enable us to become masters over our drives, so that the negative feelings do not translate into negative behavior.

Thus, when a child says, "I hate him," he should be helped to understand that hatred is a negative emotion which is a component of our physical bodies, but since we are humans rather than animals, we must work upon ourselves so that these primitive feelings not cause us to act improperly. The same is true for greed and envy and all other such emotions, whose existence within us does not make us bad, and it is only when we allow ourselves to act out these feelings that we are derelict. The statement "Good children do not hate" can be misconstrued to mean that the very presence of the feeling itself makes a person bad, and this can contribute to a child's developing unwarranted feelings of shame and unworth.

By the same token, we must stress the capacity of every person to be in control of one's actions. Torah does not accept the concept of "irresistible impulse," which sometimes appears in a legal defense. A person is always responsible for his actions. When a child who hits his sibling says, "I couldn't help it. He made me so mad!" he should be told, "That's not quite right. I can understand that your brother made you very angry and that it may have been difficult for you to control your urge to hit. But difficult does not mean impossible. You do have the strength to overcome even strong feelings of anger and to avoid acting on them. There may be times that you do things that make others angry, and you certainly would not want them to hit you and claim that they couldn't help it."

When an impulse is repeatedly controlled, it withers by the process of attrition. Thus, if one restrains oneself and does not act out on the negative feelings of hatred and envy, the latter become attenuated and may be eliminated. As a person grows spiritually, he may rid himself of these undesirable emotions, but this is something that comes with time and maturity, and is too much to expect of a child. Thus, rather than reprimand a child, "It is wrong to hate," he should be taught to avoid acting out his hostile feelings. Total elimination of hate will hopefully come about as he matures.

As we exercise restraint over our physical drives, our quality of mastery improves, and being in control is no longer as formidable a task. We can teach this to our children, but of course, primarily by setting an example for them.

Chapter Eighteen

Problem Solving

learly, one of the parental responsibilities is to teach children how to identify and solve problems. There will be no dearth of these in their lives. Problems come in all shapes and sizes, from the most simple to the most complex, from difficulty in opening a jar of pickles to what to do when one loses one's job.

As mentioned earlier, a phrase that should be avoided is "Let me show you how it's done," which, although it may sound perfectly innocent, may be interpreted by a sensitive child as, "You are too stupid to figure this out yourself," or "I don't expect you to figure it out."

Suppose the child is putting all the pieces of a toy back into the box, but can't get the box to close. Instead of "Let me do it for you," which is a no-no, or "Let me show you how," a better statement is "Let's see if we can figure out what's wrong here." After taking out a few pieces you say, "I wonder what would happen if we put these in this way?" and then let the child discover that proper arrangement and stacking will allow the box to close. When he achieves this, the statement "There, you've done it!" or even "There, we did it, didn't we?" will usually elicit a smile of pride.

This approach should serve as a prototype for all problem solving. The Talmud says an impatient person cannot be a teacher (*Ethics of the Fathers* 2:6), and although doing something for the child may be the fastest way to get it done, it may undermine his self-confidence.

Some children may skip over word problems in arithmetic, having concluded, "I can never figure these out." I know of one teacher who uses figures of optical illusions to point out that sometimes we may see things in different ways, depending on our perspective. The same picture may appear to be the top of a staircase as well as the underside of a staircase, depending on how you look at it. Then she says, "Sometimes we look at a problem and it appears to be too difficult to figure it out because we are looking at it the wrong way, but if we look at it another way, it becomes quite simple. Let's see how we can look at this in a different way."

The basis of cognitive psychology is that many problems are rooted in our "cognition," i.e., how we see things. A person with paranoid tendencies may see someone leave the room just as he enters, and may conclude, "He is leaving because he saw me coming in. He does not like me," while the real reason the person left the room was to make a phone call. A person with poor self-esteem may interpret many things as relating to him in a negative manner.

Errors in cognition are common, and parents can serve as models to demonstrate that we are all susceptible to these. The father may say to the mother, "Guess what? I said 'Good morning' to Mike today and he just ignored me. I couldn't figure out why he was angry at me. Then I found out that his son is in the hospital and the doctors aren't sure what's wrong with him. Mike was just preoccupied with worry, and wasn't angry at me at all. Let's call him up and find out how things are." Such revelations of "I too misinterpret things" may help a child realize the pitfalls of errors in cognition.

An intense fear of failure can result in anxiety so severe that it may paralyze a child's problem-solving capacities. A young man was referred to me for psychological evaluation, because although he had been an A student in high school, he was doing very poorly in college. The interview reviewed that he came from a family of coal miners, and that he was the first member of the entire family to complete high school and go onto college. His father was very proud of this, and made no secret of how much he was sacrificing to put his son through college. The young man was made to feel that he was responsible for redeeming the family honor, and although he studied well and knew the material, his mind went totally blank when he took a test. Why? Because the possibility that he might not do well on the tests and thereby disappoint the family caused him so much anxiety that he was unable to recall anything he had learned.

Our children should know that we are proud of their achievements and wish them to succeed, but that failures may occur and are not disastrous. I have often related to my children that although I did well in college, I once received a D in a course on Shakespeare's Prince Henry IV, and it was as a result of this failing grade that I sought help on how to study literature properly. The Talmud goes so far as to say that a person does not fully understand a *halachah* until he first makes a mistake in its application (*Gittin* 43a). The aphorism "Experience is a hard teacher but fools will learn no other way" is wrong. Fools are those who do not learn from experience. It is the wise who learn from their mistakes, and we should help our children realize that whereas failure is something that is unpleasant for the moment, it can be a valuable lesson for the future.

Some problems cannot be solved alone, and require assistance from others. Some children may be reluctant to ask for help, just as some adults may consider it a sign of weakness to ask for assistance, and they try to tackle a task which is clearly beyond one's own capacities. Unfortunately, such heroic efforts often result in failure. The skill of asking for assistance when appropriate needs to be taught and valued in and of itself.

The Torah tells us in the process of Creation G-d said, "Let *Us* make man" (*Genesis* 1:26). Rashi explains that although G-d is Omnipotent and does not need the help of anyone, He nevertheless consulted the heavenly angels, in order to teach us that no matter how great and powerful one may be, one should not hesitate to seek and accept help from others.

Here too, parents may provide valuable teaching by serving as models. When occasions arise where they have to enlist the help of others, they should share this with their children when it is appropriate to do so.

Not all problems lend themselves to solution, and sometimes we must learn how to live with conflict. Inability to live with conflict may result in any variety of escapist techniques such as relocating (geographical cure), denial and self-deception, or recourse to alcohol or drugs. It is understandable that parents may wish to intervene to eliminate conflict from their children's lives. At times this is necessary, but one must give this serious consideration, perhaps with expert consultation, because reality is fraught with conflicts, and children must learn how to live with conflict. Parents cannot be around forever to extricate their children from conflicts, nor is it their role to protect their children from all and any harm. Wise parents allow their children to be exposed to conflict so that they learn to tolerate stress and get a chance to practice coping and problem solving. We need to "expose" our children to appropriate stressors or problem situations in order for them to become hardy and skilled. The parent who wants or needs his child to be happy all the time is doing the child a disservice and is ultimately gratifying his own needs to view himself as a perfect parent.

Putting It All to Work

Chapter Nineteen

What About Anger?

ne of the most difficult challenges facing parents is teaching children proper management of anger. In all probability, anger is the most difficult emotion a person must deal with, and mismanagement of anger may well be at the root of many physical symptoms as well as psychological disorders. There is evidence to implicate anger in migraine headaches, high blood pressure, skin disorders, and a variety of other physical conditions. Before approaching teaching our children how to cope with anger, we must do a personal inventory, because we ourselves may not be handling anger optimally.

There are some conflicting and confusing ideas about anger. Some ethicists appear to be saying that a person must subdue all feelings of anger. They quote Rambam (Maimonides) as saying that anyone who is angry is equivalent to one who worships idols (*Daos* 2). That would indeed be an alarming indictment, and anytime an individual felt anger, he would have to consider himself most sinful. At the other extreme are some psychologists who say that because repression of anger can cause a great deal of emotional, physical and psychological harm, a person should therefore discharge his anger. They appear to advocate shouting it out, pounding a punching bag, or in some similar fashion getting it out of one's system. With such a wide variance of opinions, what is one to do?

The fact is that there is not a shred of evidence that discharging anger by beating a punching bag or the like eliminates any of the anger. To the contrary, such behavior may aggravate the anger rather than mitigate it. On the other hand, the teaching of the ethicists has been misunderstood. Much hinges on a correct understanding of the Hebrew word *ka'as,* which indeed means anger. But we must divide anger into three phases: (1) the initial feeling of anger, which occurs when one has been personally offended, or when one perceives injustice, even when not personally involved; (2) the expression of anger, how it is manifested and conveyed; and (3) the harboring of the feeling after its initial occurrence. To avoid confusion we must understand how the term *ka'as* is used in all three.

There is a principle in Torah that G-d does not make unrealistic demands of a person (*Avodah Zarah* 3a). When a person is offended or hurt, he automatically feels angry at whoever or whatever hurt him. This feeling can be directed even at inanimate objects; for example, it is not uncommon for one who has bumped his head into an open cabinet door to hit the door as if to punish it. This is a carry-over from childhood days, when, if the child bumped her head against the edge of a table, her mother comforted her by hugging her and hitting the table, saying, "Bad, bad table. You hurt my little Rivkie." Incidentally, this is a rather foolish thing to do. The table is not going to change its nature. It would be wiser to soothe Rivkie and then tell her to be cautious not to run about recklessly. If you blame the table, Rivkie may not learn to be more careful at age 2, and even at age 32 may continue to blame others for her own dereliction.

At any rate, the initial sensation of anger when one is provoked appears to be a reflex action, which, as a rule, is not under voluntary control. It is therefore improper to adjudge this initial feeling as being morally and ethically bad, since this is a term that should be reserved only for behavior which is subject to one's control. Hence, the ethicists who condemn *ka'as* are not referring to this initial *feeling* of anger, since G-d would not demand of us something which is beyond the average person's control.

You will note that I said that "as a rule" the reflex reaction of feeling anger is not under one's control. There are exceptions, as with some of our great *tzaddikim* who were able to achieve voluntary control even over reflex reactions, and in modern times, our electronic genius has developed the technique of biofeedback training, whereby a person can learn to control such actions that have always been assumed to be completely involuntary. But with the exception of great *tzaddikim* who achieved their self-mastery by enormous self-discipline and intense prayer, the average person experiences anger as a reflex reaction and has no choice whether or not to feel it.

In contrast to biofeedback training, which teaches voluntary control of traditionally involuntary reactions, there is a psychological mechanism that can eliminate the *awareness* of the feeling of anger, that is *repression*. A person can be so impressed with, or better yet, so intimidated by the evil of anger, that his psyche represses the feeling and does not let it come to his awareness. This is distinctly unhealthy, because the feeling is not at all dissipated, but rather driven deep into the recesses of the unconscious mind, where it festers and seeks expression in any one of many circuitous ways, and may even result in triggering a depressive reaction.

There is a difference between subduing or *sup*pressing the anger versus *re*pressing it. Suppression is a conscious process. For example, my boss has provoked me, and I am angry with him. I do not disown my anger, but I know that if I ventilate my feelings, he will fire me, so I decide to keep silent. This is suppression, and is not as likely to result in various symptoms the way unconscious repression is.

If a person fails to feel anger when provoked, something has gone awry (with the rare exception of the accomplished *tzaddik*). It is as if someone who is pricked with a sharp instrument does not feel any pain. Failure to feel pain on appropriate stimulation is a signal to the doctor that something has gone wrong with a patient's nerve conduction or brain perception. The same is true of failure to perceive anger when it is reasonable to expect that a provocation should have elicited anger.

It is therefore clear that what the Rambam refers to when he uses the term *ka'as* as being equivalent to idolatry is what the Talmud says (*Shabbos* 105b), "One who tears his garments in rage, or breaks things in rage, or throws about his money in rage, is equivalent to an idolater." Whereas we may not have control over the initial feeling, one has much control over how one *expresses* anger. Losing control as a result of anger is not permissible, and since exercising restraint is well within a person's capabilities, one is held responsible for how one expresses anger.

To avoid confusion, let us agree on terms: We will use the word "anger" to refer to the pure *sensation* of *feeling* angry, and the word "rage" to the *expression* of anger. In addition, there can be an entire spectrum of rage, from a very mild expression of rage to a violent, explosive fury. So let us keep our terms clear: anger = feeling; rage = expression.

Having defined phases (1) and (2), let us move on to phase (3). Whereas we may not be able to avoid the *initial* feeling of anger, one does not have to hang on to this feeling. This is what the wise Solomon is referring to when he says, "*Ka'as* rests in the bosom of fools" (*Ecclesiastes* 7:9). Granted, we are not in the position to prevent the reflex arousal of feeling, but why hang on to it?

Again, to avoid confusion, let us agree on the term "resentment" to refer to the *feeling* of anger that *continues to persist* after it is initially evoked. We thus have:

(1) anger — the initial involuntary feeling

(2) rage — expression of anger

(3) resentment — retention of anger

It may not be easy to get rid of resentments. After all, if somebody has offended you or committed a grossly unjust act, it is only natural to continue to feel negatively toward him. Now, while the Torah does not ask us to love our adversaries, it does ask us to exercise restraint in how we act towards them. There is probably nothing in the world that is sweeter than revenge, getting back at the scoundrel who behaved in so hostile a manner. At the very least, if one cannot take revenge, one can wait for the opportunity when that person needs your help, and then say to him, "Look, you good-for-nothing. I'm going to go out of my way to help you, even though you don't deserve it because you treated me so rashly. I will show you that I am a real *mentsch*, not an inconsiderate person like you." But, alas! The Torah forbids this, stating explicitly, "You should not take revenge nor carry a grudge" (*Leviticus* 19:18). Any acting out of negative feelings towards an adversary is forbidden.

If you cannot act on your resentments, what good are they? All they can do is eat away at you and cause you much grief, if not ulcers. The person that offended you is not going to be punished by your harboring your resentment towards him, since you are restricted by Torah law from doing anything in retaliation. Why hang on to a feeling that can only harm you and be of no retaliatory value?

In my work treating alcoholics, I found that they place great emphasis on divesting oneself of resentments, contending that resentments are probably the single greatest factor responsible for relapse. One recovered alcoholic said it simply: "Carrying resentments is like letting someone whom you don't like live inside your head rent free." Why would anyone allow that?

All logic and reasoning notwithstanding, ridding oneself of resentments is not that simple, and one must look for ways to accomplish this. My father used to say, "I never carry a grudge. There is no valid reason why any sensible person should wish to harm me. I do not pose a threat to anyone, and I wish everyone only the best. If someone nevertheless wishes to harm me in any way, whether by word or by deed, he is either misinterpreting things or is acting on wrong information about me, or is simply lacking the capacity to think sensibly. If so, I should feel sorry for this person. How can I be angry at someone who acts foolishly, when I feel sorry for him for being a fool?"

I can personally testify that this kind of reasoning is effective. I know of times when my father was a victim of very unkind words and deeds; yet he never bore a grudge against anyone. As one might gather, the very people who had offended him later became his friends.

I know that there have been times that I have acted in haste or otherwise used poor judgment, and said unkind things about other people. I have genuinely regretted doing so. In cases when I have had the opportunity to apologize for my behavior, I have done so. In those instances where it was impossible for me to make amends,

I have continued to feel distressed for what I did, and I wish I could make amends to those people. Is it not possible that people who have offended me have similarly regretted their behavior? Perhaps they are ashamed to apologize to me, or perhaps they are afraid that I might rebuke them. But why should I not give them the benefit of the doubt that they too acted in haste or used poor judgment, and now wish that they had never done so? If I hope that others would think of me in a favorable light and not hold a grudge against me, should I not extend this consideration to others?

One does not have to be magnanimous to forgive others. All it takes is a bit of clear thinking to get rid of resentments, which are nothing but an emotional burden. Ridding oneself of resentments may not occur overnight, but with the passage of time it can be accomplished.

To recapitulate, there may be nothing that we can do to avoid the initial reflex-like feeling of anger, but we can restrain ourselves from acting on this feeling (rage), and we can eventually divest ourselves of resentments.

If all this is clear to us, we can try to find ways to convey this to our children. Obviously, they must be able to observe how their parents restrain themselves from acting in rage, and how they do not harbor resentments. Needless to say, children who see their parents acting in rage or detect that their parents bear grudges are not going to be impressed with didactic lectures to the contrary.

Let us take an incident where a child feels both hurt and angry. Shani comes home from school angry, throws her schoolbag on the floor, runs up to her room and slams the door. What do you do? Go up to the room and say, "Now, young lady, we don't tolerate that type of behavior here"?

That will get you nowhere and will only generate more anger. Instead, *acknowledge*, *empathize* and *identify*.

"Shani, I'd like to come into your room to talk with you."

"No! Go away."

"I'm sorry, Shani, but I am coming in. You don't have to say anything if you don't want to."

You enter the room and sit on the edge of the bed. Shani has her head buried in the pillow crying.

"You wouldn't be crying if you weren't hurting, honey. If you had fallen and scraped your knee there might be something I could do to make it feel better. But when your feelings have been hurt there's not too much a mother can do. All I can do is tell you that I can understand how you may be feeling, and if you're angry at whoever made you feel this way, I understand that too."

"Never mind, it was nothing. Just leave me alone."

"Honey, I remember when I used to cry into my pillow and Bubby would try to comfort me and I would tell her to go away. That's the least thing I really wanted her to do."

"You never felt this way. Nobody in the whole world has ever felt the way I do."

"That's funny you should say that. You seem to be a perfectly normal person in every other way. What makes you think you are so different now?"

"Because."

"Well, I don't think you're different at all. Maybe you think I was always a grownup person. Sure, you couldn't have known me when I was 10, but I can assure you that the same kind of things happened to me at 10 as you are going through now (pause). We don't have to talk about it now, and it can wait until you feel like sharing it with me. If you're really interested, I can tell you about why I know what you're feeling like, the kind of things that happened to me at 10."

Shani may or may not wish to continue the dialogue. If she does, it should not be too hard for you to remember being deeply hurt, whether at 10 or 12 or 14. I really doubt that you grew up in a sterile environment in which you were never offended. If Shani does not wish to continue the dialogue, respect her wishes. Kiss her on the back of her head and say, "You can have your privacy now. As soon as you're ready, come down for supper."

In all probability, children will eventually share with their parents what happened. Invariably, someone said or did something that hurt Shani deeply. The narrative of the personal insult may be accompanied with, "I hate Bruchie. She's mean. I'll hate her till the day I die."

Now the opportunity for identifying with resentments has presented itself. Assuming that the parents have practiced ridding themselves of resentments, they can share some of their own experiences with their children, how they eventually divested themselves of their anger even though they too may have initially felt, "I'll hate him for the rest of my life."

The Shabbos table again provides an excellent forum for discussing how we are supposed to deal with our emotions. Recourse to our rich literature about the great women and men in our history will provide appropriate anecdotes of their lives and reinforce your point.

One of my favorite stories about self-restraint is that of Rabbi Mordechai of Neschiz, whose love for *Eretz Yisrael* knew no bounds, but in the 1700's it was impossible for him to get there. Rabbi Mordechai had a fervent desire to acquire a piece of wool cloth from the Holy Land to make himself a *tallis katan* (a four-cornered fringed garment) so that he could fulfill the *mitzvah* of *tzitzis* with wool woven from sheep that had grazed on the land of Abraham, Isaac, and Jacob.

This was not an easy task. Not much wool was being manufactured then in the Holy Land, and communications to and fro were most difficult. But after many months, the long-coveted piece of cloth arrived, and Rabbi Mordechai kissed it, held it close to his heart, and then gave it to one of his students to shape into a *tallis katan*.

For whatever reason, the student was a bit careless, and when cutting out the hole for the head, he folded the cloth once too much. Instead of one hole there were two. Horrors! The piece of cloth that the rabbi had waited for so long was irreparably ruined!

Trembling, the student brought the ruined cloth to the rabbi, expecting a sharp dressing down for his negligence. Rabbi Mordechai looked at his demolished hopes, and his face reflected his anguish. But he quickly wiped away his tears and smiled.

"Quite right," he said to the student, "this piece of cloth was supposed to have two holes."

The student sat there dumbfounded, not even able to utter a word to ask why, and Rabbi Mordechai continued.

"This cloth required two holes. One for putting over the head, and the second to test me whether I could be in control of my emotions.

"True, *tzitzis* is a great *mitzvah*, but flying into a rage is a great sin. The intention to do a *mitzvah* should never result in committing a sin."

Children can be taught how to manage anger properly, and they can learn much from the works of *mussar* and the anecdotes of our great personalities, but only if they can see that their parents have learned these lessons well.

I can assure you that in your lifetime there will be adequate opportunities for you to show your children how you manage anger.

Let's assume it is summer and in the midst of a torrid heat wave, your air-conditioning breaks down. Or perhaps it is winter, and in the depths of a frigid spell, the furnace breaks down. These conditions are intolerable, but of course, if it has happened to you, it has also happened to others. You call the repairman, who does not return your call for six hours and you plead with him for mercy. He has had many calls and cannot possibly make it until the day after tomorrow. You grudgingly resign yourself to your fate. This is serious enough to take priority over your dental appointment for that day, so you cancel the appointment and either wilt in the heat or shiver in the cold, being kept alive by the awareness that relief is only 36 hours away.

On the day of the hoped-for salvation, you wait impatiently for the ring of the doorbell. When it rings at 11 a.m. you jump to open the door, only to find someone who wants to sell you a subscription to a magazine. It is all you can do to avoid slamming the door in his face. After all, it's not his fault that your equipment failed.

When the serviceman fails to show at 1 p.m. you call, and the answering machine requests your message. "Please!! I'm calling at 1 p.m. Don't forget me." At 3 p.m. you call again, and again the same lack of response.

At 6:30 p.m. the serviceman calls. There were unexpected complications at earlier service calls and he could not get to you. He hopes to be there tomorrow afternoon.

You wasted a whole day having canceled a dental appointment, let alone sweltering in the heat or freezing in the cold. This is enough to drive a person into a near-homicidal rage. You want to scream at the serviceman and hurl invectives.

Just pause for a moment. What do you *really* want? Relief from the heat or cold. The equipment repaired. How is screaming going to contribute to that goal? Do you really believe that shouting at the top of your voice will bring him to your home five minutes sooner? Why do something that serves no purpose whatever? In fact, if you really lose your cool, he may just say, "I'm sorry, sir/ma'am. I don't take that kind of talk from anyone. Please call someone else (click)." Now where are you? Back to where you were two days ago.

Let's apply a bit of *sechel* (logic). Suppose he was repairing your equipment and found that it's much more than a broken fan belt. The motor needs to be replaced, which requires a trip to the shop and three hours labor. Suppose he were to say, "This is a bigger job than I thought. I have other calls to make. I'll come back in a day or two when I have more time." You would hardly accept that. You have a right to expect him to finish the job. Well, that is exactly what happened on the call prior to yours. He did for that client what you would have wanted him to do for you.

Your child hears you say, "I'm awfully disappointed that you couldn't make it today and it is terribly uncomfortable here. But I can understand that unforeseen things can happen. Please make every effort to come as early as possible tomorrow." In all likelihood, the serviceman is not a sadistic villain and if he was delayed by things beyond his control, he appreciated your understanding and he probably will try extra hard to come early. It is pleasant to work for nice people.

There were two options: (1) to scream and accomplish nothing, or (2) to be sensible and make the best of it. If you take the second option, you have taught your child that (1) yes, you were angry, and (2) you controlled it and (3) you let go of your anger by understanding that the serviceman did not act out of meanness, but much like yourself, was a victim of circumstances. This is a powerful lesson, more effective than countless lectures. Actions speak louder than words. Show your children how it is done.

Anger rests in the bosom of fools (*Ecclesiastes* 7:9).

Chapter Twenty

Motivation

*T*here is general agreement that motivation is the key element in both learning and character development. Motivation is a broad concept and there can be a great variation of motivation much of which is phase related. I.e., at different levels of maturation, there are different types of motivation. What is proper at one phase may be totally inappropriate at another.

For example, there is a tradition that when a child reaches his 3rd birthday, he is taught the *aleph-bais*. Some people have a chart with the Hebrew letters, and put a drop of honey on each letter. The child is then taught the name of the letter, and when he repeats it, he gets to lick the honey. Others throw pieces of candy to the child, telling him that the angels from Heaven threw these candies because they are so pleased with his learning the *aleph-bais*. Whatever technique is employed, the intention is to use reward as a motivation for learning. A small child cannot understand the intrinsic value of Torah knowledge, so an extrinsic reward in the form of sweets is used to provide motivation.

Obviously, if one were to approach an accomplished Torah scholar and say, "If you study this piece of Talmud you will get some candy," this would be the height of absurdity. It is true that even an accomplished scholar may still be motivated by the desire to be acknowledged as a great Talmudist, in which case the motivation is still one of reward, but even if so, the reward is more subtle and sophisticated.

The ultimate in motivation is to do what is right and proper because it is right and proper rather than because of some external reward. But while this is the ultimate, it cannot be the way one begins. The Talmud recognizes this when it says that a person should learn Torah even if not for its intrinsic value, because the knowledge acquired will eventually lead one to learning for intrinsic value (*Pesachim* 50b). Both approaches have their place. One must recognize that we are to strive for doing what is right and proper for its intrinsic value, but that en route to that goal, we may have to utilize reward for motivation.

By the time we have become parents, we have already achieved the ideal motivation for many things, while there are still others that we may be doing for reward. One of the measures of maturity is how much of what we do is for intrinsic value and how much for reward. Needless to say, the more parents can do for intrinsic value rather than for reward, the greater is the impact on the child to follow suit.

All books on childrearing address the concept of motivation. The book, *Make Me Don't Break Me* by Rabbi Moshe Gans (Mesorah Publications 1994), is entirely devoted to motivational therapy and is highly recommended. I wish to call attention to just a few highlights regarding motivation.

We can readily understand that positive motivation is far superior to negative motivation, and that while fear of punishment may occasionally have to be employed, and while rebuke and reprimand are a necessary ingredient of discipline, every attempt should be made to emphasize the positive. The Talmud states it so well. "Rebuke with the left hand while embracing with the right" (*Sanhedrin* 107b). Moses, as he began delivering his sharp reprimand of the Israelites, first introduced his subject by hinting at the subject matter (*Deuteronomy* 1:1, *Rashi*), and then said, "May G-d increase you a thousandfold and bless you as He had promised" (ibid., 1:11), and only then did he rebuke them. When children do wrong it is necessary to correct them, not because they have angered us with their behavior, but because persisting in acting improperly is to their own detriment, and we discipline them out of love for them. We must therefore look for ways to convey this to them.

A most effective motivation for a child in terms of reward is *praise*. Children, very much like adults, like to be praised, and because of their small stature and associated feelings of inferiority, are even more thirsty for praise than adults. But while praise is an excellent motivator, there are a few precautions to keep in mind.

Some children, when praised by being told that what they did was good, may react somewhat differently than expected. They may look upon the complimentary statement, "That was very good," as a judgment or evaluation, and they do not like to be judged, even when it is a favorable judgment. The reason for this is that they may be very apprehensive about how the parent will react if what they do is *not* good.

When my 4-year-old grandson was learning the *aleph-bais*, I reviewed a page with him, and as he pronounced each letter to which I pointed, I said, "Good!" After several such comments, he said to me, "Zaidy, stop saying 'good' all the time." I think the reason for this was his concern about what my reaction would be if he mispronounced the letter. If I was sitting in judgment on each performance, then just as each correct pronunciation received a positive evaluation in terms of "That's good," then a mispronunciation would elicit a comment, "That's bad," and that is something he wished to avoid.

What then is a parent to do? This is a bit tricky, and our vocabulary may not be varied enough to provide us with nonjudgmental terms of approval. In the case of the *aleph-bais*, I did want the child to know that his pronunciation was correct, so I switched from saying "Good" to "Uh-huh," which indicated that he had pronounced the letter correctly. Whereas "good" is a value judgment, "okay" or "yes" or "uh-huh" is not.

Sometimes things lend themselves more easily to nonjudgmental approval, as when I told my 7-year-old violinist that I recognized the tune he was playing instead of saying, "That was beautiful." Sometimes it is possible to show approval by describing the child's performance, as when the child displays his crayon drawing which is supposed to portray the sun and the sky and grass. Instead of saying, "That is a beautiful picture" (probably not true), which would be a value judgment, and may cause apprehension that the next picture will not be as favorably judged, you can affirm his performance by saying, "This is the bright sun that you colored yellow, and the blue sky is clear without any clouds. Now sometimes you might want to draw a picture of the sun just as it rises or sets, and maybe you want to show some clouds. Then you have to add a little bit of orange to the yellow and leave some blank spaces in the blue which would be the clouds. Would you like to draw me a picture like that, too? Then I will have two pictures of two different days." By doing this, you have offered your appreciation of his work without rendering a value judgment.

This may seem like nit-picking, but it is important to at least bear it in mind. Firstly, things that may appear as trivia to adults may be of great importance to a small child. Secondly, it would be well for parents to reserve value judgments for when they are really necessary. There are enough times in a child's upbringing when a parent must sit in judgment on his behavior, when making value statements is unavoidable. Wherever it is possible to get along without these, it is preferable to do so.

We often "catch" children doing something wrong and scold them for it. We must learn to "catch" them doing things that are right and praise them for it. Too often the things that they do right are taken for granted. It is an established fact that behavior that is rewarded is reinforced, and if we praise them for doing what is right, they will be motivated to continue to do right. Most of us expect G-d to reward us for giving *tzedakah*, or for doing any of the other *mitzvos*, even though all we are doing is what is our duty. If we keep on the alert for things that warrant praise, we will find many of them.

When we invest money, we often allow the accrued interest to be automatically reinvested, so that the interest begins to earn interest. It is much the same with children who may be motivated by success. If we praise a successful performance, regardless of how trivial it may seem, we motivate the child to try something a bit more advanced and challenging, and in this way success feeds upon itself. It is much like learning how to walk. When the child takes his first step, the parents clap their hands and declare how thrilled they are. "Look," they exclaim, "Chaim'l took a step!" The infant who finds he can take one step now tries for two. Even if he should fall, the glee the parents manifested on his taking his first step overcomes the defeat of falling, and the child continues to try again. The way an infant learns to walk should serve as a model for other desirable behavior.

Children may try to do something right but end up doing wrong, as when they wish to surprise their mother by preparing a meal while she is asleep or away from the house, and end up with a kitchen that looks like it's been hit by a tornado. Looking at the horrible mess, the mother might well exclaim, "What's been going on here? Why is everything in such a mess? Who's going to clean all this up?"

Before making any such comments, try to find out what was going on, and if it indeed was a well-intentioned venture, think about how you felt or would feel when you did your best to avoid bumping into a parked car when you skidded, and ended up with a body-repair bill of several hundred dollars. Remember the formula: **acknowledge, empathize,** and **identify**. If your memory serves you well, you should be able to come up with a similar incident, and instead of screaming at them, acknowledge their good intentions. "Kids, I know you meant well, and I appreciate your intentions. This reminds me of when I . . . . I meant well, but it ended up being a fiasco, and I cried my eyes out. So, let's call the governor to get the kitchen declared a disaster area. The next time you want to surprise me by preparing supper, let me join in on the surprise, okay?" Then you give the kids a big hug and you say, "That's for your good intentions and not for the chocolate goo that's all over the cabinet." Years later you will be looking back at the incident and laughing at it, so why not begin laughing now?

Motivation can succeed only when the child believes that the task at hand or the expectations of him are realistic and when he understands them. Parents may tell the child to do something, taking for granted that the child will understand just what it is that they want, and this may indeed be within the child's capacity. However, if the assignment is not spelled out clearly, the child may not understand what it is the parent wants, and may even be confused or mistakenly assume that what was asked of him is beyond his abilities. In either case, the child may not comply with the parent's instructions, and this may be misinterpreted as defiance. In other words, when giving a child an assignment, *be specific.*

A simple statement, "I want you to clean up your room," should not cause any confusion, should it? But think for a moment: Are there not many levels of "cleaning up?" Even among adults there are varying concepts of what constitutes "cleaning up." Some housewives are satisfied with the house being more or less orderly, others are more meticulous about having everything in its proper place, and still others want their floors to be gleaming if not surgically sterile. Why then should we assume that the child knows what we mean by "cleaning up?" Suppose a mother inspects the room and finds that the room was "cleaned up" by shoving almost everything under the bed and stuffing whatever didn't fit under the bed into the closet. She then shouts, "Just come here at once, young man!" and then sternly says, "Is this what you call cleaning up? You ought to be ashamed of yourself."

I'm not at all sure that the child should be ashamed of himself. First of all, even if the child was derelict, the words "ashamed of yourself" are improper, as we note in our discussion of guilt and shame, and really should not be in a parent's vocabulary. Secondly, is it possible that Daddy's desk is not "cleaned up" any better than the child's room? Finally, how is the child to know that removing objects from sight by putting them under the bed or in the closet does not constitute "cleaning up"?

It would take just a few seconds more to tell a child, "Here's what I would like you to do. Put the dirty clothes in the hamper, the books back into the bookcase, and hang your jacket in the closet. The toys can go under the bed, and then straighten up the bedcover. I'll help you with anything you can't do yourself. Call me when you're finished." With more specific instructions and an offer to help with anything he might think he cannot do, compliance is much more likely.

Sometimes children will complete an assignment "satisfactorily," but may do it in a different way than the parents would have done it. Parents who are rigid may say, "I want you to do it my way." Unless there is really a legitimate reason for insisting on a particular way of doing something, rigidity for the sake of rigidity is rather pointless. Furthermore, allowing children to be innovative may stimulate their creativity. It might be wise to acknowledge this and say, "Look at this! I've been doing it this way all the time, and Chani has found another way!"

There is probably nothing in parenting that is as responsible for parents graying prematurely as *homework.* If I had to choose the most common phrase parents have uttered in desperation, I would vote for, "My kid with his homework is going to drive me out of my mind!" Parental attitudes and management of the homework issue can make the difference between success and failure. I know that some of my suggestions may be received with the comment, "How does he expect me to do this? I've got my hands full with *kein ayin hara* eight children!"

My response to this is recourse to a comment by the Rabbi of Gur on the verses in *Numbers* 11:4-13. The Torah relates that some of the Israelites demanded meat in the desert, and Moses turned to G-d, crying out, "Where am I to get meat for this multitude? Did I conceive this nation or did I give birth to it, that You tell me I have to provide for them?"

The Rabbi of Gur asks: Why did Moshe add the second statement? If he cannot provide meat for such a multitude, what difference did it make whether or not he conceived or bore them? If he doesn't have meat, then he doesn't have it.

The Rabbi of Gur answered, "For children whom you conceived and whom you bore, the claim, 'I cannot provide for them,' is unacceptable. Children are the parents' responsibility, and they must find a way to provide for their legitimate needs."

Every child has the legitimate right to have conditions conducive to doing homework; i.e., a table, adequate light, and an absence of distracting noise. If a parent will say, "But we live in such cramped quarters, and I have little children that are crying. There is just no way that I can give him such conditions," I will fall back on the words of the Rabbi of Gur. No, you do not have an obligation to buy your child designer clothes, but you do have an obligation to provide him with a proper environment for homework. When a child sees the effort that parents make to provide him with these conditions, he is much more likely to take his homework more seriously.

Children may complain that their homework is too hard and that they don't understand it. "My teacher did not explain it well." This is usually not true. The child may have been daydreaming or was otherwise distracted and did not pay sufficient attention.

It is important to note at this point that some children may have learning disabilities of one kind or another, and these are too often overlooked. There have been more than a few instances where a child's hearing difficulty went unnoticed, and if he sat in the rear of the classroom, he may not have heard the teacher. Similarly, some children cannot see the blackboard clearly, but their visual disability has gone undetected. Attention-deficit disorders are not infrequently overlooked. Any difficulty in absorbing subject matter warrants an evaluation to insure that the child's system is functioning properly. We will elaborate on some of these conditions in a subsequent chapter.

A child's comment, "I just can't get these arithmetic problems. They are too hard," may elicit a parental comment, "I was just like that. Arithmetic was my worst subject." This is one time where identifying is not appropriate. The child may assume there is a hereditary disorder in grasping arithmetic and resign himself to failure in this subject.

With some children, especially in the lower grades, it may be necessary to offer a reward for doing homework, but this should be discontinued as early as possible. Giving a reward implies that they are doing the parents a favor by completing their homework, and children must be taught that doing homework is for their own advantage. Indeed, this may be the prototype by which the child learns that when he does things that he is supposed to do it is for his own benefit. Thus, even when the young child is offered some type of reward for doing his homework, he should be told, "Now this is only to show you that when you do your homework, you gain by it. The real gain you will have is that it will enable you to understand the subject better, and you will get better grades. All kinds of good things are a result of better grades.

"It is also important to make your homework paper neat. When we serve your food on the table, we try to make it appear tasty, because a pleasant appearance of the food makes eating more pleasant. When you have a birthday cake, it is not only the cake that is nice, but you also enjoy the pretty trimmings. The same is true of your homework, which should look nice and neat."

What about helping a child with homework? This can be constructive, since it indicates that a parent shows interest in a child's schoolwork, and also enables the parent to detect if the child is having any difficulty in understanding the teacher and why. Helping the child should be in the form of stimulating the child, showing him that he really has the ability to do the work. For example, some children sign off on word problems. "They're too hard. I can't do them." With a bit of patience, the parents can help the child see that he can figure out what the problem means and how to work at it to arrive at the solution. At each step, when the child has the correct insight, a comment like, "See! You *do* know it. You just have to study it a bit, and then you discover what is being asked for and how to do it. Sometimes we look at things and can't figure out how to do them, but if we just persist a bit, we get the right ideas. Just a few moments ago you thought that was terribly hard, and now you figured it out. So let's go on. You can figure out the next step too."

Great caution must be exercised not to do any of the work *for* the child, because this only confirms his opinion that he is too dull to do it himself.

Sometimes a parent is unable to help the child with the homework, as for example when a child learns the "new math," with which the parent is unfamiliar. In such instances, one may get a student from a more advanced grade to help the child with the homework, if this is necessary.

What if the child returns with a poor grade on homework or a test? If the child has tried, he should be praised for the effort in spite of the poor grade. The parent might say, "A baseball player that hits .300 gets $3 million a year, even though he makes an out seven out of ten times. You get an A for your effort. Now let's see what needs to be done to get the grades for your effort."

As was noted earlier, parents should be aware of their own needs to have a star student. If these feelings are recognized, parents can avoid pushing the child in order to satisfy their own ego needs rather than the needs of the child.

I want to reemphasize the role of parents as a model. Mature motivation should be for the inherent good in doing things that are right and proper, and the seeds for a child developing such motivation should be planted early. When children see parents behaving in a manner that conveys to them that we should not be limited to doing things for reward, they will learn from that and apply it to other areas in life. For example, when parents visit a sick person, or make a condolence call, or give *tzedakah*, or do any other act of *gemillus chesed* (kindness), it is appropriate to find a suitable time to discuss these *mitzvos*, not in a sense of boasting that they are *tzaddikim*, but as examples of the *mitzvos* that they are learning about in school. Stories of acts of *chesed* by our great personalities can be related at the Shabbos table, and may be followed with, "Now there are many opportunities every day to do *chesed*. Helping another child who may be carrying a heavy load of books is *chesed*. Next Shabbos I would like each of you to tell me what kind of *chesed* you were able to do during the week. Okay?"

The connection between acts of *chesed*, homework, and cleaning up one's room may not be immediately evident. However, a number of *mitzvos* in the Torah are followed by the phrase, "And you will do what is good and proper in the eyes of G-d." The Talmudic principle of "one *mitzvah* leads to another" has broad application. Every single proper act serves as a precursor for another proper act.

I must digress a moment to reiterate why the demands on parents are greater today than in the past.

The Torah relates two incidents where populations were so utterly corrupt that they were destroyed. The first was the generation of the Flood, whose immorality had exceeded even the infinite tolerance of G-d, and the second was Sodom and Gemorrah, whose corruption consisted of legitimizing all evil by legislation.

Our model civilization has combined both of the above. The world population is at risk of being destroyed by diseases secondary to unbridled lust, and our legislative bodies are constantly passing laws decriminalizing behavior that had previously been condemned. One does not need to be a party to the controversy over abortion to realize a simple fact: An act that just several decades ago was considered criminal and tantamount to murder is now considered a basic human right which should be funded by tax dollars.

Bringing up children in today's world is a far greater challenge than for any of our forebears, and this is why so much more extra effort and even sacrifices are necessary in parenting.

Chapter Twenty-One
Unconditional Love

*L*ove of a parent for a child should hardly require much discussion. There is obviously a powerful biological component to parental love, since it is present in so many forms of animal life where we assume intellectual activity to be sparse.

But even parental love is not without its problems. Firstly, love is not a well-defined concept. The term is frequently used to describe a feeling that is self-centered rather than outwardly directed. Thus, we can "just love" a particular garment, and one often hears people describe various kinds of delicacies that they "love." In these instances the term clearly refers to the gratification one receives from the love object. Even in human relationships, love can be based on self-gratification. I "love" that person because he/she satisfies my needs.

There is also an altruistic love whereby one adores someone else beyond the gratification one receives. People who willingly sacrifice their belongings, their personal comfort, and even their lives for someone they love are placing the love object above their personal needs.

Parental love, both in animals and man, is often altruistic. Animals are known to sacrifice their lives when an attacker threatens their young, and humans frequently set their own needs and desires aside in favor of their children.

Problems in this love relationship may arise when children generate negative feelings in their parents. This is particularly true of anger, as when children defy their parents. Many people assume that anger and love towards the same person cannot coexist. Children, particularly, who do not have the biological love towards the parent that the parent has towards them, may feel that if the parents are angry at them, this means that they do not love them.

This is not true, and a very powerful example of this is described in the Torah. King David had a rebellious son, Avshalom, who was overtly defiant of his father and was exiled. After he returned, he organized a coup and pursued his father with the goal of killing him, causing David to flee. He publicly violated his father's wives. Yet, when David learned that Avshalom was killed in battle, he wept bitterly in grief over this renegade child. "Avshalom, my son, my son. I wish I had died instead of you" (*II Samuel* 19:1).

In my work with drug-addicted youngsters, I have had to counsel and provide support for parents who have had to take a "tough love approach" towards their children. This attitude is essential because parents cannot be a party to or condone a child's self-destructive behavior. Tough love may therefore necessitate discontinuing financial support of a drug-addicted child, and even evicting him from the home and turning him out to the mercy of street life. The agony these parents experience is heart rending. They are forced to take drastic steps because of their love for the child and in their desperate efforts to save him. Yet the child who is treated thusly perceives this as rejection and believes that his parents do not love him.

Whereas parental love may be biological and unconditional, children may not be able to understand this. As a rule, we do not understand anything that we have not experienced ourselves. A child's concept of love is not altruistic, because he has never experienced this. Juvenile love is self-centered, with the child loving those things that give pleasure, and despising those things that cause him displeasure. The child therefore thinks that his parents' feelings for him are of the same character, and he has no way of knowing that parental love is of a different quality. Inasmuch as the child despises things that cause him to be angry, he may interpret his parents' anger at him as indicating that they do not love him.

A child may favor one friend over another and may relate to this friend differently than to others. He may spend more time with this friend and more willingly share his things with him. For the child, preferential treatment is an indication of greater love, and of course, the child lacks the maturity to distinguish self-centered love from altruistic love. If he believes that a sibling is receiving preferential treatment from the parents, he concludes that his parents love the sibling more than him.

Statements like, "You gave Penina a bigger piece of cake than me," or "Nachman always gets to go with you and I never do," or any such similar assertions of parental discrimination are an expression of the child's feeling unloved or less loved. As a rule, it is not the particular incident that generates the feeling of being unloved, but just the reverse. It is because the child feels unloved that he is sensitive and interprets, or better yet, misinterprets parental behavior as being indicative of their greater love for a sibling. The statement, "You gave Penina a bigger piece of cake than me," is thus a *symptom* of a child's low self-esteem. The underlying statement is "I do not feel I am as lovable as Penina." It is the latter implied statement that should draw parental attention. Responding, "That's not true. Your piece of cake is just as big as Penina's, but it was just cut differently," or any other response relating to the cake is totally irrelevant. The child is revealing a painful feeling about himself, and this needs to be acknowledged. The immediate response should be something like, "Mommies and daddies love all their children. Just because one piece of cake looks bigger than another has nothing to do with how much mommies and daddies love their children."

This response has at least addressed the issue and informed the child that the parents know he has felt hurt. However, the response in itself has done nothing to resolve the underlying feeling of being unloved, and parents should realize that this is how this child feels, and direct their efforts to helping the child overcome the negative feelings about himself. It might seem that taking the child aside after supper and telling him how much he is really loved and that his observation of the preference for Penina is fallacious should do the trick. The fact is, however, that while such reassuring statements may be pleasant and helpful, they are not sufficient to change the child's self-concept, and parents should look for ways to enhance the child's self-esteem, whether with some of the suggestions in this book, or by supplemental readings on the subject, or by getting some direction from someone with expertise in child psychology. Again, while the parents may know that their love for the child is unconditional, the child may not perceive this, and may feel that because he is undeserving of parental love, he is indeed less loved by them.

But let us not deny reality. The fact is that biology notwithstanding, parents sometimes do favor one child over another. We have noted earlier that parents do have an ego investment in their children, and if one child shows great promise in being valedictorian while another is barely squeaking through with passing grades, the parents may indeed favor the one who will bring honor to the family. The reasons why parents may favor one child over another are legion. The Midrash is critical of the patriarch Jacob, stating that the Egyptian captivity and enslavement was due to his showing his favoritism for Joseph.

It is futile for a parent to try and deny his special feelings for a particular child, because children are very sensitive and can see right through the pretense. Furthermore, contrary to what we might think, children can grasp the fact that they are all differently endowed. A child who is tone deaf can understand very well why a sibling who is musically inclined will play at a recital, while he is unable to do so. He may not be too upset by the fact that the parents are proud of the sibling's performance, while he cannot give them this particular *nachas*. However, the child wishes his parents to appreciate him for what he is and for his efforts.

The disaster with Jacob's children did not occur during the years that their father devoted more time in transmitting his knowledge to Joseph. The brothers recognized that Joseph was a prodigy and deserved having more teaching time invested in him. But when Jacob made Joseph the multicolored silk coat, that is when the brothers were provoked. Joseph did not need to be rewarded for his greater innate talents. As far as their efforts were concerned, they were all equal, and it was the unwarranted demonstration of favoritism which led to their envy of him and the tragic aftermath.

The Chassidic master, Rabbi Zusia of Hanipole, used to say, "I have no fear of being asked on Judgment Day why I was not as great as the Baal Shem Tov, because I will respond, 'That is an absurd demand. How can you expect me to be as great as the Baal Shem Tov?' Nor am I worried that they will ask me why I was not as great as my teacher, the Maggid of Mezeritch, because I will say, 'How can you expect me to be as great as the Maggid?' But if they say, 'Zusia, why weren't you as great as Zusia should have been?' for that I will have no answer."

The message of this anecdote is that each person is supposed to live up to his own potential. Indeed, a child who has only the intellectual capacity of getting C's and who does get C's is more deserving than a child who has the capacity to get A+'s and gets only B's. The latter's grades are indeed superior to the former's, but he is lacking in performance.

The ideal parental attitude is for each child to maximize his own potential. The child's efforts towards this goal should be appropriately acknowledged. Parents should be able to set aside considerations other than this, and the fact that one child was born with greater skills and talents should not affect their love for other children nor result in the more talented child being shown favoritism.

Chapter Twenty-Two
Whose Fault Is It?

*S*ometimes I have the feeling that there are four essentials for human survival: (1) food and water; (2) clothing; (3) shelter; (4) someone to blame. The need to blame someone for what has gone wrong is so universal that it seems to be a basic component of life.

Some things enjoy wide popularity because they serve a function. I therefore ask, "What function does blaming someone serve?" Identifying someone who has committed a crime or an assault against a person or one's property may serve the purpose of punishing the criminal or suing for compensation, but when these factors do not apply, what purpose is there in placing blame?

I believe I have found the answer in my work treating alcoholics. These people are notorious for their propensity to ascribe blame. "I drink because . . . my boss is hypercritical; or, my wife nags me; or, the neighbors make too much noise and do not let me sleep at night, etc." It became obvious to me that the function of placing blame was not only to rationalize one's behavior, but even more importantly, *to avoid having to make changes*. In other words, the person argues, "It is not my fault that I drink. My drinking is a consequence of my wife's nagging. If she were to stop nagging, I would not drink. Therefore, *she* is the one who must make changes in her behavior rather than *me*." If there were no one to blame, the alcoholic would have to seriously consider discontinuing his excessive drinking, which is certainly a difficult ordeal. Blaming eliminates the need to undergo the distressful experience of stopping drinking. Blaming is thus a defensive maneuver whereby a person tries to justify continuing a particular behavior which really requires modification. Blaming thus preserves the status quo.

Obviously, preserving a status quo which should be changed is destructive. It is therefore important to impress children with the futility of finding fault. Mother hears screaming in the dining room and rushes in to discover Yanky beating Ruchi. "Look what she did! She spilled chocolate milk all over my homework paper!" Yanky has every reason to be angry, but should be told that beating Ruchi will contribute nothing to completing his homework assignment. He should be told that whereas his anger is legitimate, the first order of business is to complete the assignment. If the paper cannot be salvaged, he will have to recopy it on another sheet. After this is done, Ruchi's offense can be dealt with.

This approach accomplishes several things. Firstly, it acknowledges the legitimacy of the anger. Secondly, it permits getting the assignment done. Thirdly, it allows a cooling-off time for dealing with Ruchi. After all, Ruchi may indeed have been a bit careless, but it is hardly likely that she intentionally spilled chocolate milk over Yanky's paper. Hasn't something like that ever happened to Yanky? The anger can be defused, but it is difficult to do so when the passion is at its height.

The tendency to blame and react rather than first attending to the problem is not limited to juveniles. Sometimes our better judgment does prevail, as in the case of a fire, when we first put out the fire and then investigate the cause. Or, if someone has caused you to fall and break an arm or leg, you first attend to the medical problem, and only later file suit against the assailant. This is how we should deal with all problems: First correct whatever has gone wrong, and then attend to the cause.

This rule has often been violated in dealing with psychological problems. For many years, the theory prevailed that the way to overcome a symptom of an emotional disorder is to dig into the past in the hope of discovering the cause, and by gaining insight into the cause, the symptom should disappear. The theory is reasonable enough, but the catch is that very often it does not work. It is common to hear patients say, "I understand everything perfectly, but I just don't feel any different."

More recently, an increasing number of psychotherapists have adopted the approach of first correcting the behavior, and only afterwards investigating its cause. Thus, the success of Alcoholics Anonymous is due to its avoidance of considering the drinker's rationalizations for his use of alcohol. The message is, "Don't pick up the first drink and be sure to go to meetings." The pathology is the drinking and that must be eliminated first. Once the sobriety has been achieved, one can then look for underlying causes for the drinking.

Our analysis of the defensive character of blaming fully justifies this approach. Looking for the cause of any behavior may be nothing other than a delaying tactic to avoid making changes in one's customary behavior.

Proper upbringing should prepare children for the life ahead of them. If we can teach them to first correct the problem and deal with its possible causes later, we will have contributed immensely to their welfare.

It is common for siblings to fight. "He hit me first." "I did not! He threw that book at me and look at my arm where it hit me." "He called me a bad name," etc.

Parent may try to intervene by seeking to get to the root of the problem. This is usually futile. Each child will come up with an account of how the other provoked him first, and that his response was in self-defense or retaliation. Trying to ascertain the facts makes everyone dissatisfied. The only approach that can succeed is "Stop this bickering. I don't care who did what to whom. The fighting stops *now!* Each of you go on with what you are supposed to be doing. A bit later we will get together to try to get to the bottom of this so it shouldn't happen again."

Do not be surprised that perhaps in a half hour when you wish to convene court to deal with the fracas, the two siblings are playing together, having forgotten the whole incident rather rapidly. You may offer to hold court, and if they still wish to do so, you may set up a hearing in a quasi-humorous fashion.

"Okay, I guess I have to be the judge. Now you don't have any lawyers, so each one of you will have to plead his own case. In a court, the prosecution goes first but then the defense, but since we cannot establish who is the plaintiff and who is the defendant, the only fair way is to toss a coin. Heads, Sender goes first; tails, Rafi goes first. Okay?

"Now in a courtroom, everyone gets a chance to plead his case. You can't interrupt to present your side, and all you can do when the other person is talking is say, 'I object,' but you have to let the other person finish, and then you get your turn. Now we'll do this according to the rules of court. If you're good at this, you might even decide to become lawyers."

This quasi-humorous approach defuses the anger and allows the children to participate in a reasonable debate. When both sides have been presented, you have several options.

"Okay, I've heard both sides. I think we should first try for an out-of-court settlement. Why don't you both talk it over and see what kind of compromise you can reach that will be fair?" Or, "I must take this under advisement. Court will be recessed until tomorrow, at which time I will hand down a decision." Or, "I don't think I can deal with this by myself. This case requires a jury. We'll have to pick several outsiders to form a jury."

It is rather unwise for parents to try to settle a dispute among children. Firstly, it is next to impossible to get at the real facts. Secondly, children have to learn how to settle disputes on their own. In their future lives, the parents are not always going to be there to settle their differences with others for them, and training a child how to get along with adversaries is an important preparation for life.

Correcting the problem first and postponing looking for or dealing with the cause until a later time is an excellent formula for adjusting to real-life situations. We can successfully convey this to our children, but if, and only if, we practice this in our own lives. Children who see parents indulging in blaming, whether they blame each other or outsiders, are likely to adopt the defensive blaming tactic themselves. When parents correct whatever needs correction instead of blaming, and point this out to the children, they are providing them with an invaluable method of coping with the many stresses they are sure to encounter in their adult lives.

Chapter Twenty-Three

When Am I Supposed to Do All This?

ou may say, "Yes, my 7-year-old is in the house moping while his friends are playing, and I would just love to implement your suggestions and have a conversation with him. It is easy for you to write all these brilliant ideas in the peace and quiet of your study, but my 7-year-old has four younger siblings, the two youngest both in diapers. They are, thank G-d, all very active children, and they happen to be at the peak of their activity. I just heard a scream from upstairs, and I dread to find out who did what to whom. Yesterday the baby got a haircut from her 4-year-old brother. I would like nothing better than to have the conversation you recommend with my 7-year-old, but please be realistic. You must be kidding!"

I hope I am not ignoring reality. I am not suggesting that you do the impossible. But even a house with five children under age 7 is not always mayhem, and there are times when you can implement the recommendations for acknowledging feelings, empathizing, and identifying. Do it when you can.

But we really should take another look at the "impossible" situation. Not all impossible situations are as impossible as they may seem.

A man once entered a large hotel and requested a room. When the clerk told him that they had no vacancies, he said, "There must be one available room out of 400," but the clerk insisted that all rooms were occupied.

"Don't tell me if the president of the United States came here now, you wouldn't find a room for him," the man said.

"Well, I guess we would have to find something for the president," the clerk said to him.

"Good," the man said. "Now the president is not coming, so you can give me the room you were going to give him."

I know that a busy parent may have his/her hands full, but if the 7-year-old had a doctor or dentist appointment, or had to be driven to his violin lesson, somehow time would be found to get this done, even with the four other active children doing their things. Well, he does not have a doctor appointment or a violin lesson, so let's use that time to talk with him. His emotional well-being should rank right up there in priority along with other appointments for which time would somehow be found.

There is no question that both fathers and mothers may be overburdened. The father may be holding two jobs to make ends meet, and the mother may indeed have her hands full with several active children. Yet even with these real demands on their time and energies, slightly more judicious timing and priority setting can help parents find a bit more time for their children. For example, it is not unusual to see a mother trying to serve supper to several children, some of whom may be fighting at the table, while she is talking to a friend on the cordless phone. It really would be much better to carry on the conversation with the friend after the children are in bed, and give the children the attention they need.

While the demands on a parent's time may make it impossible to carry out some suggestions at any specific time, the fact that they are not carried out at all, even at a later time, may be due to the parent's not being willing to deal with the problem and hoping that it will just go away. A parent may not feel competent to engage the 7-year-old in a discussion about his withdrawal from his friends, and may use the scarcity of time as a rationalization for not doing so. If parents will recognize the importance of acknowledging feelings, empathizing, and identifying, they will try to find some time to help the 7-year-old. If it cannot be at that particular moment when the children are screaming, then it can be done later.

Parents should carefully consider their priorities, and perhaps seek consultation even when they are certain that what they are doing is proper. For example, I have spoken with some young children of alcoholic fathers, and they have essentially said, "I really don't feel so angry at my father, because I know he's sick, but it's my mother that I can't understand. Instead of giving us any attention, she's spending all her time trying to control my father's drinking." There's no question that in such a situation the mother is certain that she's doing the right thing, whereas in fact she is expending energy in futility while the children are being deprived of the attention and guidance she could give them. Similar improper allocations of time and energy occur even in the absence of alcoholism.

Let's recapitulate. Our great-grandparents may have had fewer time-saving gadgets, and in some way their lives may have been more difficult. However, as far as raising children was concerned, the street and environment was not polluted with immorality the way it is now. During the past two generations there has been a progressive deterioration of the environment, and street morality is now at an all-time low. Even in some tight enclaves and ghetto neighborhoods, there is no keeping out the toxic immorality of the prevailing culture. Nor can the school be relied on to form character, and we should be happy if they get the subject matter taught properly. Character training remains almost totally the responsibility of the parents, and if we just realize the magnitude of this responsibility, we will give it the highest priority.

Bringing Basics Together

Chapter Twenty-Four

Back to Basics

*I*n this section we would like to bring together some basic knowledge that is essential for today's Jewish parent. Even the most skilled parent who is in possession of a well-stocked parenting toolbox is dependent on factual information about the nature of children, common problems in childhood, and some of the worrisome signs of our times. While we do not expect that our children will have problems with drugs and alcohol, it is foolish to assume that because we have given them a Torah upbringing, such problems could never occur to them. We cannot be in total control of our children's associations, nor do we understand everything about why some youngsters may experiment with drugs, and furthermore, why some become dependent upon regular use of drugs or alcohol. The doors to our educational institutions are open, and one cannot frisk every person who walks through the open doors of the yeshivah. The approximation of one vulnerable child with one purveyor of drugs can be the beginning of a most serious problem.

There is still a prevalent attitude that whereas dysfunction of the eyes, ears, lungs, or any part of the body is an "illness" which may require expert treatment and which is no reflection whatever upon one's character, any *behavioral* dysfunction is a moral failure or character weakness which requires discipline. We now know that learning disorders and other behavioral or psychological problems are not moral weaknesses, but conditions that are no less respectable than other physical diseases, and which are amenable to and require appropriate treatment. Similarly, whereas parents do not feel guilty if their child has, for example, an asthmatic problem, they tend to blame themselves if the child has any type of psychological problem. This self-incrimination may contribute to a denial of the child's problem and failure to identify it and seek expert evaluation and proper treatment.

There was the case of a child who simply could not sit still, was highly distractible, constantly fidgeted, and could not attend to the classwork. The teacher naively assumed the child to be the victim of a battle with the *yetzer hara*. This child's behavior is a classic example of Attention Deficit Hypertension Disorder. The approach is not to make the child feel guilty and to discipline, but to help him medically and with proper counseling, to treat this condition.

It is also a mistake to dismiss as insignificant the very real stresses of a mother who may be overwhelmed by the care of five or six little ones. While we advocate large families and we see each child as an additional blessing, we must also be considerate of and empathize with the mother who has three children in diapers, and the two oldest of the five are home from school with colds. There is also no guarantee that even a good parent will not lose his cool, or that children will not tax their parents' skills and drive them to distraction.

While we have no difficulty seeking medical assistance for physical conditions, even from secular physicians, we are much more sensitive when it comes to behavioral problems. There is good reason for our defensive attitude, inasmuch as some psychological schools based their treatment approaches on concepts that were antithetical to Torah values.

In recent years there has been a major change in psychological theory and practice, and there are schools of psychology, such as the "cognitive school," whose ideas do not conflict with Torah concepts. We are also fortunate in having competent psychologists and psychiatrists who respect Torah values and will not challenge them.

One must not have immediate recourse to a psychiatrist or psychologist for every problem. The judicious use of self-help books, scientifically well-grounded books about child development, a conference with an experienced mother, the child's physician, or a school counselor can often provide the necessary information for a given problem. It is important that we have an awareness of our own needs as people as well as our role as parents, and overcome our inhibitions to ask for help.

There is particular danger in the assumption that children will outgrow all their problems. There are indeed certain phases in juvenile behavior that are age specific, and which the child does outgrow. But there are other conditions that, if left unattended and untreated, may leave permanent scars. There are some types of childhood trauma that can have a devastating effect that may extend throughout the child's adult life. There is no substitute for alertness, awareness, and knowledge. We hope to enhance these in the following pages.

Chapter Twenty-Five

Don't Undermine Your Authority

Chezky: Boy, was our teacher ever crazy today. Two of the kids were fooling around. We couldn't help it and we all laughed. The teacher just lost his cool and yelled at the class, and then he kept us all after school. The whole class!

Mother: That was stupid. I can't imagine a teacher doing anything like that. He could have just kept the two boys after school.

Chezky: Yeah, pretty dumb, huh?

Mother: I'm going to call the principal and give him a piece of my mind. Teachers should have better judgment than that.

You just blew it, mother.

Or perhaps this scenario.

Father: You should have been at *shul* this morning. The rabbi's *drashah* (sermon) would have given you something to think about. He said that ... (comment on a controversial issue).

Mother: He said that? I can't believe it. Rabbi Goldberg never would have said anything like that. Where do these young rabbis get such weird ideas?

Father: That's the kind of rabbis they're putting out now. They're still wet behind the ears and already they consider themselves capable of telling people twice their age what's right and what's wrong.

Mother: Isn't anyone going to set him straight? Didn't anyone have the courage to challenge those remarks?

Parents, you have just dealt yourself a severe blow.

Authority is authority is authority. When you indiscriminately attack authority, you are undermining your own authority. If the teacher is stupid and the rabbi is reckless and therefore they are not accorded the respect of their positions, then perhaps parents can be treated likewise.

Are teachers and rabbis always right? Of course not. But then again, neither are parents. The *halachah* is quite clear on how one may disagree with a parent, and this should be a model for all authorities (*Yoreh Deah* 240).

In the scenario with Chezky, parents should be aware that their child's description of the incident may not be quite accurate. Even when it does not involve an authority figure, it is wise to withhold reacting to a reported incident until one has determined what the facts were. *Halachah* requires that a judge listen to both sides before rendering an opinion, and it is only fair and reasonable that we apply this principle to all judgments we make. An investigation of the incident may reveal that the teacher did initially discipline the two boys, and that the class then joined in an uproar, jeering the teacher, and yes, dear Chezky may even have been one of the leaders of the rebellion.

In the scenario with the rabbi, it would be wise to check with the rabbi regarding what he actually said. I have often heard myself misquoted, and things have been attributed to me that I never said.

People have a way of taking things out of context or simply hearing partial sentences and filling in the empty spaces with their own ideas. But even if the rabbi was correctly quoted and you happen to disagree with him, it would still be appropriate for you to make a personal inquiry and listen to the reasons for his statement. The second scenario would then go like this:

Father: You should have been at *shul* this morning. The rabbi's *drashah* (sermon) would have given you something to think about. He said that ... (comment on a controversial issue).

Mother: I have great respect for Rabbi Cohen, and I'm not at all sure that he came across with what he really wanted to say. I don't happen to agree with what you're quoting him as saying, but I'd like to find out what he said, and if he does take that position, I'd like him to explain it to me.

There is nothing wrong with disagreeing with someone, even with authority, but if one does so in a disrespectful manner, this is considered *letzanus* or mockery, which is soundly condemned in Jewish ethics. In his lectures on ethics, Rabbi Chaim Shmulevitz cites various incidents of defiance of authority, all of which had tragic consequences, notably that of the Korach Rebellion (*Numbers,* Chapter 16). There was no substance to Korach's rebellion, yet he was able to incite 250 of the elders against Moses by means of *letzanus.* Rabbi Shmulevitz quotes Luzatto's comparison of *letzanus* to a well-greased shield, which causes all objects to slip off and not make any impact. Similarly, an attitude of mockery results in the person not taking things seriously and dismissing them without adequate consideration (*Sichos Mussar* 5731:21). If parents promote or condone this attitude toward other authority figures, they should not be surprised when their children exhibit a similar attitude toward them.

By the same token, it is important for authority figures to own up to having made a mistake. The Torah states that when Moses reprimanded Aaron for what he felt was a violation of ritual, and Aaron explained his actions, Moses conceded that Aaron was right (*Leviticus* 10:11-20). Admitting a mistake is not a sign of weakness.

To the contrary, it is the obstinate insistence that one is always right that betrays weakness. The Talmud states, "Fortunate is the generation where the greater ones can accept the opinion of the lesser ones" (*Rosh Hashanah* 25b). Teachers, principals, rabbis, parents — none are infallible, and they will gain stature when they admit having made a mistake.

It is sometimes difficult to accept the authority of a younger person. The mother in the second scenario appealed to the authority of the venerated previous rabbi, and saw his young successor as being incompetent. The Torah is very clear on this issue: "You will come to the judge who will be in those days" (*Deuteronomy* 17:9), which leads the Talmud to comment that we must have recourse to the Torah authorities of our generation. True, today we do not have a Reb Moshe to decide on halachic issues, but there were those who had been hesitant to accept Reb Moshe's opinion because he was not the Chofetz Chaim, and so on all the way back to Moses.

In a generation where authority of all kinds is under fire, parents should try to support authority rather than to disparage it, if for no other reason than the fact that to undermine any other authorities also results in undermining their own.

Chapter Twenty-Six
Say "Thank You"

*W*e teach our 3- and 4-year-old children to say thank you when someone gives them candy or cookies. Some children respond immediately, but other children seem to be resistive, and the embarrassed mother may have to repeatedly coax them to say the magic words. Why should there be any resistance at all to saying "please" or "thank you"?

Saying "thank you" is more than a polite gesture. The feeling and expression of gratitude occupies a central portion in Judaism. Indeed, the very first words a person utters on awakening each day are *modeh ani*, an expression of gratitude to G-d for another day of life.

Our daily prayers are replete with expressions of gratitude. We recite many *brachos* (blessings) during the day for the food we eat, and there is a vast array of *brachos* for various things we experience. Indeed, there is even a *brachah* for unpleasant things, in accordance with the Talmudic dictum that a person is required to express gratitude to G-d for the bad he experiences as well as for the good.

The Talmud is extremely critical of someone who fails to acknowledge a favor (*Avodah Zarah* 5a,b). Apparently it is not only children who may have difficulty in expressing gratitude, and the fact that this reluctance appears in children of 3 and 4 indicates that it must be related to some very primitive feelings.

Some people sense that receiving a favor from someone obligates them to that person, and they do not wish to feel beholden to anyone. If the latter feeling is sufficiently unpleasant to them, their unconscious mind may play one of its cunning tricks and cause them to deny having received a favor. Indeed, in extreme cases, receiving a favor from someone may elicit resentment instead of gratitude! I know of one rabbi who said, "I cannot understand why that person resents me. I do not recall ever having done him a favor."

And what if gratitude does obligate somewhat? Is it not right and proper that one good turn deserves another? Should it happen that the person who did a favor for you asks something of you which is unrealistic, you should be able to explain to him why you cannot do it, his previous kindness to you notwithstanding.

The psychological consequences of gratitude can be far reaching. Gratitude is a positive affect; hence, it cannot co-exist with a negative affect, anymore than light can co-exist with darkness. If gratitude can be adequately developed, it can be the single most effective method for eliminating distress of various kinds.

For example, a person who had a narrow escape from a traumatic occurrence may suffer considerable anxiety, as has been found in "Post-traumatic Stress Syndrome." If the person can sincerely pronounce the *brachah*, "Blessed is the One Who miraculously saved me at this site," the gratitude can actually extinguish the anxiety that would otherwise occur.

Anxiety can virtually disable a person, and taking anti-anxiety medications is hardly a long-term solution. These drugs accomplish their effects by depressing brain function, which is not conducive to optimum functioning. Furthermore, many of these drugs are dangerously addictive. Suppressing the anxiety by introducing a counteracting feeling of gratitude is far superior to drug-induced tranquility.

Most of us may lack the spirituality of the Talmudic sage Nachum Ish Gamzu, who accepted everything as being for good and was grateful for it. However, if we can be grateful for those things that warrant gratitude by anyone's standards, we will have enough positive experiences during the day that should obscure many distressful feelings.

It is indeed important to teach children to say "thank you," but the teaching of gratitude should go beyond that. Parents should always acknowledge their gratitude when a child does something for them, and the few words of an elaboration of the concept of gratitude can be most helpful.

For example, "Esther, could you please bring me the telephone book from the study?" ... "Thank you, honey. I appreciate this. It makes you feel good when something you do is appreciated, doesn't it? You should remember to show other people your appreciation of what they do for you, just as you like to know that your actions have been appreciated." As with other appropriate acts, it is wise to comment on such behavior; e.g., "I was proud of Esther. She called her friend to thank her for dropping off her books for her, and that was very thoughtful." And again, the Shabbos table provides a forum for elaboration on the virtue of gratitude, and for explaining the folly of people who are reluctant to express thanks for favors received.

An 8-year-old child can write a few words of thanks to the friends who attended his birthday party and for the presents they may have brought, and to grandparents who send Chanukah gifts. Rather than being a perfunctory task, these should provide opportunities to emphasize the importance of gratitude.

Parents should not take each other for granted, and should serve as models for expression of gratitude. When one serves another at the table, it is appropriate to say "thank you," and when one runs an errand for the other, it should be acknowledged with an expression of gratitude.

The concept of gratitude is related to the dependence-independence issue. Difficulty in feeling and expressing gratitude because of the wish to avoid feeling beholden may result in fierce independence which may be destructive. Furthermore, some people are so anxious that accepting help is an indication of weakness on their part that they reject help when it is legitimate and essential. Yet the realities of life are that no person can be completely self-sufficient, and trying to get through life on one's own is being reckless rather than heroic. I have known of cases where a patient who suffered a heart attack disconnected his intravenous and monitors and walked out of the intensive-care unit because he could not accept that he needed care. Less extreme cases where people refuse to ask for warranted help abound.

The Talmud is equally critical of someone who accepts charity when he does not need it, and of someone who refuses to accept charity when it is essential for his survival (*Mishnah Peah* 8:9 and *Jerusalem Talmud Peah* 8:8). Again we encounter the Rambam's principle, the delicate balance between two extremes, which parents should adopt themselves in order to appropriately teach their children. They should show the child that it is appropriate to accept help gracefully and with gratitude when this is necessary, and to try to avoid imposing on others when one can be self-sufficient. This requires much thoughtfulness, and it is another reason why parenting cannot be left to whim or intuition.

The latitude within which parents must function is not quite as narrow as that of a tight-rope walker, whose acceptable margins of error to either side are very slim. However, the analogy to a tight-rope walker is justified in that if he fails to concentrate on what he is doing and is distracted by the prize he will get for completing his feat, he is likely to lose his balance. Similarly, parents must keep their eyes focused on the delicate task of raising the child properly and not allow themselves to be distracted by extraneous motives that can result in inadequate parenting.

Chapter Twenty-Seven

But I'm Only Human

ood! That's what parents are supposed to be. But how are children supposed to know that? Children think their parents are perfect. The sooner they discover that their parents are indeed their protectors, but are by no means perfect, the better it will be for them.

As we noted earlier, children who think their parents are perfect are likely to be extremely self-critical. If something has gone wrong in the home, and it can't possibly be the parents' fault, then the child must accept it as his fault. What other option is there? This self-degrading attitude may be the source of many later problems in life.

I have suggested that parents try to avoid screaming when angry. This is indeed ideal, but the parent may be exhausted and tense after a full day of work laced with various aggravations, and may be beset with financial worries as well as several other nagging concerns. Just at this inopportune time the child does something that he has been told numerous times not to do, and the parent loses it. He screams at the child and perhaps even spanks him, perhaps assuming that the child was acting out of defiance.

Give children the benefit of the doubt that they are only children, and may be behaving according to juvenile abandon rather than with hostility toward the parents.

Okay. So you were taut as a guitar string and you lost your cool. Indeed, you are only human. How about letting the child in on this secret?

A bit later in the day, perhaps at bedtime, you can walk in and sit down on the child's bed. "I'm sorry I screamed at you the way I did. Even though you did what I had told you not to do so many times, I should have just sent you up to your room (or whatever other disciplinary measure you use) instead of screaming. I always tell you that it is not right to scream, and if it's not right for you it's not right for me either. I did have a very hard day and was just on edge, but that still doesn't make it right." Let's face it, the screaming was a mistake, so own up to it.

I once had a patient in the psychiatric hospital who asked for permission to leave the hospital for a few hours to attend a farewell party for his fellow students who were going to disperse at the end of the semester. I authorized the pass and wrote the order on the chart. When I returned the next day, he was irate because he had not been permitted to leave the hospital. "You promised me, and you backed out on it! I will never have an opportunity to see some of these friends again."

I traced the problem and found that I had been indeed written an order for a six-hour pass — on another patient's chart! I then explained my mistake and apologized.

This was one of the most therapeutic things that could have happened. The young man realized that the doctor had made a mistake, and had written an order on the wrong chart, which could conceivably have been disastrous. Yet, he was still functioning as a doctor, and his authority had not suffered. Making a mistake is not a capital crime after all! It does not destroy one's reputation. This was something this patient needed to know.

Much the same holds true for children. They need to know that parents retain their authority and respect even after having made a mistake.

Is a young child really able to grasp all this? Let me assure you that even if he doesn't fully understand all the words, the feelings will register. He will know that Daddy was tense, that Daddy is sorry that he screamed, and that Daddy is very human.

Children do not have to be privy to everything that worries parents, but as a whole, the fewer secrets that are kept, the better. Children have a rich fantasy, and if they do not know what it is that parents are worried about, they may fantasize, and their imaginations may be far more anxiety provoking than reality. If you don't tell them what is bothering you, then it must be something so terrible that you can't even talk about it. You may be worried because your bank returned a check for insufficient funds when you believed you had adequate money in the account, and you will not be able to find out what went wrong until after the weekend. You had assumed that you had adequate funds, and you also wrote several additional checks, and these too will be returned. This is obviously very aggravating, but why bother a child with it?

There happened to be a great deal in the news that particular day about layoffs in various plants and the downturn in the economy, with many people losing their jobs. This may have resulted in some discussion at the supper table. Seeing the father's worry, the child puts two and two together, and concludes that his father had been fired. The next morning he shares this terrible news with his friends, and that evening the father receives several calls from neighbors sympathizing with his misfortune and offering to help in whatever way possible.

This is just one possible scenario. I know of one case where a father happened to be away on business, and the mother was very depressed because she had been notified that her sister's child was gravely ill. She did not want to impose this worry on her child. However, that day there was a great deal in the news about the police search for a serial killer, and the child began thinking that perhaps his absent father was the sought-for villain, and that was what was worrying his mother. If at all possible, try to explain to children just what it is that is worrying you.

A not uncommon problem is a child's protestations when the parents go out in the evening, leaving him in the care of a babysitter. The child may express fear of monsters in the closet or under the bed. Incidentally, whereas childhood fears have probably always existed, there is little doubt that the graphic portrayal of violence and fiendish creatures on television has intensified such fears.

Children who exhibit such fears will be less frightened when the babysitter is a mature adult rather than a young adolescent. It is also advisable to establish a familiarity with the babysitter, so that she is not a stranger to the child and he can feel some trust in her.

But let us look at this problem from another aspect. The child's expression of fear of monsters may be the only way he knows how to emphatically declare his protestation about his parents' leaving. Rationally, he knows he is safe, and even though he may "believe" in the monsters, this may be the only way his underlying emotion emerges. The underlying emotion may be due to the child not being able to understand why in the world the parents have to leave the home. The small child, who since infancy has been the recipient of his parents' attention, may have come to believe that the parents exist in order to care for him — period, end of matter. The fact that the father may have to leave home to learn or work makes sense, and that the mother may have to go to the supermarket also makes sense. After all, these activities are all directed toward his support and well-being, and that is how things should be. But what is this business about their going out in the evening? That doesn't serve the child's needs in any way. That can only be for the parents' needs, but since when do parents have needs?

This is why it is important to let children know that parents are humans, and indeed, they *do* have needs of their own.

The juvenile concept of parents is often that they are G-dlike. We often refer to G-d as our Father in Heaven, and to small children the reverse may also be true. Not only is G-d our Father, but our father and mother are G-d. They are great and powerful and perfect, and like G-d are immune to all distress and have no needs of their own.

It will help in many ways for children to realize that while parents are indeed strong and loving and will care for them and protect them, they are nevertheless human, and that they do have needs. The child should be helped to realize that parental needs may be similar to his own, which he can easily understand.

"Honey, you know how you like to be with your friends? Well, Daddy and Mommy like to spend time with their friends just like you do. During the day we are all busy with our work, so Daddy and Mommy get together with their friends in the evening. When you get together with Motty and Danny and Itzi you have a good time and talk about interesting things. Daddy and Mommy are going to be with Danny's daddy and mommy tonight, and we're going to talk about things that interest us, just like you do."

I have a childhood memory of having said at age 5, "A mother is not a *mentsch* (a person). *A mother is a mother*." I don't remember the context in which I said it, but I do recall saying it, and my mother thought it was worthy of repeating, so I heard myself quoted several times. But this indicates to me how I felt about my mother at that age. She was a mother, which is a unique being, far superior to a mere *mentsch*.

If we understand this, it is no longer surprising why a child insists that when his mother is sick in bed with a high fever and aching all over, she should come down to prepare his breakfast. He just may not be able to grasp that parents are mortal.

Letting children know that parents are indeed human may have many dividends.

Chapter Twenty-Eight

Painful Recollections

It is not uncommon for children to be angry at their parents. After all, responsible parents must often turn down children's requests — ice cream before dinner; neat $65 sneakers like Shimmy just got; an expensive electronic game — the list is endless. As a rule, these juvenile disappointments and frustrations are soon forgotten, and indeed, as children mature, they generally realize that the parents had reason for refusing these requests, and they may even recognize that the parents were right in their reasoning. Certainly when they grow up and become parents and are placed in the position of having to deny some of their children's wishes, they can then identify with their parents. These disappointments may produce severe anger outbursts at the time, but have virtually no long-term effects.

On the other hand, there are things which may not produce a severe or even any reaction at the time, but are remembered for decades, often with much bitterness. One of the most painful recollections is that of being humiliated, sometimes even resulting from well-intentioned parental behavior.

One patient, a gentleman in his 60s and a highly successful executive of a major corporation, had great anxiety in making a presentation at a board of directors' meeting, even though his report was excellently prepared. Throughout his life he had been haunted by a fear of making a mistake and being humiliated, and he related this to a childhood incident which had retained its intensity even after many decades. His mother had been dissatisfied with his report card and had concluded that the teacher had discriminated against her child because they were newly arrived immigrants. She came to school, and in the presence of his classmates, screamed her rebuke at the teacher in a very fragmented English. He was deeply humiliated by his mother's performance, and this feeling of being embarrassed plagued him all his life.

One of the most distressing feelings a person can have is that of being abandoned. This is a theme which recurs in fairy tales, and perhaps the function of these stories is to validate a child's feeling or to provide a happy ending in the hope that it will mitigate the anxiety if a child should feel abandoned. The source of such fears in later life may have been a childhood trauma, as when a child detached himself from the parent in a crowd, or when a mother took sick when the father was away on a business trip and the small child suddenly found himself in a strange home, or even when parents left the child with a babysitter without adequately preparing the child for the separation. In any of these situations the child may not only retain the painful effect, but may also harbor resentment against the parent whom he felt abandoned him.

A frequently recurring resentment is not having been shown affection. There are some people who believe that parents should not be demonstrative. I recall a young man of 34 who was treated at our rehabilitation center for alcoholism. He was a very pleasant person and we grew quite fond of him during his stay with us. On the day he left, some of the staff embraced him warmly, and one person kissed him. He broke down in tears, saying, "That is the first time in my life that anyone has kissed me."

Affectionate physical contact between parents and young children is essential for optimum emotional health. There is a classic study by Rene Spitz, which shows that infants who do not receive the warmth of adequate physical contact during the first six months of life may be severely disturbed emotionally, and in some aspects, irreversibly so. Adults may recall very tearfully how they had craved being embraced or kissed by a parent, but the parents were rather mechanical and did not show them affection by physical contact.

On the other hand, people have fond memories of warmth shown by parents or other significant individuals. One representative of a yeshivah defied all advice and went to solicit a very wealthy man who had been totally alienated from Judaism. He was warned that he might find himself forcefully expelled from the premises. He later reported that he was welcomed warmly and was given a generous donation for the yeshivah. The man related that as a young boy he had been sent to Radin to learn at the Yeshivah of the Chofetz Chaim. Since he initially had no place to stay, he slept at the humble abode of the Chofetz Chaim on the first night. During the night the Chofetz Chaim entered the room, covered him with a blanket, and patted him gently on the head. Although he subsequently defected from Torah observance, the reassuring feeling of affection conveyed by the gesture of being covered and patted on the head had remained with him for six decades.

The impact of demonstrative affection is indicated by the Midrashic comment on the episode of Jacob disguising himself as Esau in order to receive the patriarch Isaac's blessings. "Isaac said, 'Come near and kiss me, my son.' He approached and kissed him, and he smelled the scent of his garments and blessed him" (*Genesis* 27:26-27).

The Midrash comments that the word *begadov* meaning "garments" can read phonetically as *bogdov* meaning "defectors." In other words, Isaac prophetically saw that some of Jacob's descendants would be defectors. The Midrash relates that when the Romans conquered Jerusalem, they told Joseph Meshisa, an avowed heretic and traitor, to enter the Temple and take any of the spoils for himself. When Joseph emerged with the Menorah, the Romans said, "That is not meant for anyone's personal use. Go take something else," whereupon Joseph responded, "It is enough that I have angered my G-d once. I will not do so again." The Romans then put him on the torture rack, and he died the death of a martyr, professing his devotion to G-d by uttering *Shema Yisrael* with his last breath.

Whence comes such heroic loyalty in someone who had for so long been defiant of G-d? From the embrace and kiss of Isaac and Jacob. This was the patriarch's message of how the core of loyalty may be preserved even in the most deviant Jew, by an affectionate parental caress.

Parents should show their affection for children by appropriate embrace. Unfortunately, however, we live in a world where perversions are not uncommon, and unfortunately, incidents of molestation do occur. As the child grows older, therefore, fathers must be cautious how they embrace their daughters, and mothers must be cautious how they embrace their sons. Given the inroads of the decadent general society, even the most innocent and sincere expressions of affection may lead immature children to fantasize and impart an exaggerated or distorted intent to wholesome parental embrace. Hence it is important that parents observe a delicate balance, providing affectionate physical contact, but being cautious not to provide grounds for a distortion of their show of love.

Children may also harbor resentments if the parents did not accord them priority. There is often much residual anger in cases where a father or mother gave more importance to their own family, i.e., to their parents or siblings, and the children felt that they played second fiddle to these relatives.

These feelings of anger may well be justified. A father's and mother's prime responsibilities are to each other and to their children. Other relatives may be attended to, but not at the cost of depriving the spouse and the children of their legitimate needs. It is true that the Torah requires that we honor our parents, but the Torah also says, "Therefore a man shall leave his father and mother and cling to his wife and they shall be as one" (*Genesis* 2:24), and the same holds true for a wife. Parents must always be honored, but if an irreconcilable conflict arises between one's duties toward one's parents versus those toward the spouse and children, the latter should be accorded priority.

As was pointed out earlier, children may resent having been "used" by the parents and having been asked to do things which were not to their interest. A number of middle-aged people have recalled how they were coerced to go to after-school Talmud Torah where they learned nothing of substance, but they had to attend so that their parents could throw a *bar-mitzvah* party. When they recall how their friends were playing football while they were sitting in a classroom, totally bored by having to read words they did not understand, with the full awareness that this was not to increase their knowledge but simply to permit their parents to fulfill their social obligations, they do so with much bitterness. They say that their homes were neither kosher nor *shomer Shabbos*, but they were deprived of four years of playing with their friends just so the parents could show-off at a *bar-mitzvah* extravaganza. This was too much for them as children, but they were too small to resist, and the anger remained with them throughout their lives. Had these parents truly wished to give their children the rudiments of a Jewish education, this desire might have mitigated the resentment and per-haps even had a positive effect on their later lives.

Resentments may also be the result of feeling that one's progress or welfare was sacrificed because of another sibling. A 60-year-old grandmother recalled that she was not permitted to advance her education after high school because her mother was protective of her older brother, and did not wish her to surpass him. Deprivation for a plausible reason (even if not understood at the time) is acceptable, but "I could not have something because he/she did not have it" is angrily resented.

Parents should be cautious not to make demands that are not within the capability of a child to fulfill. A man in his 50s recalls both shame and rage that when he was 6 years old and still a bed-wet-ter, his father reprimanded him, "We can't go on vacation and stay in a motel or at friends' homes because you still wet the bed. You are ruining the summer for all of us." This was a totally unfair rebuke, because he was unable to control his bed-wetting, and he said that his father's vicious criticism drove a stake into his heart. What was even worse was that this was said in the presence of his siblings. Thoughtless remarks such as this can have untold impact on a child, with long-term residuals of acrimony.

This is a good place to point out that there is a rather limited latitude within which parents should expect or demand performance from children. If parents demand tasks which the child does not have the capacity to perform, it may result in confusion, anger, and depression of his self-esteem. A child may think the parent was justified in making a particular command, and that his inability to perform is an indication of his inadequacy. This can seriously impact on the child's self-confidence. On the other hand, if parents do too much for the child and do not stimulate him to do that which he can, the child may not develop his potential. Like inactive muscles, skills that are not activated may atrophy. Furthermore, this too can depress a child's self-confidence as he may reason, "I must be lacking the ability to do this, since my parents are doing it for me." Parents need to observe the child carefully, and to provide the necessary stimulation and motivation for him to do what he can, and to provide well-measured assistance when necessary.

Our children's lives may not be exact replicas of our own childhood, yet if we reflect upon feelings we had when we were children, we may be better able to understand how our children feel, and by empathizing with them, help them adjust to difficult situations and forestall the negative consequences that may arise from misunderstandings and distorted perceptions.

Chapter Twenty-Nine

You're Going to Give Me a Heart Attack

*S*ome people may say foolish things, especially in moments of desperation, and parents are no exception. Statements such as "You're going to give me a heart attack," or "You're going to make me lose my mind," or "Over my dead body will ..." are all very foolish, and comments such as these should never be made.

Firstly, there is a principle in Judaism which discourages saying anything malevolent, whether about oneself or others (*Berachos* 16a). Profanity, swearing, or cursing — especially invoking the name of G-d — is a sin, but even expressions that in anyway forbode evil or harm should be assiduously avoided. In my book *Generation to Generation* I recalled the worst expletive my father could utter (and even this is after he was provoked beyond his virtually infinite patience), which was "May he have soft, fresh bread, and cold, hard butter!"

Secondly, it is important to realize that the human mind may retain ideas, unconsciously, if not consciously. Remarks such a those cited above, said to a 6-year-old child, when a parent feels he has reached the end of his rope, may remain imbedded in the child's mind long after the parent's anger has subsided and he has forgotten that remark. Years later, if the parent does suffer a heart attack or an emotional illness, the son or daughter may experience intense guilt, believing that they were the cause of it. As an example, a woman of 33 was obsessed with the guilt over her father's death. When she was 11, she had behaved in a juvenile manner not too unusual for youngsters of this age, which elicited the comment from the distraught parent, "You will be the death of me yet." The father died of a heart attack at age 60, when the young woman was 27, but the remark made 16 years earlier came back to haunt her. No parent would wish such torment on a child, and parents should therefore be cautious not to be carried away with emotion to say things they might regret. Ramban, in his famous letter to his children, states, "Always consider what you are going to say before letting the words escape your lips."

There are some threats that are not anxiety provoking. For example, telling a child that if he runs into the street he may be hit by a car is not a threat, but a simple statement of fact. Explaining to a child that there is harm inherent in a particular act is not a threat. Children must learn about the dangers that exist in reality.

Children must learn what is acceptable behavior, and there must be a setting of limits, with clarification of what kinds of behaviors will not be tolerated. Such warnings are not threats. The particular consequences of unacceptable behavior must be just and realistic, leaving little to the imagination. Deprivation of privileges should be spelled out. We can learn from *halachah* that warning a person about the punishment for a transgression must be specific. It is not sufficient to say, "If you do that you will be punished," but the penalty must be clearly stated and there must be an indication that the person has heard and understood the warning. In addition to relating the punishment for a specific act, discipline should always be accompanied by understanding that *teshuvah* is a constant option, and that by realizing that one has done wrong and sincerely resolving not to repeat the act, one is immediately restored to full favor. Indeed, we should point out to children that sometimes the only way to grow up is by making mistakes, and that when these occur and are corrected by proper discipline, the learning experience is a constructive one.

Anxiety-provoking threats are those that are open ended or ill defined. "Just wait until your father gets home. You will see what will happen" is a very unwise remark. The child is left with unlimited capacity to fantasize the worst. Furthermore, an improper act that was committed at 9 a.m. should not be punished at 7 p.m. If punishment is to be effective, it should follow the act as quickly as possible. There is also the probability that by the time the father gets home from work, the mother may be occupied with other things and forget to mention the offense. This places a child under tension for days, or may cause him to dismiss the mother's threats as meaningless.

Threats which are excessive or are incapable of being carried out are worthless at best. "If you do that again we will just throw you out of the house" is an absurd remark to make to an 8-year-old. Just where will you send him if he repeats the improper behavior? He will either be flooded by the anxiety of abandonment or will dismiss the comment as silly patter, either of which defeats the purpose.

Young children are apt to take things literally, in a manner which the parents may not consider. For example, I recall that as a child I heard my father tell my mother that a certain person had been fired, and for days I imagined him being burned at the stake. To me "fired" was a derivative of the word "fire," and it was only after I once cried bitterly and told my mother that I was having nightmares of this man being burned that she explained the meaning of "fired." It is well to remember that children may not be hearing what we think we are telling them.

While it is not necessary to talk to children according to the simple words "See Jane run" of the first-grade primer, it is nevertheless important to bear in mind that vague statements in particular are subject to distortion, and that figures of speech may be misunderstood. It was rather embarrassing for parents when a child brought a visitor his hat, saying "Show me how you do it. Daddy says you talk through your hat."

If we watch children's facial expressions, we may detect their confusion or bewilderment about something that was said, and be able to clarify it for them. If we practiced the teachings of Ramban and thought a bit about what we were going to say before we said it, we may eliminate sources of confusion and anxiety from our children.

Chapter Thirty

Personal Memories

*I*nasmuch as my memories are all pleasant, and since I have never been involved in any anti-social behavior, I must assume that (1) my parents' method of discipline was effective, and (2) it was not traumatic. In *Generation to Generation*, which is essentially memoirs of my childhood, I recalled some childhood memories that relate to parenting, and I will cite several of them here.

As I began to focus on the problems of low self-esteem that I found in the majority of my patients, it occurred to me that my father's primary disciplinary method was probably helpful in preventing my developing a full-blown self-esteem problem. Inasmuch as he was a great person, a highly respected Chassidic *rebbe* with a large following, an excellent counselor whose advice was sought by Jew and non-Jew alike, a very charismatic person, my standing in his shadow could have resulted in a devastating depression of self-esteem. That it was not worse than it was can be attributed to some very clever tactics on his part.

I recall that when I did something that he did not approve of, his reprimand consisted of *es past nisht*, Yiddish for "that is not becoming of you." In other words, "Why are you doing something that is beneath your dignity? You are too good for that." Never did he tell me I was bad, because that would have been deflating. He achieved the purpose of letting me know that what I did was wrong by elevating me rather than depressing me. The three-word phrase *es past nisht* is valuable enough in its own right, but even more than this, it reflects his attitude toward me, one of appreciation and approbation.

I am not particularly proud of this story, but since it does make a point, I feel I must relate it.

At age 9, I was not too fond of *davening*, yet I knew my father expected this of me. When my father left to go to *shul*, I took a *siddur* from the bookcase, placed it on the table to give the impression that I had indeed used it, and then went about doing whatever I wanted to do. This ploy worked for a short while, until one day, upon returning from *shul*, my father asked me to bring him the *siddur* I had used for *davening*. When I did so, he showed me that the pages I should have been reading were clamped together with a paper clip. I had been caught red-handed.

"You cannot fool Hashem," my father said, "and as you see, you have not been fooling me either. That leaves only you, and you have been deceiving yourself. Now tell me, how does a bright young man like yourself allow himself to be fooled by a 9-year-old child?"

My father did not yell at me, nor tell me how evil I was for having lied about my *davening*. I have never, thank G-d, missed *davening* since. Although I did not fully appreciate it at that age, I later came to realize that when we try to deceive others, we are actually the victims of our own cunning. At that time, however, I did realize that *es past nisht* to let myself be duped.

Some parents may think that in order to socialize properly, a child must blend into his environment. Being different may create problems. This type of thinking was also responsible for those who thought that Jews would be more accepted in a non-Jewish culture if they dropped their distinctly Jewish appearance. The tragic fact is that this strategy has led to disastrous assimilation, while anti-Semitism has remained robust and vibrant.

If my childhood experience is any measure at all, it certainly repudiates this ideology. I was as different as different can be. I grew up in Milwaukee, which in the 1930s did not have a day school, and there were few, if any, observant children my age. In absence of a day school, I attended public school, and my *payus* (long earlocks) elicited mocking from my non-Jewish classmates. In the lower grades, children had birthday parties in class, and I could not partake of any of the goodies. I did not associate with any of the children after school, because there was no one to associate with. My after-school hours were spent with a *melamed* (a Hebrew tutor) or playing chess with some of the attendees at *shul*, or reading. I did not have the companionship of siblings, since my next older brother left to yeshivah when I was 7, and my younger brothers were born when I was 8. I was in every way alone and different. Very, very different.

One might predict that this kind of upbringing would invariably result in a person becoming a loner, being unable to relate to others. Being the only one of a kind, raised totally within the narrow confines of a Chassidic home, precludes any kind of adjustment with a secular world or with non-Jews.

That is not quite what happened. The boy who did not eat at the birthday parties, had no non-Jewish friends, and whose earlocks elicited much taunting turned out to be chief of a department of psychiatry of St. Francis Hospital of Pittsburgh, and received honorary doctorate degrees from Duquesne University and St. Vincent's College, all of which are Catholic institutions.

How did this happen? Why did the sharp differences not result in irreparable isolation?

There was an important positive ingredient in being different, which was so powerful that it totally obscured and obliterated all possible negatives. *I knew who I was.* I was not lost in the shuffle. *I was me*, and my parents helped me to feel proud that I was me.

The words "alone" and "lonely" are by no means synonymous. You can be the only one in a huge auditorium, totally alone, but not necessarily lonely. On the other hand, you can be in a stadium with 60,000 other people, not at all alone, but terribly lonely. *"Alone" is* a state where you don't have anyone else. *"Lonely" is when you don't have yourself.* Yes, I was very much alone as a child, but I was not in the least bit lonely. I had *myself*, and I was proud of who I was. I owe it to my parents who gave me that pride.

Messages are conveyed in many ways. Indirect messages may have an even greater impact than direct messages. For example, when I was a child, my mother told me that when she was 5, she watched her grandfather, the *tzaddik*, the first Rebbe of Bobov, as he sat silently in front of the Chanukah lights, deep in meditation. With a curiosity of a 5-year old, she did not hesitate to interrupt him. "Zaidy, what are you thinking about now?"

The saintly grandfather said to her, "I am praying that you have good children."

What does this anecdote tell us? Firstly, it told me that when my mother was age 5, she was not only blessed by a *tzaddik*, but also commissioned, given an assignment to have good children. What an awesome responsibility to give to a 5-year-old! Doctor Spock would never condone it! Yes, it was an assignment, accompanied by a blessing that would empower her to do so. This is exactly what the Torah says in so many places. We are instructed to do the *mitzvos*, and given the Divine blessings that empower us to perform them.

Secondly, I was told of this assignment and the accompanying blessing when I was just about the same age. My mother expected me to rise to the challenge, and assured me that I could do so. She did not say, "I expect thus and so of you." That would have been an order, and people, even children, generally do not like being commanded to do anything. Rather, the message was in a story, a brief, rather uneventful story, with a most powerful message.

The Talmud says that one who diligently observes the *mitzvah* of the lights will be rewarded with good children (*Shabbos* 23b). What *mitzvah* of lights? Why, the Chanukah lights, and the Friday evening lights!

The Chanukah lights convey the miracle of how the one vial of pure, undefiled oil lasted for eight days. Could not the victorious Hashmoneans have compromised and used less pure oil for the Menorah service? Yes, they could have easily justified using impure oils, but they didn't, and thereby taught us that when one is staunch and refuses to yield on principles of purity, one can achieve miraculous results.

The Friday night lights? Read the prayer that mothers say after reciting the blessing for lighting the candles. "... and may I merit to see children and grandchildren to be wise, understanding, loving, and revering G-d, people of truth, sacred children, who will illuminate the world with their Torah study and good deeds."

There is a tradition in many families to add one candle for each child that enters the family. How edifying it was for me to know that our home was brighter on Friday nights because I was in existence!

A mother's profound prayer is reinforced by the father, who in his blessing says, "May G-d make you as great as Ephraim and Menashe," and for girls, "May G-d make you as great as Sarah, Rivka, Rachel and Leah."

My mother conveyed my great-grandfather's assignment and blessing to me. There was never any question what was expected of me, nor was there any doubt that I had the capacity to realize these expectations.

In my book *Life is Too Short* (St. Martins Press 1995), I share my own history of low self-esteem feelings. Such feelings are universal, and as our ethical writings teach us, are the tactics of the *yetzer hara*, which tries to crush us and disable us from fulfilling Torah and *mitzvos*. I was not immune to this attack by the *yetzer hara*, but that I was able to triumph over it is due to the techniques my parents used in raising me.

As a good parent you must discipline your children, but as I look back upon some six decades earlier with pleasant memories, I can assure you that if you make a concerted effort, your children will have pleasant memories of their childhood. We must certainly observe Torah and become spiritual people. We have the heritage of Abraham, Isaac, and Jacob; Sarah, Rivka, Rachel, and Leah. We have the ingredients that enable us to achieve our assigned goal. The basic formula is a simple one. Let children know what is expected of them, and help them realize that they can achieve it.

Chapter Thirty-One

Guilt and Shame: Their Role in Parenting

"G uilt" and "shame" are terms that are often interchanged as though they were synonymous. One might say "I feel guilty for what I did," or "I am ashamed of what I did." At the risk of being pedantic, we must distinguish these two terms and define them, so that when we refer to each of them, we will know precisely which emotion we are discussing.

Guilt is related to action. It is the distressing feeling that is associated with doing something wrong. Guilt can be healthy or unhealthy.

Healthy guilt is what keeps us from doing things we should not do. We may be tempted to do something improper, and the knowledge that we will later suffer guilt for having done so deters us from the particular act. If we have indeed done something wrong, the pain of guilt is what causes us to do *teshuvah*, whether this is making amends to whomever we offended or asking forgiveness from G-d.

Unhealthy guilt occurs when we feel bad about something we did, even though we were right in doing so. For example, a mother who was overprotective of her child refused to allow him to ride a bike for fear of an accident. The child complained that he could not keep up with his friends, and the mother was told that she was being overprotective and that riding a bike is a legitimate activity whose risks are minimal. The child did indeed have an accident which resulted in facial cuts requiring stitches, and the mother felt guilty for having yielded to the child's wishes. Although her distress at the child's being hurt is normal, there is no reason for guilt, because to have deprived the child of a normal childhood activity would have been wrong. She made the right decision, and there should be no guilt for correct decisions, even if the consequences are unpleasant. When one retains guilt for right decisions, this is unhealthy guilt.

Shame, however, as we will use the term, is not related to any action, but to a feeling about one's *being*. "I did something wrong" is an expression of guilt, whereas "I am a bad person" is an expression of shame. Put in other words, guilt is "I *made* a mistake," while shame is "I *am* a mistake." Whereas healthy guilt is constructive, shame is never constructive. Guilt can lead to corrective action, but there is nothing one can do about shame. If one feels that one is inherently bad, inherently inferior, made out of defective material as it were, there is nothing one can do. Healthy guilt can lead to growth, whereas shame results in giving up and in depression.

Understanding these concepts is vital for both parents and children. Parents should know when to feel guilty and how to avoid unhealthy guilt and overcome shame. Similarly, parents must be careful to avoid inflicting unhealthy guilt and shame on their children.

We often hear that constructive criticism consists of condemning an improper action but not condemning the person. Expressions such as "You *are* bad" are therefore not constructive, since one is making a statement about the person rather than the act. We may wonder, just how can we separate the act from the person? How can we convey to the child that what he did was wrong while maintaining that he is a good child?

This is not as difficult as it seems, but it does require some thought. If we think a bit about how to react to a child's misdeeds, we can find a way to discipline him properly. Too often we react in haste, and make unwise statements that are not the optimum discipline.

My favorite example is a personal one. As a young child, I learned to play chess from several men who came early to *Minchah* (afternoon prayer services). They were first-generation immigrants from the Ukraine and many were excellent chess players. I became somewhat of a prodigy, was triumphant over veteran chess players and enamored with the game.

One Rosh Hashanah a rabbi from Chicago was our guest, and in the afternoon when everyone else was resting, he asked me to play chess. "But it's Yom Tov," I said. The rabbi assured me that I was wrong and that playing chess was permissible on Yom Tov, whereupon we played two games, both of which I won.

That night I was told that my father wished to see me. When I entered his study, he was engrossed in a *sefer* (volume of Torah), and I stood by respectfully silent, awaiting his recognition. After a few moments he looked up and said softly, "You played chess on Yom Tov?"

"Yes," I said. "Rabbi C. said it was allowed."

My father said nothing. He returned his gaze to the *sefer*, and slowly, barely perceptibly, shook his head in the negative. The message was clear: Even if technically not forbidden, it was not in the spirit of Rosh Hashanah to play games. I felt terrible. I had desecrated the holy day.

I remained standing respectfully, waiting to be dismissed, digesting the reprimand I had received. Then my father looked up, with a twinkle in his eye, and said, "But you did checkmate him, didn't you?"

"Twice," I said, softly but happily.

My father returned to his *sefer,* and after a few moments smiled. "*Geh gezunterheit.*" (You may leave now, literally, "Go in good health.") This scenario was nothing but a stroke of genius. His disapproval was conveyed to me forcefully, albeit very gently, by a slow negative gesture. No screaming. After I had been permitted to absorb the reprimand, he gave me the opportunity to redeem myself. He *knew* I had defeated the rabbi in chess, and he wanted me to know that he knew. The Talmud says that to disciple effectively one should "reject with the hand and embrace with the right hand" (*Sanhedrin* 107b). I am certain that this is the technique the Talmud was referring to.

While healthy guilt should lead to rectification of a wrong, the anger at oneself for being derelict may sometimes preclude the proper amends, and instead result in a negative reaction. People who are unable to accept and deal with healthy guilt may project onto others and blame them for what goes wrong instead of taking corrective action.

Yankel's family gets a call from school that their son has been acting up during class. He is disrespectful and does not pay attention, and the principal has called him the "class clown, disruptive and disrespectful." Yankel's father knows that he should be spending more time with this child, but he has been avoiding it. He finds it more rewarding to study at home with his older son and they have a closer relationship. Yankel loves baseball and would love his father to spend some time pitching balls to him. The father knows that he needs to spend some time and thought on this younger son, but to avoid the painful feelings of guilt and to block his awareness of his own shortcomings, the father gets angry. When Yankel comes home, he blasts him and takes privileges away, saying things that he later regrets. "Why can't you be like your older brother? You'll end up a no-good bum. How can you do this to me and your family?" Later that night the father is remorseful and tries to make up with the boy, restoring his privileges. A few days later the principal calls again, stating that nothing has changed and the cycle has repeated itself.

In this case, the father ignored the sign that his guilt tried to give him: Take a look at your relationship with your son and correct it.

A parent's pre-existing sense of shame and inadequacy may result in negative reactions to the child's behavior. A mother gets a call from school: Her first grader, Gitty, does not have a lunch — again! The mother feels embarrassed. Yes, Gitty is easily distracted and needs an extra eye in the morning. Transition from kindergarten to first grade is difficult for her. However, the mother starts to imagine what the principal and teacher think of *her*, namely, that she is careless, uncaring, disorganized, and incompetent. She brings the lunch to school in an angry mood, and when Gitty gets home she reprimands her: "Do you really want to bring shame on your family? Don't you care for your mother, giving her this extra work?" The mother's tense behavior may affect the way she reacts to the whole family that night. Her unjustified and unwarranted feelings of shame have provoked an improper reaction to a rather simple childhood forgetfulness.

If parents can separate guilt from shame, identify healthy versus unhealthy guilt, use healthy guilt to correct mistakes, and avoid shame in themselves, they are in a much better position to help their children do likewise. They can avoid inflicting shame on their children, and can apply proper discipline while enhancing the child's self-esteem by affirming the positive aspects of the child. Yes, I was wrong in playing chess on Rosh Hashanah, but that did not diminish my father's pride in my success.

Chapter Thirty-Two

Charting: Awareness of Change

*H*elping our children grow means helping them change. Physical growth is one kind of change, which parents help primarily by providing nourishment and other necessities, a relatively simple (although not always easy) task. Assisting children in character growth and development is another kind of change, a much more complex one.

The process of change is facilitated when we consciously choose our goals and are aware that we are moving in a positive direction, even if the steps are small. For example, someone who wishes to lose weight has a specific goal, and so he notes even a slight reduction in weight and that he has adhered to the recommended diet, and is thus encouraged to strive further to reach the goal. By the same token, a clear awareness of the goal alerts us to "danger spots," such as high-calorie deserts.

Young children are generally not fully aware of just what it is that they need to change. In truth, parents may also not be aware of precisely what it is that they want their children to learn. For example, parents do not want Yankele to hit his siblings, but they may not have a clear idea of what they want him to do instead of hitting when he is angry at them. Change means going from A to B rather than from A to not-A. An effective substitute for hitting when provoked is much more effective than simply commanding the child, "Do not hit!"

We must be alert for opportunities that permit growth and change to occur, and be cautious not to stifle them. The latter may occur when we rush to fix a problem for the child rather than help him find a solution. As purely objective teachers we might more easily allow the child to find his own solution, perhaps with our assistance, but as parents who are emotionally involved we may momentarily forget that our job is to facilitate our children's growth and development, and try to fix things for them.

Problems can be approached in either a negative or positive manner. When the Psalmist says, "Veer away from evil and do good" (*Psalms* 34:15), he is dictating policy: It is better to achieve something by a positive rather than a negative approach.

Suppose Yankele does not do his homework: "Let's take his bike away." Or Rochel refuses to babysit: "Let's ground her for two days." Or Sara is impudent: "Let's put her in time-out for five minutes." While none of these methods are inappropriate and they do have a place, parents may not realize how much more powerful and tool for change they have at their disposal if they *combine the negative with the positive.*

To help a child change we should always combine negative strategies with positive strategies. The balance between positive and negative strategies should be such that the *positive outweighs the negative approximately 70 percent to 30 percent.* Similarly, the amount of words, energy, and attention spent on the negative versus the positive should be approximately 30-percent negative and 70-percent positive.

Shlomo tends to whine a lot when he does not get his way, and his mother is tired of it. She feels that Shlomo needs to stop this babyish way of dealing with frustration. She knows that it has "gotten to her" and has occasionally led to angry words on her part that she later regretted. But now she may tackle this challenge in a new way, by thinking over the situation in terms of positive and negative strategies and goals. What are her positive goals? What does she want Shlomo to learn instead? What are her negative goals and strategies?

The mother's positive goals are to help Shlomo express his feelings in a more mature way. "Look, honey, I'm interested in listening to what you have to say, but when you say it in the whiny voice, it just turns me off and I can't hear what you're saying. So, let me hear you say it again, this time in a regular tone of voice, just the way big people do." Shlomo then repeats what he says, and his mother listens attentively to it and responds to it.

His mother may also plan to help him tolerate frustration better and to be able to come up with good ideas on how to solve the challenging situation. She will try to "catch" her son whenever he masters frustration by himself, and pay special attention to the positives, catching even his partial successes, and letting him know that she values such "great kid" stuff. Of course, she will model for him ways to master frustration. Negative interventions will focus on ignoring him for pestering and whining, and making sure that she does not give in out of exasperation. Before this miniprogram starts, the mother meets with Shlomo and tells him what she plans to do. It is important that her son be part of the change process.

This lopsided balance of positive and negative strategies ensures that the child perceives the new way as a positive one. The child can identify with the new skills that he is learning, and ultimately his self-esteem is nourished and enhanced. Interventions that are primarily or exclusively negative are experienced as punitive, and children often revert back to old habits when the program is stopped.

Let's go back to Shlomo's mother. Because she sees the child as a partner in the change process, she wants him to know how he is doing and how things are progressing. She wants to build up in him an awareness of change and an interest in the change process itself. This goal is in and of itself worthwhile. People have trouble changing because they are afraid of change and may easily become disappointed if they encounter setbacks. Most of us want instant cures and instant success, and we may shy away from working on things systematically and persistently. Being interested in change and appreciative of the small steps that lead us to the goal enables us to see a problem as a challenge instead of as a sign of failure or an unwelcome defect.

The mother can accomplish this by designing a feedback system that monitors Shlomo's progress and tells him where work remains to be done. This gives the mother and father a chance to celebrate his successes. This is done daily, and the "weekly review" becomes a focal point of the Shabbos table. It also helps them focus the child to what he needs to pay special attention.

A feedback system also gives the child much needed information about his behavior. This is true not just for young children but also for teenagers, who often seem to suffer from temporary memory loss when it comes to remembering difficulties. Children need concrete and specific feedback that focuses on their actions and skills.

Vague feedback that focuses on "goodness" and "being good" may be confusing, and often results in feelings that things are either good or bad. This dichotomizes reality into extremes. A child may report that he was either "good" or "bad" in school, whereas in actuality, he may have accomplished many commendable things in addition to managing to get himself into trouble. There is not a single day, even in the life of the most difficult child, where there are not at least a few positive behaviors. Sometimes we may have to look for them with a microscope, but it is essential that we should find them. It is also vital that we not only tell the child what *not* to do, but also let him know in great detail and with great specificity what he *should* do.

Feedback charts do not have to be complicated. A parent can simply note every day three positive behaviors, or "*mitzvah* stuff." In Shlomo's case it might read something like this:

> Shlomo handled it well when his sister knocked part of his building down.
>
> Shlomo waited five minutes while his mom was on the phone.
>
> Shlomo used a regular voice to tell about too much homework.

Such *mitzvah* notes can be reviewed on Shabbos or before bedtime. Furthermore, his mother may also track the whining, simply noting how many times it occurred at different times in the day. This is not to be a record against the child or for the parent, but *for* the child and supportive of the change process. For example, it may be pointed out to the child, "See, you do more whining in the evening than in the morning. What is it that happens in the morning that enables you to avoid whining?" This helps focus the child on the positives in the morning rather than on the negative behavior in the evening.

Parents often tend to reward children for success with money or other material things. Rewarding a child with prizes means that we are using means that are extrinsic to the task to motivate the child. A candy bar or a trinket do not have a direct relationship to doing homework or taking out the garbage. The goal has to be to help the child become intrinsically motivated; i.e., the ultimate reward for succeeding at new skills should be one's feeling of mastering and self-enhancement.

The principle that we learn in *Ethics of the Fathers* that one should not serve G-d with the intent of being rewarded (1:3), or that the "reward of the *mitzvah* is in the *mitzvah* itself" (4:2), can be applied to young children as well as to mature adults. When children are growing up, parents can help them develop this attitude by showing their pride at the child's accomplishments and efforts. There is nothing as rewarding for a child as seeing his parents really impressed or amazed, happy with his progress. Giving the child our time and attention to go over his accomplishments shows him that we value what he does. Helping a child understand his mistakes and helping him focus on how to reach his goal tells him that the tasks that he is struggling with are important and that mastery is an asset to his person.

Parents serve as models and as a mirror for the child: The child sees his reflection in their favorable responses to his accomplishments and in their interests in his efforts. As parents, we are essentially telling the child who he is and what he can become. Over the years, the child incorporates his parents' responses and becomes capable of deriving joy, healthy pride, and renewed motivation by himself. He internalizes his parents' joy in his progress and the tasks themselves become motivating. The child learns for the sake of learning, helps for the sake of helping, and does *mitzvos* for the sake of the *mitzvos*. Let us not forget that accomplishments and competences, whether partial or complete, are the best sources for building and enhancing self-esteem. Behaviors that are reinforced by tangible items tend to be fragile and often collapse when the material reward is withdrawn. Giving a child money for brushing his teeth may result in the child expecting to be paid for breathing.

Being Jewish is a lifelong process of learning and ascending. We must teach our children to be comfortable with self-change and seek self-improvement. Avoiding change means that we are only deceiving ourselves, and avoiding taking a good look at ourselves. To live in this constant upward striving mode, we need to be aware of self-change and to be able to celebrate small movements in the right direction. As parents, when we make our children partners in their own self-change process, we teach them to become change agents themselves, and to live life for the rewards that it offers in and of itself.

Chapter Thirty-Three

Individual Differences: Temperament and Styles

*A*s any mother can tell you, not all children are born the same. Having the same father and mother does not mean that they are all packaged alike. At times the variation is surprising and even challenging. It is not by accident that we talk about "easy" babies and "difficult" ones. The only problem with these labels is that they say more about *us* than about the baby.

What is an easy baby? It is a baby that gives us little trouble, sleeps well and eats well, is good at being *schlepped* around, and is overall hardy and does not get bent out of shape easily. In contrast, difficult babies are often those with colic, difficult to feed, very reactive to changes in routine, and quick to fret and fuss. One mother called her challenging baby the "two-second bottle kid." For this child, hunger was an intense feeling that demanded quick action. It is *we* who determine what or who is easy and difficult for us. Only too quickly, moral judgments may be added which actually do not help, but rather mark the child for the future. To call a baby "stubborn" is missing the point.

It is important for us to be aware that there are vast temperamental and stylistic differences, and that what is normal is not the textbook baby. Scientists talk about a "normal range" in all areas of functioning. Some babies walk at 18 months, others at 15 months, but both are within the normal range. Some children talk with many "action" words — hello, bye, in, out — while others prefer to label "things" — table, mommy, dog — but both children learn to talk well. Some children jump promptly with both feet into a circle of other children playing, while others are slow to warm up, observing at first and only entering gradually. Both of these children are just fine.

When it comes to parenting, it is important to have a sense of the child's natural predisposition or temperamental style. Let us again recall the wise words of Solomon, "Train the child according to his way" (*Proverbs* 22:6). Two babies explore their world. One moves throughout the house opening cabinets and taking everything out. The other sits on a blanket and carefully examines toys with different types of shapes. Both of these children are learning, both may be equally bright, but their styles of doing things and of approaching tasks differ. Later on the stylistic differences persist, and we might have two different Talmud learners.

Temperament is something like the initial wiring of the child's nervous system. There are a number of dimensions that make up a child's temperament. We have already mentioned differences on how tasks and situations are approached, with some children being more cautious than others and slow to warm up. They are reflective and take their time before they join a play group or new activity, while others are eager to get into things and show no hesitance when faced with new situations.

Children also differ in their natural activity level. Some children are "movers," while others are less physically active. A child's arousal system may show wide variations: Some babies sleep through sirens, phones, noisy siblings, while others are easily overstimulated and get highly upset from loud noises. Some babies can soothe themselves easily: They find their thumb early in life and settle down quickly after being upset. Others are less adaptive and more intense: They have difficulties during transition times or changes in routine. Such babies require more parental shielding from stress and are more "labor intensive," putting a greater demand on the parents.

We know from research that temperamental differences persist as the child grows up. The active "go-getter" will continue to approach new situations — sports, learning, artistic skills — without much hesitation and anxiety. At times he may act without enough thought and may make mistakes that could have been avoided with more deliberation. He may need help to learn that he must stop and think. The more cautious child continues to show a more reflective and hesitant style as he grows older. He is more leery of novelty and tends to avoid new tasks unless he is first given time to prepare himself. He may practice roller-blading in the hallway of the apartment before joining his peers in the park. He may need some help from his teachers to "get over the hump."

Why is it important for parents to be aware of temperamental differences? Parenting is not a canned activity. It is not something that even the best-programmed robot could do. Parenting consists of creating a relationship with a child and connecting with him in a deep and harmonious way. Healthy relationships in parenting show parent and child in synchrony. This does not mean that there are no conflicts or difficulties, but the relationship is one that works and that is constructive. The child feels understood, his needs are met, and discipline is constructive. The child thus develops a healthy self-esteem. When the partners in the relationship are mismatched, the relationship becomes dysfunctional and counterproductive. Many problems that start in childhood are due to mismatches in the parent-child relationship and unrecognized temperamental factors.

At times, parents who do very well with one child may encounter great difficulties with another. Zippora, a young mother of two, delights in her oldest child, a lively, spunky 3-year-old girl. Sarah reminds her of herself, and together they have much fun. Her second daughter, 15 months old, is much calmer and can keep herself busy with simple things that she deliberately explores and appreciates. She seems physically less skilled, and this worries Zippora, although her doctor assures her that Mindel is doing just fine. At times, the mother feels guilty because she feels that her second child is less close to her heart than her oldest who delights her with her lively nature. When Aunt Bina visits, Zippora is amazed to hear her comment so favorably on her younger daughter. Mindel is playing with a napkin, carefully opening it and spreading it out on the floor. She pays attention to the pattern and tries to fold it in several different ways. Aunt Bina points out that Mindel is into the "micromechanics" of things, while Sarah is into the "macromechanics" of life. Unless Zippora can recognize that she is dealing with two different temperamental styles, she runs the risk of seeing her second child as somehow not as good as her oldest. She may feel frustrated and may get into the habit of continuously comparing the two girls. She is able to reflect her delight and love to her older daughter, and for Sarah, this becomes a source of early self-esteem. It is much more difficult for her to do so with Mindel, because she cannot mirror pride and joy at this child's activity. Recognizing the stylistic differences in her daughters would allow mother to learn to appreciate the qualities in her second child. It gives her a chance to stop comparing and to let each child develop along her own natural lines of development.

I previously noted the case of Rabbi and Mrs. X who have 10 children. It is a busy and happy household with much activity. When Yankel was born, both father and mother were surprised, because unlike their other nine children, Yankel cried all night long and only seemed to be comfortable when he was held. Yankel was very sensitive and fussed easily. At times he seemed to be inconsolable unless he was rocked. The doctor said there was nothing wrong with the child physically and told them that Yankel is probably one of those "super-sensitive" kids. Father and mother decided that they would take turns holding and rocking Yankel if that is what he needed. After one year, Yankel became much easier to manage, and by 18 months he was able to sleep through the night. He remains more sensitive than their other children, but father and mother consider that to be no different than their other children's many qualities.

It is our job as parents to create a bridge to our children so that we can connect with them and fulfill our duties. The bridge spans the inherent separateness between us and the child that we are given. It is important to remember *that it is primarily our obligation to reach the child and it is not his obligation to reach us.* When we have trouble extending ourselves, there is the tendency to blame it on the child. We may see him as unteachable, unreachable, unresponsive, ungrateful, un-this, and un-that. The mature parent can look at the same situation as a challenge: It is his job to find ways to connect, and if necessary, change himself. G-d gave us children as much for ourselves as He gave them us as parents for their benefit.

Chapter Thirty-Four

Talking to Children

*W*hen we mention discipline in parenting, we generally refer to the ways in which parents guide, regulate, and influence their children's growth. One of the most important and calmer ways to regulate behavior in children is through the use of words. Too often, discipline is exclusively associated with loss of privileges, physical punishment, or behavior modification. Yet, talking to our children is probably the most widely used way for us to communicate our intentions and expectations. We need to talk to our children to let them know where they are going, what they are supposed to do, and how.

Parents are the captains of the ship and need to be in charge. Commands are frequently used to prevent problems, correct a child, or guide his behavior. "Don't touch the stove!" "Turn your sweater around!" "Pack your lunch!" When commands are used within limits, are brief, precise, and to the point, they can be an effective and important tool in childrearing. However, when commands are overused, they tend to backfire on the parent. If a parent does not "ration" his commands, the child tends to become flooded with commands. Very few of these commands can actually be enforced, because the parent does not have the energy to follow up on each and every command. As a result, the child obeys only a fraction of the parent's orders, and becomes accustomed to disobey or ignore adults.

Equally important is the effect that the overuse of commands has on the overall atmosphere in the home. Parents who overuse commands create a climate of tension and jumpiness. Commands, by their nature, are incisive and sharp verbalizations. Think for a moment about the difference between telling a story and issuing commands. It is important to realize that we can direct and guide our children with just as much firmness and authority without having to turn our home into a bootcamp with rebellious juvenile recruits. We also need to realize that too many commands may be a sign of the parent being overwhelmed and stressed. Parents need to assist each other in decreasing this stress. While it is surely important for a father to *daven* with a *minyan* in *shul,* it is equally important for him to lend a helping hand to a tired and overwhelmed wife.

Often, parents who overuse commands fall into the trap of constant negative disciplinary interactions with their children. These are the parents who feel that they run from one emergency to the next, who feel that they never get a breather, and for whom the entire day from morning to night is an endless tug of war. Such homes are full of lecturing, arguing, scolding, correcting and overcorrecting, reprimanding, hollering and yelling, and commands, commands, commands. Most of us have at least had moments like this or times that we have come close to "losing it."

Let's look in on one scene. "How long are you going to stand there? Didn't I tell you to put that coat on? Put it on! Right now! No, not that way! You can do it yourself. Don't expect me to help you now! Don't whine. No, turn it around! Wait 'til I tell Bubbe about this! Okay, then don't put it on! Go ahead and catch cold. Oh, give me the coat. I'll put it on for you."

If negative disciplinary actions become a major way of interacting with a child, the parents actually end up giving their child much attention for not listening and not behaving. We can become very good at catching our children making mistakes or not measuring up to our expectations. Catching children being good is an art that needs cultivating. Furthermore, negative disciplinary interactions are rarely very instructive and helpful if they become habitual ways of relating the children. In the heat of the battle, not much is being heard, and often what is being said is not really worth it.

Apart from having an insidious way of poisoning the relationship between child and parent, habitual negative disciplinary interactions rob the parent of the constructive use of reprimands, corrections, or lectures, all of which are important tools in the parental toolbox. These strategies are effective only when they are not overused and when the parent is in control of himself. Let us realize that a reprimand is a parental statement that the child has fallen short of his and our expectations of himself, and can thus be a depressor of self-esteem.

I recall as a child my father gently reprimanding me when I did something of which he disapproved, by saying, quite softly yet emphatically, "*Es past nisht*," which means "That is not becoming of you." In other words, he was telling me that what I did was beneath my dignity, and that is why it was wrong. Rather than being a put-down, this reprimand was a builder of self-esteem, telling me that I was too good to engage in certain types of behavior.

In a home with clear rules and consistently enforced expectations, it may only be necessary to remind the child of the rule: "Remember, we don't play ball in the living room." Rules provide parents with a much needed framework for managing their children, and clear rules often make directions unnecessary, because children get accustomed to doing things a certain way. Rules also give a clear and fair framework for consequences and punishments.

Power battles can often be avoided by simply offering children more adaptive ways to implement their plans. Parents can steer their children to help them find more appropriate and nondestructive ways to express themselves. "You can't do water play on the kitchen floor, but you can have a bucket of water outside on the patio." By offering an alternative, the parent honors the intention of the child to play with water, and simply suggests a better location. Often times parents also suggest better times to do something: "Yes this is a good idea, but it's too late today. Let's make plans for tomorrow." This way parents also encourage children to show initiative, model for them how to generate options, and encourage compromising.

It is often possible for parents and children to do some tasks together. This is especially appropriate when the task is difficult and unfamiliar or not well liked. The parent can turn disliked tasks into something that becomes a chance to be together and provides an opportunity to learn cooperation.

Politeness is important, and we expect it from our children. One of the most effective ways of achieving this is for parents to be polite to their own children. When parents show respect and consideration toward the child, they set a positive tone for the interaction. "Please" and "thank you" should occupy prominent places in the parental vocabulary. We really cannot expect our children to be polite to us or to others when they are not treated themselves to elementary forms of civility.

It is preferable to use suggestions instead of commands, particularly when it is not absolutely necessary for the children to comply. Suggestions give children a choice: "Would you like to go out and play?" "How about a game of chess?" "Could you get your doll off your bed, please?" Suggestions are important parental tools because they give children a sense of control and decision-making power. Children are often more willing to comply with a suggestion, and parental approval tends to reinforce this. However, suggestions may become confusing if the parent uses them *instead* of commands. "Would you turn the tape recorder off?" is misleading when the parent really means to say, "Please turn the tape recorder off."

Some tasks that seem easy to adults may be quite difficult for children, and they may not comply with a request or command because they do not know how to go about doing certain things. It may be a difficult task for a 4-year-old to clean up his room. It may be equally difficult for older children to do certain household chores without having been taught. For example, loading a dishwasher seems so easy to us adults, but for a child it may not be so clear without having practiced it several times. In such situations, the parent needs to break the task down into smaller steps, and lead the child through the proper sequence. As the child cooperates, the parent makes sure to give much positive feedback.

Parents have many options to use words in a constructive way to guide children. It is up to us to be inventive and innovative, and to use the power of speech in the service of parenting.

Chapter Thirty-Five

ADHD

*A*ttention Deficit Hyperactivity Disorder, also called ADHD, describes a condition that is characterized by attentional and organizational difficulties. Children with ADHD have trouble paying attention and staying on task. They are easily distracted, and as a result move from one uncompleted activity to the next. They are often excessively fidgety, and tend to touch and handle things inappropriately. Sitting still for long periods or standing quietly in line is a hardship. It is difficult for them to be organized and to proceed in an organized fashion. These are the kids who habitually act before thinking, and their impulsive and disorganized style makes growing up very frustrating. Unlike children who are temperamentally very active and who fall into the high end of the normal range, children with ADHD are overly active — *hyper*active — and maladaptively impulsive. Parenting these children is a challenge and demands many adjustments and new skills on the part of the parents.

When ADHD is not recognized and treated it can become a debilitating condition that may permanently affect the child's self-esteem. In addition, we know from research that children with ADHD have a significant chance of developing conduct problems as they grow up. For example, it is quite common to find that children of 10 or 11 who are troublemakers in school and at home had initially come to the attention of their teachers in the early elementary grades because they would not listen and were constantly off task. Often their parents will report that even as young children they were a handful, being overly active and impulsive. For a child with ADHD, school is an endless stream of negativity and commands, and becomes a setting for failure and low self-esteem. Furthermore, school gets him in trouble with his parents. After a few years, the child may very well decide that he hates school and choose to be disruptive. He may feel that inasmuch as he cannot be "good," he might as well be good at being "bad."

ADHD is a condition that is most noticeable in school settings where the child has to listen a great deal and has to attend to very specific tasks. In addition, in a classroom there are many distractions: There is the noise from Yankel's pencil, a glimpse of a student walking through the hall, the teacher's voice in the back row talking to another student, and a siren on the street. There are all the books, papers, directions and folders to attend to, not just one's own but also those of other children. Often the child with ADHD may perform well in a one-on-one situation with a resource room teacher, a therapist or a parent. At home there is often less pressure to be organized and focused, except when it comes to doing homework. *Just because a child seems fine at home that does not rule out ADHD.*

Nothing is as destructive to a child suffering from undiagnosed ADHD as parents and teachers who make moral judgments about his fidgetiness and lack of concentration. We have to be careful before we tell any child that his conduct is a function of his *yetzer hara,* a lack of willpower or moral backbone. We need to be cautious before we label any child's problem behavior as simply a function of making the right or wrong choices. Choice implies that the child has a true option to select the path of good or the path of evil. As adults we should know that even in situations of true choice, temptation can be hard to overcome: How about that cookie we sneaked? How about watching TV? How about *davening* quickly to get it over with? The list is truly endless. Instead of resorting to labeling we would do better teaching our children about the workings of temptation and the ways that lead us to make the good choice.

When we take our time, children with ADHD will often describe their experiences as frustrating and discouraging. They want to acquire those "listening and attending skills" that the teacher is talking about but seem to always find themselves off task or fidgeting with a pencil, a shoelace, the page of the book they are reading. They themselves do not know why they touch other children while waiting in line for washing. By calling it the *yetzer hara* at work the child can only see this as a further indication that he is not trying hard enough at harnessing his evil impulses. Such an attitude can result in deep feelings of inadequacy and the sense that one is inherently damaged and beyond salvation.

Not every child who is fidgety or distractable is suffering from ADHD. There are a number of other conditions with similar symptomatology which can be confused with attentional problems. *It is therefore very important that qualified professionals take a close look at the child before a diagnosis is made.* ADHD is both under- and over-diagnosed by laypersons, including teachers. Children who are overly anxious are also distractable and unfocused. In response to stressful or traumatic events, such as death, an accident, or the birth of a sibling, children are often disruptive and unable to settle. Such normal adjustment phases or adaptation difficulties must not be confused with ADHD. Finally, there are children who simply reflect the chronic chaos in their homes. These are children who come from homes that are disorganized, without rules, and full of abrupt changes. Homes with a mentally ill or chronically overwhelmed parent are often devoid of routines and predictable consequences. Such situationally induced attention and organizational problems are not to be confused with ADHD. Children from such homes may do better in school because they respond to the structure of that setting.

ADHD is a condition that is medically treatable. Stimulant medication may help the youngster with ADHD focus for longer periods of time and lower his activity level. Parents may confuse this effect with being tranquilized. Stimulant medication does *not* make the child sleepy or dopey. Rather it puts "blinders" on the child, making him less susceptible to distraction, and in this way helps him improve his concentration.

About 70 to 80 percent of hyperactive children respond to medication. A psychiatrist, pediatrician or skilled family physician can prescribe the medication. It is best to monitor the child's progress by keeping track of his response to the medication. There are several rating scales that can be filled out by the teacher or parent to monitor the effect of the medication. Depending on the result, the dosage can be increased or leveled off. It is generally best to start with a low dose, maintain a close and careful observation of its effects, and adjust the dosage based on these results.

In addition to the medication, it is important to teach the child ways to monitor himself better, increase his organizational and planning skills, and find ways to stick longer with tasks. Parents need to be helped to run their house in a more organized and routinized fashion, in order to provide an external structure for their child. A psychologist, social worker, or psychiatrist can help the parents accomplish this. Medication should be looked at as something that gives the child an *opportunity* to learn the psychological skills that can counteract his natural impulsive and distractable tendencies.

It is important to let children know that medication gives them a chance to concentrate better and will help them stick to tasks longer. By emphasizing the new opportunities that the medication gives them, we make sure that they do not get the feeling that taking a pill is the whole solution. Medication does not do homework, medication does not practice the new *pasukim*, and medication does not read the chapter in social studies. It is *they* who do the learning, who practice their new assignments, who do the homework and who organize and plan their time and tasks in a better fashion. When parents and professionals fail to introduce the medication properly, it often happens that the child attributes magical properties to it: i.e., he failed a test because he did not have enough medication, or he got into trouble because the medication did not work. This kind of thinking is dangerous because it elevates the medication to a level of power greater than one's own. It becomes an explanation for any kind of shortcoming and abrogates one's sense of responsibility.

The child who sees medication as a key that opens the door to many possibilities that had previously been difficult or impossible to realize, can put the medication into its proper place. It is a means to an end and nothing more. The effect of the medication is to give him the power to actualize his capabilities. Parents of a child with ADHD should see medication not as a panacea, but as opening the door for teaching the child the skills that did not naturally evolve due to the ADHD. The parents' role becomes one of supporting the child in his efforts to build up strategies and tools to counteract impulsivity, distractibility and lack of concentration.

This way of thinking about medication is true not just for stimulant medications but for the many psychotropic medications that are currently available. Antidepressant medications can be very helpful in treating biologically based depressions, but they are not magic. Rather, they open up new opportunities to a person who is otherwise incapacitated. Often antidepressants make it possible for a person to start to work on new ways of thinking and feelings that are not possible in the depth of depression. To put it in baseball language, medication allows the person to make contact with the ball and to be part of the game. But it is the *person* and not the medication who runs the bases and who executes a skillful double play. While medication can be extremely valuable and even lifesaving, we should never lose sight of the centrality of the *person*, who is ultimately the one who must make the adjustments to the various stresses of reality.

Chapter Thirty-Six

Sexual Abuse, Physical Abuse

arenting obviously involves taking care of children's physical needs and ensuring their safety. We need to ensure their physical health and take care of their health needs, including immunization and well baby checkups to treating their illnesses and accidents. But health extends beyond the narrow definition of medical health. We also need to ensure the child's safety and provide a nonthreatening environment.

Jewish parents are typically described as indulgent and doting people who could never be abusive to their children. Unfortunately, human perversity can also extend to Jewish families, and even to some who are ritually observant. It is true that the cases are rare, but we know that there are Jewish parents who have beaten their children black and blue, and there are Jewish families where sexual abuse has been tolerated by the nonabusing spouse. There are uncles and grandfathers who coerce the little boys and girls in their families into secretive "games." There are camp counselors who overstep boundaries and attempt sexual explorations with their charges. There are mothers who create overly intimate bonds with their sons and allow them to sleep in their bed until they are close to *bar-mitzvah* age.

In an abusive environment the child's physical and/or psychological safety is jeopardized and the child grows up in a family context that perverts the role of both parent and child. Parents stop being parents, adults stop being adults, older friends or siblings stop being friends or siblings, and children become victims. The abuser is always in a power relationship relative to the victim. This can be because he is older, smarter, trusted and considered knowledgeable. Abuse involves coercion on the part of the abuser. Often coercion may begin in subtle ways but advances to threats if the child does not comply. In long-term sexual-abusive situations there is often a progression from apparently innocent "secret" games to increasingly more explicit sexual involvement.

Sexual abuse has to be distinguished from the "show and tell" games of young peers who are interested in looking at each other and showing off. While such behavior needs to be corrected and channeled, there are generally no adverse effects, since the elements of coercion and secrecy are missing. In abusive relationships between a younger and an older child we will find that the older child is using his superior skills to manipulate and coerce the younger one. This may be as simple as calling the younger one "chicken," or threatening to beat him up if he tells.

Chronic physical and sexual abuse of children results in the annihilation of childhood and may affect all aspects of a child's development. Survivors of abuse have great difficulties forming healthy attachments. They are plagued by depression, self-loathing and perennial self-doubt. The are often torn between conflicting feelings about the abuser. They are at risk for substance abuse and might well repeat unhealthy actions with their own children. Psychotherapy is a must for chronic victims and tends to be long term and difficult.

Both physical and sexual abuse are assaults on the self and one's sense of integrity. Unlike abusive words, they attack the body itself and with it the very fundamental sense of self. Our first sense of our "selfs" is through our bodies; because we live in and through our bodies. The intactness of the body is a first prerequisite for a sense of trust, optimism and self-confidence. When a child's body is repeatedly abused, be this through blows, inappropriate caresses or sexual activity, the child as a whole is attacked. Healthy growth is stilted, and the child develops unhealthy compensatory coping strategies. The child may "forget" the incidents. He/she creates two different personalities, and in that way dissociates from the abusive experience. The child may also identify with the abuser and seek out others to victimize. Chronic abuse by close relatives is especially harmful and vicious. Abusive incidents that are discovered early or at the time of occurrence can often be worked through success-fully. Here the crucial variables are whether the child reports the incident and *whether he/she is believed.*

A few years ago it was reported that a Jewish mother killed her retarded child for soiling himself. Subsequently, a long history of abuse was uncovered and the failure of the social service agencies was reported. But is it really enough to blame a state-funded insti-tution? What about neighbors? What about the husband who silently stood by while his child was being abused and while his wife lost herself in abusive rages?

As conscientious and protective parents, we need to ask our-selves what we can do to prevent abuse and to protect our children from being victimized. Children can be exposed to specific informa-tion regarding abuse: what it is, that it can happen to them, and how to handle abusive overtures or experiences. Often this involves a discussion of good and bad "touching." This is most certainly help-ful, although it needs to be carefully done so that children do not get frightened and see abusers at every street corner.

However, the best prevention against abuse is not so much spe-cific information, as for a child to have a healthy sense of himself and his body. What do we mean by that?

First, it is important that our children develop a good sense and knowledge of their bodies. This means that they know how the body functions, what its various parts are called and that all of the parts of the body are special and useful. Children are curious about all parts of their bodies and as they develop, certain parts are high-lighted in their consciousness. It is hard to imagine toilet training without a child becoming interested in the workings of the body parts involved in urination and elimination. It is a mistake for a parent to avoid all talk about these parts.

Secondly, children need to make a distinction between public and private parts. This is only possible if one has a good sense of one's body. Privacy involves not only the aspect of modesty, but it involves also assertiveness. Modesty in the context of the body means that we conceal certain parts of our bodies from other people. Little children demonstrate very little sense of such modesty and it is the parents who should remind them that underwear is not for show or that we must remain covered until we are in the bathroom. This should be done without shaming the child. There is no need to yell across a room to one's little daughter that she is sitting in an immodest manner. It is much more effective to quietly remind her that big girls sit differently and that she probably forgot to pull her skirt down. We thereby also set an example for how to rebuke someone gently, maintaining respect for their privacy.

Privacy also involves development of a healthy sense of one's body boundaries: A child is entitled to preserve and defend his sense of privacy, and a child may become assertive in rebuking others when his bodily boundaries are invaded. Much of childish teasing involves violating body boundaries. It is important for parents to protect the child who does not want to be kissed by classmates, or to enforce limits when a child complains that others are picking up her dress. At times children may also be standoffish toward relatives and may refuse to kiss an aunt or uncle that they have not seen for a long time. It might be proper for parents to insist that the child say hello, but that a kiss and a hug can be held off until the child is more comfortable. Sometimes relatives or friends give children hugs that are too enthusiastic, or are in the habit of pinching children's cheeks in an affectionate way. Some children don't like this, and complain about it. If we honor a child's needs and see things his way, we affirm that he is entitled to be the master over his own body.

Thirdly, children who have found their parents to be understanding and supportive in past dilemmas or problems, be they small or big, are much more likely to confide to their parents such troubling experiences as sexual overtures or threats. Children need to know very clearly that as parents we are ready to help them and that we are competent to deal with their problems. If we tell our children that we think they are wise for letting us know when they experience difficulties, they will see us as valuable resources and supports. This does not mean that we have to jump the gun every time a child reports peer trouble. However, it is important to let children know that unburdening their hearts and seeking clarification and solutions is a vital part of the parent-child relationship. Ultimately one of the best safeguards against sexual abuse is the child's secure knowledge that his parents are there to help and can be approached when the child is confronted with confusing problems and experiences.

As parents we want our children to be physically healthy and happy. The integrity of our bodies and the healthy valuation of one's body boundaries are important precursors to a healthy lifestyle. As Jews we need to value our bodies without making them into objects of worship and adulation. Energy to do our work in this world is dependent on our bodily fitness and health. It is our job to safeguard this vessel as best we can in ourselves as well as in our children.

Chapter Thirty-Seven

The Happiness Trap

Some of the theories that have been popularized in recent times seem to indicate that it is the parents' sacred obligation and responsibility to make sure that their children are happy. If a child mopes or otherwise shows any signs of being unhappy, this triggers a guilt trip within the parents: "What am I doing that is wrong?" There seems to be a prevailing attitude that "Life is going to be hard enough on these kids when they grow up. Let them at least have a happy childhood." The logic of this attitude may appear convincing, but it is misguided. Many youngsters have picked up on this theme, and if happiness eludes them, they may try to find it through the use of marijuana or other mind-altering substances.

The true parental responsibility toward a child is not to provide him with happiness, but with *chinuch*, a preparation for life, and a preparation for reality. The Torah tells us that G-d relates to us as a Father to a child (*Deuteronomy* 8:2-10), and although G-d is Omnipotent and could certainly have given the Israelites an immediate and permanent euphoria, he nevertheless disciplined them while providing for their essential needs.

There is indeed a *mitzvah* to "rejoice . . . and be happy" (*Deuteronomy* 16:14, 15), but the word *mitzvah* means a commandment, or something which a person must *do*. Joy and happiness are something we must work to achieve, rather than something G-d gives to us. It is no different with human parents. We must provide our children with the skills and resources to enable them to function optimally in the real world, but happiness is something that only they can achieve. *Parents cannot give children happiness.*

There is a great deal of emphasis in the news these days on child abuse, and unfortunately, some parents are capable of traumatizing their children. We must be careful that in our abhorrence of child abuse, we do not go to the other extreme of overindulgence, of considering every sign of displeasure as a failure on our part to make the child happy. Such an attitude may result in a spoiled but unhappy child, and a frustrated, guilt-ridden parent.

Let us reiterate. It is the parental responsibility to provide children with the tools for an optimal adjustment to the real world, to be independent learners, and to be people who can overcome challenges and master situations they have never previously encountered, but feelings of happiness must come from within. *It is not our job to give our children happiness, but rather to allow them learning opportunities that give them the skills to gain happiness by themselves, and to regain it when it is temporarily lost.*

Since happiness is something that the child must achieve, attempts by the parents to give him happiness rob him of something that can enrich and strengthen him: mastery of difficult situations and fortitude in the face of adversity. As we have pointed out earlier, when parents do something for the child that he can do for himself, this deprives the child of the necessary stimulus for maturation and independence.

Let us look at an example of how a parent might deal with a child's obvious unhappiness. Sarah, Rivvy's younger sister, received a beautiful doll for her birthday. Rivvy, who is all of 6 years old, is jealous and upset, because she, too, wants a doll. Should the mother feel guilty because Rivvy is unhappy and buy her a doll too? Should the mother try to talk Rivvy out of her feelings of unhappiness? How should she react if Rivvy starts to cry? Should she feel guilty for giving Sarah a doll as a birthday gift? Is it possible that Rivvy feels unloved? Is it possible that Rivvy will have an emotional scar throughout her life, and be permanently scarred because she did not receive a gift equal to her sister's?

If the mother feels she must make Rivvy happy, she is in trouble. Unless she succumbs and buys Rivvy a doll, Rivvy will be unhappy. This is the wrong path to take. Instead the mother might point out to Rivvy that she received a dollhouse for her birthday just a short while ago, or she may give her some other fully reasonable explanation. The problem is that when a child is upset, the impact of words, however wise and logical, is unlikely to change the way the child feels. If the mother, like many other parents, is unable to tolerate Rivvy's distress and tries to fix it right away, which in this case would mean buying Rivvy a doll, she will have failed to prepare the child for reality, because the real world will not give her everything she wants just to keep her happy.

Children may often be unhappy because of many things that displease them, and this is perfectly normal. If parents believe that it is their duty to see that the child is happy, they may interpret this unhappiness as a failure on their part, and they may therefore become angry with the child for being unhappy and making them feel they are a failure as parents. The danger of the "happiness trap" is now evident: Parents may become frustrated and angry, and children may feel helpless and dependent, incapable of making themselves happy, which lowers their self-esteem. If they become totally dependent on their parents to make them happy, the parents' inability to do so may lead to resentment.

If Rivvy's mother sees herself as a teacher of happiness *skills*, and sees it as her job to provide practice opportunities for these skills, she may look at the situation with different eyes. This is a chance for problem solving, generating options, and emotional regulation. The mother reframes the situation for her daughter: This is a challenge, both intellectually as well as emotionally. The mother sees it as her job to lead Rivvy along the way and to facilitate her regaining her emotional equilibrium. The mother would realize that her goal is to dosage the stress and to keep the problem at a level where it is solvable both intellectually and emotionally. If Rivvy is 10, the mother will treat her differently than a 3-year-old. Regardless of the specifics, mother can turn the situation into a learning experience. How does she do this?

First, it is most important that the mother accepts Rivvy's feelings of hurt and jealousy, even verbalizing them for her. "I know you also wish you had such a doll. Yes, it is hard at times to be at a sister's birthday. I can remember when I was very hurt that I did not have things that others had." Instead of trying to fix Rivvy's feelings, she lets her know that she understands them and can accept them. Mother also has to let Rivvy know that whining or crying and trying to upset everyone is not acceptable. She can remind Rivvy that not everyone in the family gets and needs the same things. By identifying and empathizing with Rivvy, mother defuses the situation.

Most importantly, however, mother is on the alert for the first indication that Rivvy is controlling her jealous feelings, and lets Rivvy know, by a smile, a nod, or a special word, that she is truly a great girl. By *not* giving and by *not* fixing, mother is helping Rivvy develop strengths and competencies. The mother herself is not in a situation where she feels a failure because her child is unhappy. The mother thus preserves the relationship between herself and her child, and in this fashion gives her a lot more than the mother who burns herself out trying to keep her children happy all the time.

The regulation of feelings, sometimes called affective regulation, is a very important skill that underlies happiness in life. We can model this skill for our children, but we cannot do it for them. We can suggest a variety of self-soothing strategies for them and help them think thoughts that are productive and that reduce the conflict, but ultimately the job has to be done by the child himself. Children need to learn to re-align their emotions by practicing this in a variety of situations. *This means that a dose of suffering and distress has to be part of a healthy childhood. Teaching the child acceptance of the distress and sincerely celebrating the child's mastery of his feelings are the psychological task of the parent.*

The Talmud repeatedly states that when Jews are in distress, G-d suffers along with them (*Taanis* 16a). But since G-d is all powerful, why is there any need for Him to suffer at all? He can just relieve our distress so that everyone will be happy. The answer is that similar to a human parent, it is not in our best interest for G-d to make us happy. He provides us with skills and strengths and teachings, but we must forge our own happiness.

A parent has to learn to walk the delicate balance between protecting the child and letting him come to terms with his own feelings. Adults who have not mastered self-regulatory skills in childhood are often very unhappy and at the total mercy of their emotions.

Chapter Thirty-Eight

Disabilities: Challenges and Hidden Giftedness

y giving us children to raise, G-d has entrusted us with a unique gift. Children are both a challenge and an opportunity for us to reach beyond ourselves and to grow into better persons. In the encounter with every one of our children, we are asked to extend ourselves and to transcend our inherent limits to some degree. On the one hand, the gift of children translates into responsibilities and personal accountability; on the other hand, it opens the door for growth, self-improvement and self-actualization. The *nachas* that children give parents is a very special bonus, but by no means the essence of raising children. Every child contains these challenges. Even the easygoing, studious, and kind child presents us with personal tasks; whether it is the cultivation of modesty or the avoidance of false pride in the face of *nachas*.

Nowhere is this challenge as apparent, however, as in the case of children with disabilities. All parents pray for a healthy child: a child that is physically fit, mentally alert, and emotionally stable. Before a baby is born, parents fantasize about the new little person and wonder whether it will be a boy or girl. We pray that the child should not have a genetic disorder, an illness or a chronic condition, G-d forbid. The Torah tells us the Rivkah sensed and worried that Eisav and Yaakov fought in her womb and would be at odds. It is only natural for parents to worry about problems. The doctor's first words at a birth are meant to alleviate these fears: "It is a healthy boy," or "It is a healthy girl." What is it, then, to have a child that is not healthy, that is disabled, sick, brain damaged, or manifests a birth defect? What is it, then, to be told that a child, G-d forbid, had an accident and is in a coma?

The Talmud tells us of a rabbi who met an exceedingly ugly man on the road. "How ugly you are! How dare you show your face in public?" the rabbi exclaimed. The ugly man looked at him calmly and said: "Don't complain to me about my looks. Complain to the potter who fashioned this vessel!" (*Taanis* 20a).

The body and all its physical abilities are but garments that surround our souls, and we cannot conclude from looking at a person what his *neshamah* is like. There are many stories about *tzaddikim* who were told that their companions in *Gan Eden* were simple and even unlearned but very devout and sincere people, whose devotion to G-d was absolute.

We truly believe that everything comes from G-d and is good. The same way as Torah observance is not a matter of picking and choosing, the children we get are not "mistakes," but given to us through Divine providence. As parents we need to thank G-d for each child, including the child with special needs, and we should see this child as both a gift and challenge.

When things do not correspond to our expectations and violate standard norms, our model of the world and ourselves is being challenged. Our own strengths as persons can be measured by the degree to which we are able to meet those challenges. The strength of a family, a community and of a society can be measured by the degree to which they are able to include and care for *all* of their children, including those that are disabled.

A story is told of the daughter of a great *tzaddik* who was betrothed to the son of a righteous rabbi from a distant town. As the wedding party approached, the girl looked out the window, and saw her groom arrive in a coach. To her horror he was hunch backed! She was so taken aback by his appearance that she called her father and told him that she could never marry this young man. The young man listened quietly to the rabbi's news that his betrothed refused to marry him. He agreed to set her free if he would be permitted a private audience with her. When the groom and the bride were alone he asked her to stand with him in front of a large mirror. As she gazed in it she saw how his hunchback lifted itself from his body and placed itself on her back. The groom then said to her: "I want you to know that our souls were meant to be together. When we were in *Shamayim* (heaven) it was decreed that you should be born with a hunchback. I took the hunchback for you, because I knew that it would be too hard of a lot for you to bear." At that moment the bride saw him as he really was, and she agreed to marry the hunchbacked groom.

An African proverb tells us that it takes a whole village to raise a child, and it may take a whole *shtetl* to raise a Jewish child. When parents have a child with a disability, the community who welcomes this child with open arms as one of its members can make the difference between success and failure. Once a child is born, we need to accept that Hashem has decided that this very child is the perfect match for us and our family, and, by extension, for the entire Jewish people.

Although it is natural to argue, to worry, to cry and to mourn the lost dream, and although it may take time to come to terms with this unexpected turn of events, we can and need to eventually accept that this child and all that its care entails was meant for us and us alone. We need to give up our dream, because that is all it was, and accept and affirm the reality as Hashem created it for us.

Relinquishing one's dreams is hard and may feel like the loss of a precious jewel. As parents we create our own image of our children long before they are born. In a way we play an exciting game in anticipation of the child. We may recall different ancestors' names and try them for fit in our thoughts. Upon shopping we may see a pretty Shabbbos outfit that might fit the potential little, as of yet unborn, princess. When the baby kicks we cannot help it but think that the baby is trying to tell us something. We look at a *sefer* and see our little *yingele* — yet unborn — reading his first words. The image may have been that of a little *boy* learning *aleph-bais,* but reality may bring a bright little *girl* studying *Chumash.*

In the case of a child with a disability we need to radically alter the picture that we treasured during pregnancy. When a child becomes disabled later in life we need to let go of our memories of the child in his days of health. When we continue to hang on to our images of how the child was or should have been we cannot help but constantly compare the child with our dreams or memories. In a way our sense of loss never allows us to meet the child as he really is. We fail to connect with the child in all of his fullness and G-dly perfection. We never penetrate the shell of his disability to know him as a unique person who carries within him a spark of G-dliness.

A disabled baby girl was born to a rabbi and his wife in Israel. For the first few days the father walked around downcast and sad. Later that week, however, a friend of his found him to be his former joyful self. "I found the name for my daughter," the father said. "We call her Shulamith. In her name is the word *shaleim* which means wholeness. When I finally found the name for her I was able to see her in her completeness and her perfection as G-d had created her."

For months after her child was born with Down's Syndrome a mother had the sensation that another baby of hers had passed away. This imaginary baby was singularly beautiful with a shiny star on his forehead and seemed to live in the back of her mind. At times she felt guilt about this, at times she felt intense pain and longing for her "starbaby." As time passed she realized that this was her dream and her own fantasies that she needed to bury in order to fully accept a treasure — her own real child.

What is acceptance? Acceptance must not be confused with resignation or a grudging "Oh well." Genuine acceptance means the favorable reception of G-d's gift. It also means taking upon ourselves the duties and responsibilities as they come with this child. We need to subordinate our will to Hashem's will and find happiness in this in spite of the suffering. While we are unable to know

Hashem's intentions, we are able to transcend ourselves and we can find positive meaning in the fact that G-d chose us to be the guardian parents of this child.

Acceptance does not mean fatalism and complacency. As Jewish parents we want to explore all avenues of helping our disabled child. We want to take advantage of advances in medicine technology, the rehabilitative sciences, education, psychiatry and psychology. We want to be in touch with other parents who can support us and share information with us. As Jewish parents we may advocate for our children's right to a Jewish education and their rightful place in the Jewish community. Although children with special needs are considered disabled, we need to remember that their "dis-abilities" exist in our eyes as something that detracts from them.

Giftedness is mostly taken as intellectually precocious and exceedingly bright, but giftedness transcends the boundaries of scholastic excellence. Persons are gifted just by virtue of being different. Giftedness is not only what a person has to give, but also what a person enables another person to give. If we were all healthy, happy, rich and all knowing we would all be self-contained, but not gifted. One person's need is a gift for those who can satisfy this need. Similarly, it takes special care and eyes to see the gifts that are not obvious nor scintillating. If we were all the same, giftedness would not be possible. It is precisely diversity and differences among us that enable us to be both gift givers and receivers.

What could possibly be the gifts that a child with a disability has to offer? A father — whose youngest son was born with Down's Syndrome — remarked that his other sons accept the father's *brachah* on Shabbos with a sort of ennui. His youngest, however, shows a true reverence for the father's act and responds to the *brachah* with great joy and happiness. The child's simplicity and pure joy is a gift to the father, who then experiences the *brachah* as the truly precious act that it is. This same child does not talk much, but his every word is special and treasured by his parents. What they took for granted with their other children has become noteworthy and appreciated. This child opened a door for them that leads and continues to lead them into spaces of Hashem's infinite palaces that they did not even know existed. Their projected life plans changed; they changed; their community is changing.

Chapter Thirty-Nine

The Gifted Child

ost often when we use the word "gifted," we are referring to a child who shows mental and intellectual abilities beyond his chronological age. These are children that come to the attention of parents and teachers because of the ease with which they learn the material that is presented to them, the sophistication of their questions, and their hunger for more learning. Often gifted children are able to master skills without direct instructions because they have acquired the tools necessary for independent learning and thinking.

As Jewish parents, we prize excellence in Torah studies and we value outstanding achievement in both secular and Judaic subjects. Judaism looks back on a long tradition of literacy, Talmudic thinking steeped in analytic thinking, and the conscious refinement of character. Our sages and illustrious rabbis were people who possessed great minds and were able to delve into the study of Torah with singular concentration and incisiveness. To the awe and admiration of their communities, many mastered Talmud at an astonishingly early age and held their ground with their learned elders. Parents and teachers present the *talmid chacham* — the person learned in Talmud and Torah — as the ideal toward which to aspire.

All children present us with challenges, and an intellectually gifted child is likewise not without challenges. It takes thoughtful parents to nurture the assets of their gifted child and help him translate his potential into achievements. The gifted child needs his parents' guidance no less than any other child. It may be daunting to raise a child who defies age norms and who, in certain aspects, mirrors competencies associated with much older children or even adults.

One mother recalled how her little girl at 3 years of age seemingly taught herself to read and was able to tell stories with great expression and amazing linguistic agility. There are exceptional children who take to learning *Gemara* like a fish to water. Not only can they recall and reconstruct logical arguments, but their questions indicate that they anticipate cases and questions that are addressed by other commentaries. Their depth of comprehension far exceeds that of their peers, and they master the material at much greater speed. There are gifted youngsters who, as teenagers, are capable of tackling scientific problems in innovative ways.

There are certain specific abilities other than general intellectual superiority where we find gifted children. Musical and mathematical prodigies are children who perform well above age expectations in these areas. They often show an interest in these areas at an early age. Similarly, chess prodigies are children who master the game of chess with all of its logical and spatial intricacies at an early age, well above average expectations. On the other hand, we should remember that many great personalities seemed less than gifted in their childhood. Albert Einstein, who revolutionized physics and our understanding of the nature of time and space, was a mediocre student in mathematics.

What are gifted children like — other than being very bright? Often the gifted child is erroneously thought to be inherently socially awkward and maladjusted. Intellectually gifted youngsters are said to have their heads in the clouds and are thought to be incapable of managing everyday matters. It is a common misconception that the gifted child must have a shortcoming in one area of functioning to offset his superior mental skills. The fact is, however, that gifted children are often socially competent, well adjusted emotionally, and show interests and talents well beyond the narrow confines of academic performance.

Most certainly, the gifted child is not a typical child, and many preconceptions that we might have as parents need to be set aside. It may be difficult to find the right balance between a child's intellectual gifts and his emotional needs. Just because an 8-year-old can master algebra does not mean that he does not need to be part of the neighborhood baseball crowd.

Rabbi Heschel of Cracow, one of our greatest Talmudists, was a child prodigy, and at the age of 10 gave intricate lectures in Talmud to accomplished Torah scholars. One time, upon emerging from the *beis hamedrash* (study hall) after delivering a brilliant lecture, a goat passed by, and little Heschel promptly jumped on it, seized it by its horns, and went for a joy ride. He later explained, "Every child has juvenile impulses. If these are not discharged in childhood, they may emerge as immature behavior later in life."

Parents may feel unsure and conflicted as to how to guide their gifted child. Are his talents to be celebrated or are they just assets like his sibling's talent for organizing a little summer camp? For some parents it can be disconcerting to deal with a child who masters complex problems with ease and who tackles material that is beyond their horizon. The stories of our sages give us many examples of youngsters who surpassed their teachers and elders at an early age.

Rabbi Yonasan Eibeschutz was a child prodigy, and one Passover he complied with the tradition of "stealing" and hiding the *afikomen* (portion of matzah designated as desert), holding it hostage until his father ransomed it with a promise for a new suit. He then returned the *afikomen* to his father, who proceeded to distribute portions to everyone at the *Seder,* except to little Yonasan.

"You do not get any *afikomen*," the father said to Yonasan, "unless you release me from my promise." Little Yonasan smiled and, extracting a piece of matzah from his pocket and proudly displaying it, said, "I expected you might say that, so I kept a piece of *afikomen* for myself before returning it to you."

A gifted child must be stimulated and challenged. His giftedness creates special needs that have to be met by school and family. All too often we encounter gifted underachievers who managed to do very well in school by just relying on their native intelligence. School is truly easy for them and they shine, but as a result, they never acquire much needed study habits, time-management skills, and a solid work orientation. Often these students run into trouble in the higher grades when the material can no longer be mastered by innate intelligence alone but requires diligent study and practice. For some very bright kids this situation may not present itself until they pursue advanced studies and are in competition with other equally or more gifted students.

The gifted child who is challenged develops a different relationship to his studies. When his capabilities are stimulated, work and studies become truly fulfilling and self-rewarding. Academic excellence becomes a testing ground for his skills and an arena for self-expression. His love of learning for the sake of learning itself is kindled.

Superior skills allow a gifted child to be helpful to his peers. In this fashion, the gifted student does not see academic achievement as an aggrandizement but as something to be shared. This may also teach him to accept the limitations of others, to show patience and tolerance, and to see his talents as something to be shared. Since our tradition values intellectual excellence so highly, it is important for parents to put this capability into the proper perspective. Mental ability in and of itself is not a cause for pride. It becomes a source of self-esteem only when it is used well and manifests itself in outstanding performance and achievements.

The traditional view defines giftedness as "outstanding mental abilities," and giftedness has traditionally been measured by intelligence tests. Children who score in the top 2 percent are considered gifted. There are, of course, varying degrees of giftedness. A child with an IQ of 150 is considered more gifted than a child with an IQ of 135, but both of these children are classified as being above average in intellectual ability.

This poses a question. What about the garage mechanic who

can figure out the workings of a car, diagnose its problem and fix it? What about the public-relations manager who keeps a staff of 150 persons happy? What about the mother who can fix toys, juggle schedules, and meet all sorts of personal needs in her family, from those of her baby to those of her teenager, not to speak of her husband's?

It is unfortunate that we have a narrow view of giftedness, focusing exclusively on intellectual-academic excellence. Giftedness in a larger sense refers to talents of all sorts that make a person special. The youngsters who can organize and plan small summer camps display talents in practical problem solving and social intelligence. The girl who sews all of her clothes, the flags for her school's annual dinner, and dollclothes for her sister, etc. is a skilled manual worker and displays superior spatial skills. The musically gifted child learns songs with great ease and takes the lead in her school play. We need to ask ourselves: Is the child who is a "crackerjack" babysitter, or the child "engineer" in the family who can mend things that seem beyond repair, not also gifted? What about the child who can draw and express himself artistically and shows a pronounced sense and appreciation of beauty?

As parents, we need to see giftedness in all of our children and it should not be limited to intellectual excellence. The nurture of talents and the appreciation of all sorts of abilities allows us to treat each and everyone of our children as special and capable of a unique contribution. The more we become tuned into our children's individuality and discover their assets, the greater our chance to build up healthy self-esteem.

Chapter Forty

Siblings — A Microcosm of Society

he quality of a community is significantly influenced by the quality of life in the smallest unit of society: the family. Families come in all sizes and shapes, and it would be a mistake to assume that all Orthodox families are the same: Observance of Torah and *Halachah* provides a framework which leaves ample room for parents to make their family unique and distinct. Every family develops its family traditions and routines that are an expression of the parents' individuality and special talents and interests. It can be as simple as a special dish, a hobby that the parent cherishes and passes onto the children, or a Shabbos melody that has been in the family for generations. In one family the father, a researcher interested in positive and negative thinking, introduced "The best things of the week," on

Friday night during the meal. Initially his intent was to stimulate his children to remember all the good things that had happened to them during the week, since we often tend to forget the good and remember the bad. Over the years it has become a much cherished ritual and leads to many happy reminisces and discussions at the Shabbos table.

Similarly, every family develops house rules and routines that can be very varied. In some families the refrigerator is off limits, in other families it is fully accessible; in some families bedtime is strictly set, in others it is a much more negotiable matter. There variations are part of living and part of our own and our family's individuality. Yet all too often it is these trivial matters that pre-occupy our minds and get us thinking — and talking! — about others in our community. What is it then that truly matters in our families if it is not bedtimes, refrigerators, interior decorating and *cholent* ingredients?

Our sages gave us a term to describe the ideal household: *shalom bayis. Shalom* means "peace" and derives from the same root as *shaleim,* "complete or unified." A peaceful and united home is not only a goal of a Jewish marriage, but it applies equally to Jewish parenting. *Shalom bayis* has to be a goal for our families. It should form the relationship between the child and parent, as well as between husband and wife, and we need to make it a top priority for our children. Children need to see *shalom bayis* as vitally important to their relationships with siblings and be taught to strive toward getting along with each other.

Most children grow up with siblings. Siblings give the child first-hand experiences at exploring a whole variety of relationships and ways of relating. There are questions of love and attachments and there are questions of power and status. There are questions of dealing with competitors, unwanted intruders, adored mentors, or cherished protectors. There are questions of sharing, compromising, and asserting.

The Torah is replete with problems of sibling conflict as well as sibling cooperation: Cain and Abel, Jacob and Esau, Joseph and his brothers, the brothers among themselves, Leah and Rachel. There are beautiful stories in the Midrash and voluminous writings in the works of *mussar* that elaborate on these relationships. Children can be moved by the story of Rachel's sacrifice for Leah, and of Joseph's devotion to his brothers despite their having dealt so harshly with him.

Siblings give the child opportunities to form both supportive and competitive relationships with the family other than with his parents. As an older sibling the child may practice parenting and caretaking, becoming the one in charge, the leader. He may also become the one to give, guide, care and protect. In its negative expression, the status of being older opens the door for the child to become a dictator who rules with threats and oppression. In *I Didn't Ask To Be In This Family* (Henry Holt, 1996), I elaborated on several models of sibling relationships.

Some of these experiences have a profound impact not only on the sibling relationship, but also on other social interactions. It is not infrequent that in psychotherapy childhood relationships with siblings take a place on center stage. A woman recalled with much feeling how as a young child she had believed her older brother had special powers. His threat of the "evil eye" — a forceful stare — made her his obedient but resentful servant.

As a younger sibling, the child finds support and at times over-involvement in his extended family. He observes his older siblings at play and work. It is not uncommon for younger sibs to want to have homework just like their bigger brothers or sisters. In order to define his own space, he needs to learn to hold his own and to assert himself. It can be challenging to have so many helpers and bosses! There is a fine line between helping and controlling, and the youngest child is frequently the one who needs to assert his independence and his need to make mistakes and venture out on his own. The youngest, especially in a large family, has siblings that are much older than he as well as some that are closer in age. His position as the youngest puts him in the enviable position of being "the baby," but it also puts him in the often resented position of having many masters.

Middle children are often skilled negotiators because they have to learn to deal both "upwards" and downwards." At times, middle children "get lost" between the older and the younger ones. For some children this is perceived as a lack of attention; but for others the lack of limelight allows them to stand on their own two feet outside the circle of parental scrutiny and anxiety that an oldest child might feel.

Is it better to be the oldest, the youngest or a middle child? Is it better to be the only girl among several brothers? Is it better to be one of the gang of "guys"? Is being an only child an asset or a liability? Are bigger families better than smaller ones? What about the family with six children in seven years? What can we say about birth order, the influence of the sex and age of siblings on one another?

There is no easy "objective" answer. Let us face it: There are families with two children who feel overwhelmed, and there are families with ten children who do not feel overwhelmed. There are children who wish for an older sibling and others who would like to be the oldest themselves. There are "babies" in families who are tired of always being the youngest, and there are other "babies" who thoroughly enjoy their birth order. There are, however, a few points to remember than can guide us and help us promote healthy sibling relationships in the sense of *shalom bayis*.

First, we need to keep in mind that in raising a child, the relationship among the siblings in the family constitutes an important influence on development. Siblings can teach each other many things, both good and bad. Because siblings spend considerable time in each other's presence, it is important that most of their interactions be positive or neutral. Having siblings gives a child a chance to practice many social competencies and social problem-solving skills. Siblings confront each other daily with conflicting plans, needs and wishes: Who can tell mother about the school day first? Aaron thinks it should be him, and his brother Yankel thinks it should be him. Tzippi likes to sing and hum, but her sister Sheina wants absolute quiet. Chana, the preschooler, insists that a pencil with a broken point is no longer a pencil. Avi, her brother, disagrees and tries to explain, but she gets all upset.

Sibling relationships are more than just getting along, and it is not enough to tell our kids "be nice to your brother or sister." We need to make it our business as parents to teach our children to engage in interpersonal problem solving and amicable ways of relating. This takes time and may try parents' patience and ingenuity, but it is an important component of parenting.

Second, all too often parents classify their children into categories: Shlomo is the smart one, Mordechai the practical one, Ben the *macher*, and Tzvi the moody one. This sets the tone for competitiveness and at the same time boxes the children in, because if Shlomo is *the* smart one, then Mordechai cannot possibly also be smart. Tzvi has a prerogative on moodiness and needs to maintain this role in the family. Of course, all our children are different. But the kind of labeling that can take place in families is all too often limiting and a poor substitute for getting to really know our children in all their diversity and potential.

Third, and most important, the presence of physical aggression between siblings is most unfortunate. Aggression directly attacks the foundation of interpersonal relationships and creates an atmosphere of lawlessness. Parenting involves many different things, but it is also a process of civilizing our children. The society of Sodom was characterized by murder, violence and the law of the strongest. We would like to think that in a Torah-observant home, the *midos* of Torah would prevail, and that aggression and frank violence would never occur. The Talmud tells us that in the second Temple, two *Kohanim* competed for the *mitzvah* of performing a ritual sacrifice, and when one saw that the other might get there first, he stabbed him (*Yuma* 23a). It is unfortunate that in our zeal to perform *mitzvos,* we may overlook and even overstep the boundaries of basic decent behavior and even be brought to frank aggression.

When a child habitually uses physical aggression to deal with his siblings, he fails to develop more sophisticated and ordered ways of interacting. There is a fundamental difference between asking for a toy and grabbing it. There is a world of difference between the child who hits his sibling because he lost at checkers and the child who is able to comfort himself by reminding himself that his sister is three years older or that it is now taking her longer to beat him. The habitual use of physical aggression affirms the law of brute strength as the principle that governs social interaction. From a psychological perspective, the habitual use of physical aggression prevents the development of a myriad of valuable social skills, such as compromising, negotiating, being able to tolerate frustration, and being altruistic and extending oneself.

Without these competencies *shalom bayis* is not possible, and we can talk about *ahavas Yisrael* till we are blue in the face.

If we all agreed with one another at all times, there would be no place for interpersonal problems, but people, including children, do not, by any means, have the same ideas and views of matters at hand. As a result, we run into conflicts with one another. Major segments of the Talmud deal precisely with matters of conflict between humans. "I saw it first, therefore it is mine" versus "I picked it up first, therefore it is mine."

Talmudic conflict-resolution is oriented toward clarifying the situation, analyzing its parameters, and putting it in the context of relevant information so that the conflicting claims can be resolved. Let us not forget that one of the seven Noahide laws pertains to the need for courts to resolve conflicts.

In some ways, as parents we are placed into the shoes of the rabbis and judges when it comes to our own children. It is a good rule to make physical aggression in the home unacceptable under any circumstances.

Let us look at a common scenario. Yossi knows that his younger brother is sensitive when it comes to his favorite blanket, and just mentioning throwing it in the garbage gets him going. Soon Mendel is so upset, and he lashes out and punches Yossi. What now?

The mother needs to communicate to Mendel that under no circumstances does a verbal provocation justify a physical response. All too often parents make the mistake of discussing the offense at great length with the child, but this is not a time to reason with the child. In a household that has clear and consistent house rules for aggression, mother simply enforces the consequences, most likely a time-out. Time-out is a tool which enable everyone to have a cooling-off period. The child loses his privileges and is separated from the main activity for a *short* period of time. Time-out can take place on a chair, a sofa, or by being sent to his room. The older brother Yossi does not get away scot free, and he should be reprimanded for teasing his brother, also going to a time-out, especially if he tends to do this habitually. Both children need to know that further fighting, be it verbal or physical, will result in their being separated.

Chatting about the incident should not primarily focus on the problem. Questions like "Why did you do this?" are often not very useful. All too often kids do not really know why they did what they did other than that they lost control, were angry, or "felt like it." It is more important to become proactive and to look into the future. What are better ways to handle such situations? What are smarter ways to spend time with each other than teasing? Do we really want to be brothers who cannot get along? Is it perhaps better to find things to do by oneself rather than being together and not getting along?

We want to get our children thinking and help them reflect constructively on their actions. Let's make a plan on how to get along better. Let's figure out when it is better for us to go our separate ways. Maybe Yossi's teasing is just a way to get his brother to stop following him. If so, let's explore the power of words and affirm that it is not only better but actually just fine to tell the brother to leave him alone. As parents we can let our children know that we will back them up in their constructive problem solving. Children need to know that we will assist them in their attempts to manage sibling relationships in a positive fashion.

Parents often relegate teaching to problem situations. When there is a difficulty, the need to instruct and fix jumps out at us. It is generally harder to perceive teaching opportunities in situations of competence and success.

Let us then go back to Mendel and Yossi and look at an often-forgotten scenario. Yossi is playing with Mendel. Mendel is using all the green blocks to build his stable for the animals. Yossi asks for a green block. Mendel refuses, because he says he needs all of them. Yossi changes his structure a bit and uses two blue blocks instead. Here is a parent's chance to point out to Mendel that his generosity was duly noted and his ingenious way of substituting two blue for one green is a really smart way to solve the problem.

By capitalizing on their success we help the boys become more aware of what they are doing right. Awareness of one's own skills leads to greater mastery. It is one thing for the child to be able to share or compromise, and it is another, much more powerful thing to *know* that he is able to share or compromise. When children have a repertoire of social skills that they can access easily and with confidence, the resolution of social conflicts becomes less threatening. Again, the more tools, the greater the mastery.

The experience of successful interactions with a sibling leads a child to form a bond of affection and caring with his brother or sister. It is therefore not simply the elimination of problem situations that is important, but the creation of successful and mutually satisfying interactions. When siblings get along and care for each other, we create a home atmosphere of *shalom* and a context in which Torah and *mitzvos* can blossom. When siblings can resolve conflicts in a civilized manner, we are setting the foundation for *ahavas Yisrael* and healthy ways of relating to our fellow Jews, be this peers in school, friends, or, later in life, a spouse.

Chapter Forty-One
Grandparenting

*I*t has been said that being a grandparent is having children without having to go through the labor pains. There is some truth in the idea that being a grandparent gives one the possibility of having all the pleasures of parenthood without the distress that fathers and mothers must endure. Grandparents can play with the children, kiss them, give them candy and toys, and take them to the ball game, while leaving the discipline to the parents, who also have to stay up nights with the infants during the feeding phase, care for the children while they survive chicken pox, argue with them to get them to bed, drag them out of bed for school in the morning, etc. Grandparents can be the "good guys," while the demands of reality that the children be taught right from wrong sometimes necessitate the parents being the "bad guys."

While this enviable arrangement may sometimes be enjoyed by grandparents, it is by no means the norm. The prevalence of two working parents and the increasing occurrence of single parent families often results in those parents who live in the same community being called on to provide much of the care for the children, and they must then assume many of the parental responsibilities.

When grandparents must provide parenting, there are a few important rules to follow. Let us remember that children are very clever and are most astute at playing one person against another to get what they want. They do so even with their parents, but fortunately many parents do communicate with one another and see eye to eye about the children's upbringing. This is not always true of parent-grandparent, and the generational gap occasionally results in difference of opinion. Thus, being raised by both parents and grandparents may allow a child to pit one against the other.

It is therefore important that parents and grandparents come to an understanding as to how the child is to be raised. Two sets of values can be chaotic and children should not be subjected to such confusion. Whatever ideational differences exist should be worked out in advance, so that the child can be guided by a unified approach. Grandparents had their opportunity to raise their children, and would not have tolerated anyone interfering or undermining their teachings. They should give their children the same courtesy. If grandparents feel that they cannot possibly adjust to the parents' guidelines, then it is better for the child to have other arrangements made, and pretend that the grandparents are living thousands of miles away. In such cases, let the grandparents kiss the children and give them sweets, but refrain from being involved in their upbringing.

For example, there are many instances where young people who were raised in homes which were not strictly Torah observant have become *baalei teshuvah* and have adopted restrictions and practices which their parents do not observe. The parental home may be strictly kosher, whereas the grandparents' kitchen is off limits only to pork. Parents may be meticulously Shabbos observant, whereas the grandparents' Shabbos observance is limited to lighting candles Friday evening.

I have seen such families function very harmoniously, each respecting the other's way of life. Such an arrangement need not be confusing for the children, and to the contrary, they may have the opportunity to learn how to live in a pluralistic environment. The grandparents understand that the children attend day school and are taught rules which should be respected. There is a great deal of love between all three generations, and when the grandchildren visit the grandparents' home, they are told, "Honey, before you take anything to eat, check with me whether it is okay for you." The grandparents have adequate "*nosheri*" with kosher supervision, and when the children eat meals at the grandparents' home , the meals are either "take out" from kosher restaurants or prepared by the parents, and served on disposable plates. No one expects anyone else to change their way of living, and they fully enjoy each other's company. The grandchildren see their parents respecting the grandparents, even though it is made clear to them that they are living a Torah way of life with which the grandparents are unfamiliar.

Children who live in a home where the parents have wisely decided that exposure to television is not a healthy influence on children may visit the grandparents' home, where there is television. Grandparents should respect the parents' wishes, and after embracing the grandchildren, say to them "This is not for you, honey," and without any fanfare turn off the TV.

The Talmud describes an interesting episode. One of the Talmudic sages, Rabbi Meir, heeded the words of Elisha ben Avuyah, even though he had defected from Torah observance. One Sabbath, Elisha was riding on his horse and Rabbi Meir walked alongside him. When they reached the city limits, Elisha said to Rabbi Meir, "You are a Shabbos observer. You are not permitted to walk beyond these limits on Shabbos." Even though Elisha was not observant, he respected Rabbi Meir's observance and called to his attention that he was at the city limits and to be cautious not to violate the Shabbos.

Unfortunately there are situations where such understanding does not prevail, and grandparents who disapprove of their children having become *baalei teshuvah* are openly critical of them and refuse to respect their principles. This results in an alienation of the grandchildren, who cannot be exposed to influences which undermine the way of life that the parents have adopted. If grandparents take the attitude, "If you want the children to be at our home, then they have to eat what we eat," this can lead only to the conclusion that the children will not be permitted to be at the grandparents' home. This is unfortunate, because children are unnecessarily deprived of a source of love.

When grandparents care for grandchildren, it is crucial that parental authority should not be undermined. Parental authority should be reinforced and supported, and any disagreements worked out between the parents and grandparents, rather than presenting the children with conflicting ideas.

Care-giving grandparents should also follow the formula to acknowledge, empathize, and identify. Indeed, they are often in an excellent position to provide comfort and assurance to the grandchildren, even more so than the parents.

For example, Batya comes home from school, crying because she got a failing grade on a test. "Mommy's going to kill me when she sees this."

"Don't worry about Mommy killing you," her grandmother says. "I didn't kill her when she flunked a test either. I did want to know why it happened so that she would know what to do to prevent it from happening again. So let's see if we can figure out why you missed these questions, and then see what you need to do."

This kind of response may be more constructive than the response her mother might have had, perhaps reacting out of anger. Batya is reassured that although failing a test is regrettable, it hardly warrants a death sentence. After all, her mother is alive and well, and holding a job in spite of the fact that she, too, had failed a test. What needs to be determined is why the test performance was poor. Had Batya not studied adequately? Does she not understand the teacher? There is no disguising the disappointment over the poor grade, but corrective actions can be taken, and life does not have to come to an end. Grandparents may be even more effective in this way than parents.

Children like to see pictures of when their parents were little and hear their grandparents relate things about their parents' childhood. Adults may not realize this, but little children may not be able to conceive of their parents ever having been little and then having grown up. As with Batya's discovery that her mother survived and is functional and loved in spite of having failed a test in her childhood, so children can be encouraged and reassured when their grandparents tell them about their parents' foibles.

Dovi was severely reprimanded when he was two hours late coming home from school, and his parents were beside themselves with anxiety. All that happened was that he had stopped off at a friend's house for a few minutes and became so involved with a new electronic game his friend had that he lost track of time.

"It's natural for children to become so interested in something that they lose track of time, but you have to remember your responsibilities. This should help you avoid such forgetfulness in the future. Always call home when you are delayed. Your daddy once went to a ball game with his friends, and didn't come home until very late at night. The score was tied and the game lasted much longer than expected. I didn't know this and I almost worried myself to death. But after that he always called if he thought we might be concerned. You always have to think about how other people might be feeling, and just because you're having fun doesn't mean that you can be inconsiderate."

Dovi's reprimand was well deserved, but the lesson in consideration given by his grandparents may have made a greater impression than the scolding he received from his father. Furthermore, Dovi had just been given even more reason to identify with his father, which is usually quite constructive.

Grandparents may be able to provide a measure of serenity which the parents may not have. Experience is a powerful teacher, and life provides lessons which cannot be found in books. Parents may react to things with alarm, while grandparents have learned the hard way that we can survive many traumas in life, and they can provide a valuable moderating effect.

Western civilization worships youth, and often gives only lip service to revering the elderly. However, I recall one baseball game when an outfielder, in the last year of his career, made a spectacular leaping catch, which elicited a comment from the excited announcer, "Can you believe that? Wow! A man of his age being able to make that leap and take away a sure home run!" The other announcer said, "I don't believe a younger person could have made that catch. It took 22 years of experience to know just how and when to jump to catch that ball." The second announcer was right. There is no substitute for experience.

Grandparents have that experience. They have usually experienced many joyful moments in life as well as many sad ones. They may therefore be able to put things in a perspective for the grandchildren that can help them adjust to both the ups and downs in life. The Torah tells us that we must seek guidance from our grandparents as well as our parents. "Ask your father and he will tell you, your elders (grandparents) and they will relate it to you" (*Deuteronomy* 32:7). A careful analysis of the grammar in this verse will indicate that the Hebrew word referring to how a parent will respond connotes a tone of harshness, whereas the word referring to the grandparents' response is one that connotes a much gentler tone of voice.

Although there are many exceptions, parents are likely to be busier and under greater pressure than grandparents. Parents are more apt to be caught up in the rat race of trying to get ahead in the world. Grandparents, who are at least 20 years older, may be past that stage, and even if still actively working, are at a more stable stage, not pushing as hard to get promoted or to start another business venture. They may therefore have more time. Grandparents may be able to provide constructive help with school work, perhaps by listening to a book report or reviewing some material for a forthcoming test. Grandparents, just as parents, should never do homework for the child, but may be very helpful when they listen to the child read his book report, or help him with some of the review questions in the text or the preparatory sheet that the teacher distributed.

Some parents believe that the real world is harsh enough, and that children will have to face their share of hardships when they grow up. Quite true. But the conclusion they draw from this, i.e., that therefore "let them enjoy life while they can," may be misguided. Making things too easy for children fails to prepare them for those harsh aspects of reality. Parents may therefore not be able to indulge the children as much as they would like to. However, if parents do their job well, being firm when this is called for, setting proper limits, and being just disciplinarians, then the grandparents may have more leeway in indulging the kids.

At a novelty store, I saw a paddle which was very well cushioned on both sides. Embroidered on it was, "Grandma's paddle." That's what grandparents are for, isn't it?

Chapter Forty-Two

The Single Parent

The challenges facing the single parent warrant an entire volume rather than just a chapter. Indeed, it is questionable whether even a whole book, regardless of how comprehensive, can address all the needs of a single parent. The only reason I raise the topic here is to call attention to these enormous needs, and to urge single parents not to try to be "supermoms." Single parents should avail themselves of assistance, and I believe the community should be alerted that it has responsibilities in assisting single parents. Inasmuch as in the majority of cases the children remain primarily under the care of the mother, we will assume for the purposes of this discussion that the single parent is the mother.

If a marriage has been terminated by divorce, a number of issues arise. Frequently divorces are not amicable, and there may be both overt and covert hostility between the parents, with the children being caught in the middle. The children may have feelings of fondness for the father, even in those situations where the children sympathize with the mother, and certainly in those situations where the children did not see the father as being the villain. Because of their fear that any show of affection for the father may upset the mother, the children may suppress positive feelings for the father. Returning from enjoyable visits with the father, the children may feel it necessary to please the mother by describing the visit as unenjoyable.

In an intact healthy marriage, the father serves as role model for the boys, and as the type of husband to which the girls aspire. In absence of the father, the children lack this role model, and if the father's behavior has been inappropriate or if the mother vilifies the father, distorted concepts of masculinity may occur in the children. If the girls sympathize with the father, they may be unable to look up to their mother as a role model. In any of these situations or in combinations of them, there is an increased potential for incomplete or defective character development.

The single mother may have the responsibility of being the primary provider for the family, especially in cases where the father fails to provide adequate support or where she must be involved in costly and time-consuming legal action to obtain the support money. The mother may be both physically and emotionally exhausted at the end of the workday, yet have to take care of the household duties. She is left alone to deal with the children's school problems, homework, and hassles. Sometimes there are grandparents that can assist in whatever way, or uncles and aunts, or even close friends. On the other hand, the single mother who may have a need to prove that she is a "supermom" may fail to ask for the assistance she needs.

Although divorce is hardly a rarity in the Jewish community these days, there is still a stigma attached to it, and children may feel badly about the parental separation. They may deny it to their friends and fabricate stories about family activities and vacations, in order to keep pace with the adventures of their peers. It is not unusual for children to feel a greater or lesser degree of responsibility for the parental separation, and the mother may have to deal with the child's anger for the divorce, or with his feelings of depression and guilt.

When the loss of a parent is due to death, another set of difficulties arises. In this case, the children are in the custody of the surviving parent, and if the loss was of the mother, the father has the task of being the breadwinner, while trying to make a wholesome home environment for the children. If at all possible, the children should remain together rather than being distributed among relatives, and the father should try to find time to be with the children to whatever degree possible.

Grief over the loss of a spouse is not easily dealt with, yet the mature adult can come to accept the loss and make a reasonable adjustment to reality. In contrast to divorce, death is not a rejection, and the suffering of the loss is not complicated by an insult to the ego. This distinction is not equally valid for young children, who may not understand illness and death, and may indeed feel that they are somehow at fault for the parent's death. Irrational as it may seem, psychotherapists often encounter feelings of unresolved guilt in adults who never overcame the juvenile feelings of guilt and responsibility for a parent's death. Grief is thus complicated with guilt, and the grieving husband or wife, who are struggling with their own pain, may not have the resources to deal effectively with the children's feelings. Often there is just a tacit understanding not to talk about the deceased person, as though denying the reality is beneficial.

It should be assumed that both young children and adolescents will have difficulty in coping with the death of a parent. Children should be provided with someone to whom they can ventilate their feelings, and who will be able to help them in this difficult adjustment. A rabbi who has expertise in bereavement counseling can be an excellent resource.

Additional difficulties may occur when the boys do not have a father to accompany them to the synagogue, to sit with them and supervise them during the services. The mother may not be in a position to review the Torah portion of the week with them and assist them with their Hebrew studies. There may be "father and son" events at school or at the synagogue, which cause the children to feel awkward and this may lead to social withdrawal.

An entirely new set of problems occurs when the mother considers entering a new relationship. The children may be apprehensive of anyone who threatens to drain the affection from the one functional parent they have, and the mother may feel herself caught between looking after her own needs versus upsetting the children. Should she remarry, there may be a period of adjustment to the new composition of the household, new rules, and new authority.

The single mother should not hesitate to enlist the help of family, friends, and rabbis, and not allow her pride and drive for self-sufficiency to prevail. "Supermoms" do not get the Nobel Prize. The community should be aware that a single mother may need help, and should offer it with sensitivity and consideration for her dignity. The rabbis should not wait to be called upon for their assistance, but should be proactive in helping the single mother manage with the responsibilities which may be overwhelming.

The emotional needs of children of divorce may require the attention of a competent professional. There may not be a need for long-term therapy, but in virtually every case, the children may need to ventilate to a competent, empathic person. Sometimes the single mother may resent this, misinterpreting any need for counseling as an indication of her dereliction or incompetence. In other situations the mother may wish to obtain counseling, but cannot afford it on her limited budget. The rabbi, as a representative of the community and as a respected authority, should exercise his position to enable the single mother and the children to make an optimum adjustment.

The Torah repeatedly instructs us to give extra consideration to the orphan, and the *halachah* explains that this principle applies to any disadvantaged person. Children of a failed marriage may not be actual orphans, yet may be psychological orphans, and the Torah places the responsibility of caring for them on the entire community. Teachers, rabbis, relatives, and neighbors should keep in mind that they have a Torah obligation to give consideration to the needs of children of divorce, and also to those of their parents.

Chapter Forty-Three

What About the Street?

On several occasions we have alluded to the deleterious influences that prevail in the environment in which we live. The principles of freedom of speech and freedom of the press have been exploited to permit unrestrained dissemination of violence and immorality. While environmentalists exert much energy to reduce industrial pollution, nothing is being done to reduce moral pollution, which seems to be protected by the Constitution. In order to avoid provocation and stimulation of the drives that are part of the human being's physical makeup, we would have to walk down the street with our eyes closed and ears plugged.

Some people have a delusion of immunity. From my clinical experience I must shatter this fantasy. Some of the finest families have been stricken with the incidence of society's most abhorrent evils. Desperate situations call for intensive countermeasures.

Rambam states that the influence of the environment are so great that if a person cannot find a community free of immorality, he should live in a cave in the wilderness and not subject himself to the toxicity of corrupt surroundings (*Deios* 6). Today this may not be a viable option, and although some people have settled in villages where they hope to be free of the prevailing moral decadence, it is questionable whether one can successfully insulate oneself and one's family. We must therefore search for strategies to counteract the toxic environmental influences.

Let us look at something that has worked. Earlier I pointed out that people are repelled by the thought of eating insects, and if we find a fly in the soup we will reject the entire bowl. Yet, if you observe tiny children, they do not hesitate to pick up insects and put them in their mouths. When mother sees a child do this, she shakes the child's hand to dislodge the insect and says, "*Feh, fui*," with such a vehemence that the child picks up the sense of revulsion. Several such lessons in infancy are enough to make insects repulsive and nauseating for the rest of one's life.

This technique can and should be applied to everything that is considered morally reprehensible. However, this cannot be a superficial, insincere act. The reason it works so well with bugs is because the parental reaction is genuine, and the feeling of disgust is therefore successfully transmitted to the child who receives and incorporates it. Condemnation of immoral practices, whether this be drugs, dishonesty, or violence, should reflect the parents' wholehearted negative attitude toward these.

Traditionally, drunkenness among Jews was a rarity, whereas in recent decades, there has been an increased incidence. Some social psychologists attribute the scarcity in the past to the abhorrence attached to the word *shikker*. No other Yiddish word carries with it the loathsomeness and opprobrium of *shikker;* hence, any tendency toward irresponsible consumption of alcohol was suppressed by this powerful social counterforce. A reaction of revulsion and abhorrence to all immoral acts can be a deterrent, discouraging young people from considering them as options.

In the light of this, failure to react with profound condemnation to immorality is tantamount to tacit approval. Indifference is inadequate. If responses to immoral acts will elicit an emotional reaction of revulsion in parents, and they will manifest these genuine feelings of disapproval, there is greater likelihood that the children will adopt these negative attitudes toward improprieties.

The printed and electronic media penetrate into our homes and can exert a toxic effect on our children, far beyond what we realize or are even willing to realize. For example, several years ago, in an effort to combat the epidemic of crack-cocaine, one of the networks aired a documentary which showed the disastrous consequences of cocaine: crime, imprisonment, insanity, and sudden death. Several independent socio-psychologic studies have shown that of the youngsters who watched this program, *more were stimulated to try cocaine than were discouraged.* Thus, what many thought would be a helpful educational tool against drugs turned out to have the opposite effect.

Censorship of what young people may see or read is not likely to be effective. There is no way of avoiding exposure to newspapers and magazines, and even if there is no television in the home, children may watch TV at their friends' homes. Parents may have the mistaken notion that certain material is inappropriate for the eyes and ears of their young children, but that as mature adults, they may read and see these. This double standard has been adopted by the secular world, via a method of grading material; i.e., which is appropriate for adults, and which is appropriate for children of various ages, some with and some without parental guidance. This is a grave and crucial mistake. Material that is morally reprehensible for children should be equally so for parents, and the latter's attitude should be so genuinely condemning that it should carry over to the children.

I recognize that as intelligent adults we wish to be knowledgeable about what is going on in the world: international affairs, politics, economy, etc. The popular news weeklies that present this information often have quite explicit graphic material, and this is also true of many daily newspapers.

If there is no way of avoiding such printed material entering the home, their noxious influence may be minimized somewhat by reading the essential material quickly, and then throwing the magazine or paper in the trash can. Tearing out pages is not an effective technique, since it only arouses children's curiosity, and becomes the "forbidden fruit." Again, if the parental expression of revulsion to immoral material is genuine, there is hope that this will discourage children from being attracted to it.

The ethical Torah writings emphasize the need for gaining control over one's senses. Actions are more amenable to control, but listening and seeing are passive, and it is admittedly much more difficult to avoid hearing or seeing objectionable material. Yet, difficult does not mean impossible, and dedicated Torah-observant adults should endeavor to study and implement these Torah teachings. As we have noted earlier, children are exquisitely sensitive, and if parents are sincere in growing spiritually and gaining greater mastery over their passive senses, the children will sense this and will be more likely to incorporate these parental values.

The Rabbi of Kotzk said that the real reason one should not commit sin is not because it is forbidden, but because one should not have the free time to do so. This is an excellent example of how the positive can extinguish the negative, and supports the interpretation of the verse in *Psalms* (34:15), "Avoid evil by doing good."

Our ethical works elaborate on the verse "Know Him (G-d) in *all* your ways" (*Proverbs* 3:6), which means that all of a person's actions should be directed toward the service of G-d. Judaism does not ascribe to "render unto to G-d what is G-d's and unto Caesar what is Caesar's." There is only one motivation and one loyalty: devotion to G-d.

It is a mistake to think that the Divine service is restricted to acts of ritual or specific *mitzvos*. One cannot optimally perform *mitzvos* of the Torah unless one is in good physical and emotional health; hence, everything which contributes to physical and emotional well-being contributes to Torah observance, and is in itself a *mitzvah* when it is done for this reason. A person requires adequate nutrition in order to be in good health; hence, eating can be directed toward enabling one to serve G-d. One needs to support oneself and provide for one's family; hence, working and transacting business, when done for this goal, is part of the Divine service. One cannot function without proper rest; hence, sleep and relaxation can be directed toward G-d. If a judicious amount of entertainment and amusement are essential for emotional well-being, these, too, can be incorporated into Divine service.

It is important, however, that we do not deceive ourselves, because doing so makes us the victims of our own cunning and is self-defeating. Judicious rest, relaxation, exercise, amusement, and pursuit of livelihood can indeed be incorporated into the Divine service, but one should not squander one's time in these activities and claim that it is for a sacred purpose. Certainly things that are contrary to the exalted spiritual moral ethics of Torah cannot be in anyway considered contributory to the Divine service. Just as one cannot eat *treifah* and claim that he will use this nutrient value in the service of G-d, neither can one read immoral literature for relaxation and claim that it contributes to one's emotional well-being, nor can one be physically indulgent and claim this to be in the spirit of "Know Him (G-d) in all your ways."

When parents sincerely and wholeheartedly adopt an attitude of directing themselves in all aspects of life toward the ultimate goal of doing the Divine will, the atmosphere in the home becomes one which serves as a bulwark against the destructive immorality that threatens us from the outside. While there is never any foolproof guarantee, we must do the utmost to save ourselves and our families from the decadence of the street.

Chapter Forty-Four

It Will Never Happen to Me

*W*ith every fiber in my body, I hope that it doesn't. But it is foolish to think that anyone has total immunity. Being forewarned is forearmed.

What I am talking about, of course, is drug addiction. How can it possibly happen in a fine, Torah-observant family? "My children don't even have contact with anyone who uses drugs. There is just no way it could happen."

I do not mean to be an alarmist, but I have treated young men and women from the finest families, children of esteemed Torah scholars, who fell prey to alcoholism or drug addiction. It should not have happened, but it did.

What is the incidence? What are the statistics? No one knows with any reasonable accuracy, but statistics are really irrelevant. If G-d forbid, it happens to your child, then for you the statistics are 100 percent.

How can our children ever be exposed to drugs if they are attending yeshivas and reputable girls' schools? In some yeshivas there are students who used marijuana before becoming as observant as they are today, and have continued using it because they are under the false impression that marijuana is not a dangerous drug. They may also argue that marijuana enhances their spirituality and intellectual capacity. The fact is that they may have become dependent on marijuana and resist giving it up. It is not unusual for them to offer it to their friends, and if your child happens to experience it and likes its effect, you may have the beginning of a problem.

Contrary to popular belief, alcohol abuse is not uncommon among Jews. While taking a *lechayim* at a *kiddush* or at other appropriate occasions is perfectly acceptable, there are people who are vulnerable to the addictive effects of alcohol. Problems can begin earlier than most people suspect. I have seen children of 10 or 11 at a *bar-mitzvah kiddush* and empty remainders of wine and whiskey in glasses on the table. This portends a likelihood to dependence on alcohol, as well as a vulnerability to other chemicals that cause a change in mood.

Many parents are oblivious to their children's use of alcohol or other chemicals. The conviction that "it could never happen to my child" is so strong that it can cause a parent to be blind even to the obvious.

While alcohol, cocaine, and heroin are notorious for their addictive qualities, it is important to realize that prescription drugs may be no less dangerous. While there are appropriate uses for drugs such as valium, xanax, or other tranquilizers, these do have potential for abuse. Similarly, pain pills such as percocet and percodan, while justifiable, can produce a "high" and may be the drug of choice for some addicts.

There are relatively few homes that are completely free of mood-altering prescription drugs. While they do have legitimate use, it is not uncommon for people to resort to tranquilizers when they are tense or upset, or to the pain-killing drugs for the least physical discomfort. Children who see parents using chemicals in this fashion may come to believe that there is no reason to tolerate any emotional or physical discomfort whatever. If a youngster feels ill at ease, which is quite normal in adolescence, he may go for the drugs that his parents use, or may decide that whereas the parents may use xanax to feel better, he prefers marijuana to help him feel better.

Tranquilizers and pain killers are medications, and medicine should be used only when a person is sick. Not all tension is sickness, and it is a mistake to resort to tranquilizing medication to relieve the discomforts of the normal stresses and tensions of everyday life. Parents who set an example of coping with normal stresses and tensions, insomnia, or mild physical discomfort without recourse to potent chemicals are setting an example for the child that may discourage him from abusing chemicals.

While almost all alcohol has a telltale odor and parents can detect if a youngster has been drinking, this is not true of other mood-altering chemicals. It is therefore wise to be on the alert for signs of possible drug use.

Changes in mood that are uncharacteristic for a youngster should raise the suspicion of drug use. An increase in secretiveness, isolation, concealing phone calls, a change in sleeping pattern with late-morning awakening, an unaccountable drop in school performance, association with friends of questionable character, inexplicable demands for money, and things missing from the house are all warning signs of trouble. Any of these may be attributable to something other than drugs that is troubling a youngster, but the possibility of drugs should not be overlooked. Children as young as 11 have been known to abuse drugs, so even at that tender age, the parents should not dismiss drug use as an impossibility.

If parents have any reason to suspect possible drug use in a child, the proper thing to do is to consult someone who has expertise in drug and alcohol problems among children and adolescents. Parents may have their fears allayed or be instructed what to watch for and how to handle a problem if it turns out to be one involving drugs. While there are many fine child psychologists and psychiatrists, not all of these have been trained in diagnosis and management of drug problems, and it is important to consult someone with expertise in this area.

Some parents may be extremely hesitant to consult a professional, because they fear that the word might leak out that their child has a problem and this would stigmatize the family. In those families where *shidduchim* (matchmaking) is the way their children marry, the stigma of having a drug problem or other emotional problem within the family can ruin prospects of marriage for all other children. Parents may therefore try to control a drug problem by intimidation or bribery.

I can sympathize with the parents' anxiety over the possibility of exposure of a problem within the family, but I must advise them that neither threats nor bribery will control a drug problem. And if the latter is not appropriately managed, there will eventually be exposure in a manner much more traumatic to the family than the one the parents wished to avoid. Therefore, if a drug or alcohol problem exists or is suspected, the parents must seek competent help.

But why should such problems occur at all in a Torah-observant family? Shouldn't observance of *mitzvos* prevent such problems?

The answer to this question should shed light not only on the problem of drug abuse, but on many other problems which should not prevail among Torah-observant families.

I have no way of knowing what the dominant attitudes were in previous generations, but it is clear that in western civilization today, the primary goal in life is pleasure seeking. One need only look at the covers of magazines at the supermarket checkout counters to conclude that all that is being promoted is how to gratify one's appetites. People may have different concepts of what constitutes pleasure, but there is no avoiding the fact that pursuit of pleasure is the prime and motivating drive in today's culture.

When pleasure seeking is a primary goal in life, those who feel that they have not achieved the full measure of pleasure that is their due will turn to anything that promises to provide this, and drugs do suit that purpose. The fact that drugs are dangerous and may be lethal is not a deterrent for many people, especially young people who consider themselves immune to the dangers of drugs. Billions of dollars have been spent over the years in drug-prevention programs, but there are no tangible results to which one can point, no technique or series of techniques that have been demonstrated to be effective in prevention of drug abuse among young people. The reason for this is that as long as people are pleasure driven and think themselves immune to the harmful effects of drugs, they will continue to have recourse to these euphoriant chemicals.

Many people sacrifice comforts, conveniences, and pleasures in pursuit of an ultimate goal. However, if the ultimate goal is pursuit of pleasure, it is unreasonable to expect people, especially youngsters, to sacrifice pleasure for the ultimate goal which is. . .pursuit of pleasure. Western culture with its hedonism has painted itself into a corner.

What about Torah-observant families? Let us be brutally frank with ourselves. Many Torah-observant families have been caught up in pursuit of pleasure, the one difference being that they partake only of pleasures that have a *hechsher*, which today includes almost everything.

It is not as though we were not forewarned in regard to this. The Ramban in reference to the *mitzvah* (*Leviticus* 19:2), "You shall be holy," asks, What is the requirement of this *mitzvah*? His answer is prophetic. It is possible for a person to technically observe all of the restrictions in the Torah, yet live a life of physical indulgence. The *mitzvah* of *kedoshim tehiyu*, "You shall be holy," means that a person should abstain not only from things that are forbidden by the Torah, but even from many things that are permissible, but which are unnecessary for optimum health and functioning.

Many people believe that they are completely Torah observant. Shabbos is meticulously observed, they wear *tzitzis* and *daven* daily, participate in a *daf yomi shiur*, and no food item enters their home unless it has met the highest degree of *kashrus* supervision. Their children attend yeshivas and Bais Yaakov schools. Yet the *mitzvah* "You shall be holy" is no less a requirement than any of the other 612. Can we claim to be truly Torah observant if we do not observe this *mitzvah* properly?

There is virtually no food item that is consumed by the non-Jewish population that does not have its counterpart with a *hechsher*. One might think that pork is the outstanding exception, but there is even a kosher synthetic bacon available. Kosher wine stores have an array of wines that can satisfy the most discriminating palate. Ethnic foods are available *glatt kosher*. Resorts, spas, and luxury cruises are all available with *glatt* standards. Rock music is sung to the words of Scripture, and performers sway on the stage with their long *tzitzis* floating in the air. Garments that technically comply with *tzenius* (modesty) standards are available with designer labels. All of these, within the technical confines of the *Shulchan Aruch*, are not marketed for the nonobservant consumer, because the latter opt for the secular versions. It is clear that these indulgences are provided for the Torah-observant Jew. We have thus fallen into the trap of *glatt kosher* hedonism. There are some who can afford these indulgences, and some who aspire to afford them.

Children who attend yeshivas and Bais Yaakov schools may thus be subject to the pursuit of pleasure ethos that may prevail in their environment. Their friends may be wearing designer clothes, their parents may be driving luxury automobiles, and their aspirations may be to achieve the ultimate in enjoying life. While Torah does not sanction asceticism and mortification of the flesh, neither does it sanction hedonism. The median path, the path of virtue that the Rambam advocates, is the one that Torah-observant people should adopt. We may partake of and enjoy the goods of the world, but pursuit of pleasure should not be our goal in life.

A number of years ago, a campaign was started in the United States, "Just say no to drugs." Research psychologists questioned young people about their attitude towards this, and were surprised to find 13 and 14-year-old youngsters responding, "Why? What else is there?" It should be obvious that all preventive efforts to curb the drug epidemic will be futile unless we can provide young people with a reasonable and understandable answer to the question, "Why? What else is there?"

The most effective deterrent to drug abuse as well as other destructive behaviors is the adoption of the Torah goal of *kabbalas ol malchus shamayim*, acceptance of the yoke of G-d's sovereignty, with the ultimate aspiration being the achievement of spirituality. In today's decadent, hedonistic world, it does not suffice to be technically in compliance with the *Shulchan Aruch*. Today's Torah-observant Jew must live according to the ethical teachings of the Ramchal's *Mesilas Yesharim* (*Path of the Just*), where *ruach hakodesh*, the attainment of Divine spirituality, is the goal towards which a person should strive.

Chapter Forty-Five

But What
Went Wrong

O ne of the most painful things for a therapist to experience is the agony of parents who are disappointed in a child. Such disappointment can vary over a broad spectrum, all the way from a child who is not fulfilling his potential to the extreme of a child who is antisocial or addicted to drugs. Parents who have invested a great deal of effort and had high hopes for their child are profoundly depressed when their child gets into serious difficulty or fails to make the grade.

Traditional psychology and psychiatry made a grievous error when they blamed parents for their children's problems. The overwhelming majority of parents have excellent intentions for their children and try to do their utmost to provide for them. A child's failure should therefore not be attributed to dereliction on the part of the parents. From the Scriptures through the Talmud and all the way to contemporary times there have been excellent and devout people who had a child that was deviant in one way or another.

Parents can do only that which is within their means at any given time. We achieve our maximum wisdom by experiencing the various vicissitudes of life, and we are probably at our wisest just about when we reach retirement age. However, that is not when we have and raise our children. The latter task is achieved when we are young and relatively inexperienced. At this time we can only work with whatever wisdom and tools we have, and seek the best teaching and guidance available. There is no guarantee that our best efforts will result in the success to which we aspire.

There is no way to avoid experiencing much distress when a child does not live up to legitimate expectations. While such distress is unavoidable, it is wrong to add to this the additional agony of unwarranted guilt for the disappointing result.

Similarly, in raising our children, we can only work with the facts and the capacities at our disposal. When we do our utmost for our children, we have fulfilled our ethical and moral obligations as parents. There may be many factors totally beyond our control that influence our children's behavior, and it is a mistake for parents to castigate themselves if a child turns out to be a failure.

Children can use all the help they can get, and this can be true even when they are mature adults. Parents may be able to be of great help, but they may compromise their usefulness if they are burdened by unwarranted feelings of guilt. The latter is depressing, and may drain the energy that could be helpful to the child.

It is our fervent wish that all parents see abundant *nachas* in their children. However, if reality deals us unkind results, we should maintain our composure. We should always pray to G-d for his help, and do whatever is within our means to help our children live productive lives. Let us not indulge in destructive self-flagellation, which can be of no value to ourselves nor our children.

Chapter Forty-Six

Putting It
All Together

My father used to tell a story about a Rebbe, who raised his *Kiddush* cup on the first Friday night after Sukkos, and closed his eyes in meditation. He remained in this meditative state with the *Kiddush* cup on the palm of his hand, while his *chassidim* waited for him to begin the *Kiddush*. Much to their amazement, he remained as if transfixed for several hours. The cup fell from his hand, the Shabbos candles burned out, and the *chassidim* fell asleep, yet the Rebbe remained as if in a trance. It was already dawn when he opened his eyes and proceeded to recite the *Kiddush*.

The Rebbe later explained to his perplexed *chassidim*: "When a merchant goes to a busy market, he is constantly engaged in transactions, buying, selling, trading, making inquiries, checking the quality of merchandise, etc. During this phase he is too busy to calculate just what he is accomplishing with all his frenetic activity. When he stops at the first inn on his way home, he takes out all his papers and records and analyzes just how much profit he made, what, if any, mistakes he made in his dealings, and what he must do to increase his profit next time around.

"Beginning with the month of Elul, we enter into a period of frenetic spiritual activity, with *teshuvah*, *selichos*, and then the myriad of *mitzvos* in which we engage through Rosh Hashanah, Yom Kippur, and Sukkos. During this period of time, we are so busy that we do not have the opportunity to stop and analyze the quality of our actions, and just what we have achieved. How many of our sins have we been able to exchange via proper *teshuvah*, and how many have we been able to convert into merits? What must we do next time around to make more profitable spiritual transactions? The Shabbos after Sukkos is likened to the first inn, the first opportunity to review our efforts, and it therefore took me this long to calculate what I had accomplished over the past two months."

I remember hearing this story as a child, and I was impressed that it is frequently necessary to stop and reflect on our behavior. While we are actively engaged in doing things, we may not be able to fully analyze what we are doing, and it is only in retrospect that we can evaluate what we have done.

Now that we have finished this book, it is appropriate to review its contents, to see what we have derived from our discussions, and perhaps analyze how we have been executing our responsibilities as parents. It is only with sincere and frank analysis that we can increase our efficiency as parents.

Let us also be aware that even excellent parents, who have applied the most effective parenting techniques, are not guaranteed that their children will turn out according to their wishes. From the Scriptures through the Talmud and down through all generations, some men and women who were of the highest spiritual caliber had children who deviated from the correct path, and who were a source of much distress to their parents. We can only do that which we believe to be best for our children, and when we have sought expert guidance and practiced good parenting techniques with the utmost sincerity, we have fulfilled our responsibilities. There are many factors beyond parental control that can affect a child's behavior and choices, and inasmuch as parents have no control over outcome, they should not feel guilty should their children not live up to their standards and expectations.

Unwarranted guilt is detrimental to both parents and children. Children can use all the help they can get, even when they are mature adults. Parents may be able to be of great help at every stage, but they may compromise their usefulness if they are burdened by unwarranted feelings of guilt. The latter are depressing, and may drain the energy that could be constructively applied to the children.

Let me just highlight several themes that we have stressed in this book. First, we should not assume that all parents are intuitively excellent as parents, and it is therefore important that parenting techniques be learned and developed. Secondly, there are normal and unavoidable personal interests that parents have, some of which may not necessarily coincide with what is optimum for the child, and we should be alert to these and know how to deal with them. Thirdly, while there is a need for parents to guide, teach, and discipline their children, it is always necessary to try to understand the child's perspective. Therefore, although such understanding does not mean that we must yield to the child's wishes, the feeling that one is being understood is essential for the development of a child's trust in the parent. Fourthly, in the Torah-observant family there should be a consistency of Torah values, so that the child can incorporate a value system that is relatively free of internal contradictions. Finally, parental teaching is primarily conveyed by their serving as role models for their children.

While there is no reason to expect perfection in parenting any more than in any other human activity, the awesome responsibility of bringing a child into the world and preparing him to find meaning and happiness in life does require that we do our utmost in developing the trust of our children.

The Talmudic phrase, *tzaar gidul banim*, or "Suffering in raising children," indicates that parenting is a function that is not free of misery and distress. When our children are infants and we suffer along with them as they cut their teeth and as they experience the usual childhood diseases, we look forward to the time when they will be "*mentschen*" and on their own. Yet, who has not heard their grandmother say, "*Kleine kinder, kleine tzoros. Grosze kinder, grosze tzoros*" (Little children, little problems; big children, big problems).

Let us remember that even the finest of human efforts are futile without the blessing of Hashem, for which we must pray diligently. It is our hope that by applying wholesome parenting principles, and by praying fervently, you will be able to minimize the distresses of raising children, and be blessed with an abundance of *nachas*, "To see children and children's children engaged in the observance of Torah and *mitzvos*."

This volume is part of
THE ARTSCROLL SERIES®
an ongoing project of
translations, commentaries and expositions
on Scripture, Mishnah, Talmud, Halachah,
liturgy, history and the classic Rabbinic writings;
and biographies, and thought.

For a brochure of current publications
visit your local Hebrew bookseller
or contact the publisher:

Mesorah Publications, ltd

4401 Second Avenue
Brooklyn, New York 11232
(718) 921-9000